THE INCLUSIVE SOCIETY?

Also by Ruth Levitas

THE IDEOLOGY OF THE NEW RIGHT (*editor*)

THE CONCEPT OF UTOPIA

INTERPRETING OFFICIAL STATISTICS (*editor with Will Guy*)

The Inclusive Society?

Social Exclusion and New Labour

Ruth Levitas
Senior Lecturer in Sociology
University of Bristol

© Ruth Levitas 1998

Published by
PALGRAVE
Houndmills, Basingstoke, Hampshire RG21 6XS and
175 Fifth Avenue, New York, N. Y. 10010
Companies and representatives throughout the world

PALGRAVE is the new global academic imprint of
St. Martin's Press LLC Scholarly and Reference Division and
Palgrave Publishers Ltd (formerly Macmillan Press Ltd).

ISBN 0–333–73086–0 hardcover
ISBN 0–333–73087–9 paperback

This book is printed on paper suitable for recycling and made from fully managed and sustained forest sources.

A catalogue record for this book is available from the British Library.

Printed and bound in Great Britain by
Antony Rowe Ltd, Chippenham and Eastbourne

For my father,
Maurice Levitas.
No pasarán!

Contents

Acknowledgements   ix

List of Abbreviations   xi

Introduction   1

1   Three Discourses of Social Exclusion   7

2   From Social Justice to Social Cohesion   29

3   The Optimism of Will   49

4   Staking Claims   70

5   Community Rules   89

6   New Labour, New Discourse   112

7   From Equality to Inclusion   128

8   Delivering Social Inclusion   159

9   The New Durkheimian Hegemony   178

Appendix   190

Notes   192

Select Bibliography   211

Index   216

Acknowledgements

This book is based on a project funded by the ESRC on Discourses of Social Exclusion and Integration in Emergent Labour Party Policy (R000222106). I am grateful for their support, which provided a year free from teaching and administrative commitments in 1996–7, and enabled me to give my undivided attention to the events of the pre-election period. Special thanks are due to my research assistant, Gail Hebson, who worked with dedication and flair, and maintained her sanity and good humour despite watching more television interviews with politicians than the average human being can withstand. Neither completion of the research project nor this book would have been possible without her.

The project arose from the Equity, Labour and Social Divisions Research Initiative in the Faculty of Social Sciences at the University of Bristol in 1994–5. I am grateful to members of the research group for those early discussions of social exclusion, especially Teresa Rees and Steve Fenton who made invaluable comments on the first draft of the research proposal, and Randall Smith who steered me through the arcane rules of the European Union structural funds. The interest and enthusiasm of staff and students in the Sociology Department has been a great encouragement.

Mary Bruce of the Labour Party's Information Subscription Service was enormously helpful in supplying us with relevant material. Discussions with past and present members of the Labour Party, especially in Bristol, have been vital to my understanding of the changes over recent years. I am especially grateful to Mary Southcott for explaining the workings of the Policy Forum, enabling me to make sense of the constitutional debate at the 1997 Labour Party Conference; and to Sandra Parsons and Ruairi Tobin for their hospitality during the Conference itself. Thanks are due also to Will Hutton, for finding time to talk to me about some of the issues in Chapter 3.

I have had many critical and helpful comments on papers which have fed into the chapters in this book, from participants in the British Sociological Association Conference in York; the Capital and Class Conference in London; the Third European Feminist Conference in Coimbra; the European Sociological Association in Colchester; and the Centre for the Analysis of Social Exclusion at the London School of Economics. Others have read all or parts of the manuscript, sometimes in several drafts, or sent me useful material. Among these, I would like to thank the following in particular for help, advice and encouragement: Louise Ackers, John Holmwood, Julian Le Grand, Paul Watt, Dan Finn, Gail Hebson, Carol Johnson, Maggie Studholme, Harriet Bradley, Jackie West, Stella Maile and Rob Hunter. Maggie Studholme also copy-edited the manuscript – not, in this case, a thankless task.

Particular thanks are due to Diana Levitas, for sisterhood, and for taking more than her share of the responsibilities which fall on the sandwich generation; to Gail Hebson, for commitment and friendship beyond the call of duty; to Harriet Bradley, for friendship, collegiality, intellectual rigour and gin; and to Rob Hunter, for forbearance, political commitment, food and fellowship, and fun.

List of Abbreviations

AFDC	Aid to Families with Dependent Children
ASI	Adam Smith Institute
CASE	Centre for the Analysis of Social Exclusion
CPAG	Child Poverty Action Group
CPRS	Central Policy Review Staffs
CPS	Centre for Policy Studies
CSO	Central Statistical Office
GDP	Gross Domestic Product
GNP	Gross National Product
GUMG	Glasgow University Media Group
IEA	Institute of Economic Affairs
IPPR	Institute for Public Policy Research
LSE	London School of Economics
MAI	Multilateral Agreement on Investment
NEF	New Economics Foundation
ONS	Office of National Statistics
RMI	Revenu Minimum D'Insertion
SAU	Social Affairs Unit
SERA	Socialist Environment and Resources Association
SERPS	State Earnings Related Pension Scheme
SEU	Social Exclusion Unit
TANF	Temporary Assistance to Needy Families

Introduction

On 1 May 1997 the Labour Party, led by Tony Blair, swept to power with an overall majority of 179 seats. The scale of the victory was unimaginable: 419 seats for Labour, 46 Liberal Democrats, 165 Conservatives, and 29 others. The number of Conservatives elected to Parliament had halved since 1992. Several ex-ministers lost their seats, including Norman Lamont, Ian Lang, Malcolm Rifkind, William Waldegrave, Tony Newton – and Michael Portillo, who had been widely expected to be the next Leader of the Conservative Party. Melanie Johnson's inaugural speech as MP for Welwyn Hatfield hailed a new future 'where many will benefit and we will have a society where people are included rather than excluded'. Early on 2 May Blair promised in his victory speech 'a Britain renewed...where we build a nation united, with common purpose, shared values, with no-one shut out or excluded'. The age of inclusion had arrived.

The Labour Party had undergone extensive organizational and ideological 'remaking' since 1983, under the successive leaderships of Neil Kinnock, John Smith and Tony Blair, leading to its presentation from 1996 as New Labour.[1] It was a process which provoked anxiety within and beyond the Party that traditional constituencies of support and core values were being abandoned, though some thought this change long overdue. These anxieties intensified with Blair's succession to the leadership following John Smith's untimely death, especially as Blair immediately set about changing Clause IV of the constitution. The original Clause IV was widely believed to commit the party to large-scale nationalization, although there are other possible interpretations of 'common ownership of the means of production, distribution and exchange' especially when coupled with 'the best obtainable system of popular administration of each industry or service' (see Appendix). Clause IV also stressed the link between the Party and the trade union movement, and there were concerns that Blair intended to weaken or even sever this link. Policy changes in the run-up to the election caused further misgivings, both because of their substance and because of the increasingly dirigiste mode both of their imposition and of Party management more widely. But potential divisions were muted or set aside in pursuit of the common and over-riding goal of electoral success, and amid uncertainty over how far the changes in the Party were presentational and how far they were substantive.

The increased use of spin-doctors heightened the ambiguity between presentation and substance. But so too did the new language of political debate. A major theme of this book is that the development of a new political language about social cohesion, stakeholding, community, social exclusion and inclusion was central to the creation of the 'centre-left consensus' on which New Labour's electoral success was presumed to depend. But if inclusion was New Labour's guiding value, as one future government adviser argued in his pre-election book,[2] what this meant was far less clear. It might be a code for equality, or it might be a different project altogether. When the planned Social Exclusion Unit was publicized in August 1997, and billed, together with welfare to work, as the policy defining the aims and character of the Blair Government, the meaning of exclusion was little clearer. Since social exclusion was a term often used in conjunction with poverty, perhaps addressing poverty would, in fact, be a priority. On the other hand, Labour was pressing ahead with benefit cuts announced in the last Conservative budget in November 1996, which would increase poverty for some people. This book sets out to explore what New Labour means by social exclusion and inclusion, and thus what kind of inclusion their policies are intended to deliver. What does Blair's Government mean by an inclusive society? How will we gauge its success in creating one? What is the significance of talking about inclusion and exclusion rather than equality, inequality and poverty?

The book begins, therefore, with an exploration of different meanings of social exclusion. It is a concept which originates partly in French social policy, from where it has spread throughout the European Union. But there is no monolithic pan-European definition of social exclusion; rather, there is a range of national discourses which use the idea of exclusion in different ways. As exclusion becomes an increasingly prevalent term, so there are competing discourses of exclusion within individual countries, as well as within Europe. The first chapter charts the emergence of the idea of social exclusion within British political discourse, and identifies three competing discourses within which the concept may be deployed. The first is situated in critical social policy and is a redistributionist discourse, RED, in which social exclusion is intertwined with poverty. The second deploys cultural rather than material explanations of poverty. This moral underclass discourse, MUD, originally used the term underclass, but now also uses the language of social exclusion. The third, social integrationist discourse, or SID, sees inclusion primarily in terms of labour market attachment. The identification of these discourses is principally an analytical device, although they would have no purchase if they were not also in part empirical descriptions. RED, MUD and SID are models, or in Max Weber's terms ideal types, which show how the meanings of social exclusion shift and change, and how these permutations are reflected in different policy implications. They are competing discourses, but not just in the sense that they imply a range of meanings of exclusion from which the user may choose at will. They are actively deployed as part of political projects, and the disputed meaning of exclusion is part of this political process; social exclusion is an essentially contested concept.

To talk about the language of politics as a discourse, or series of discourses, is to say rather more than that new words are being used to express new – or even old – ideas. It means that sets of interrelated concepts act together as a matrix through which we understand the social world. As this matrix structures our understanding, so it in turn governs the paths of action which appear to be open to us. A discourse constitutes ways of acting in the world, as well as a description of it. It both opens up and closes down possibilities for action for ourselves. If we can make it stick, it does this for others too. The term discourse has to some extent taken the place of ideology within social science, although there are some differences in its connotation. Ideology is itself a contested term, with meanings ranging from the non-evaluative description of a system of beliefs, to the very specific Marxist reference to ideas which serve to obscure the contradictions of capitalism and thus sustain it. Ideology was also sometimes used to imply bad faith. It could be crudely taken to imply that what is said is simply a cover for the pursuit of material interests, which are themselves unaffected by the terms of the ideology itself; discursive processes might thus be seen as epiphenomena, the outcome of material relationships. The term discourse has certain advantages. It does not imply bad faith, although discourses can be deployed in bad faith. It draws attention to the importance of the language of politics, not simply as a way of expressing the substance of political positions and policies, but as that substance. This advantage is also a disadvantage. At the extreme, the term discourse can imply that language is all, that material relations are simply the product of discursive strategies, or that the levels of the material and the discursive are indistinguishable. At best, the idea of discourse underlines the fact that the matrix of concepts through which we understand the world and act in it profoundly affects those actions and thus the world itself, without denying the material character of social relations.

Chapters 2 to 5 are concerned with the construction of the discourse of the 'centre-left' in the period between 1994 and the 1997 election, the period of Blair's leadership of the Labour Party in opposition. They look at the meanings of inclusion and exclusion in the wider debates which fed into New Labour's rhetoric and policies, including those on 'stakeholding' and 'community', and show how these relate to RED, SID and MUD. Chapter 2 looks at the penumbra of think-tanks and networks which were influential in forming the new political culture from 1994, and at three documents in particular: the report of the Labour Party's Commission on Social Justice; the Rowntree report on inequalities of income and wealth; and the Dahrendorf report on wealth creation and social cohesion. Chapter 3 examines Will Hutton's hugely influential discussion of stakeholding, while Chapter 4 outlines competing versions, from John Kay, the Commission on Public Policy and British Business, to the Trades Union Congress and the Green Party. Chapter 5 looks at the popular versions of communitarianism, through the work of Amitai Etzioni and John Gray. It also compares these with the ideas of Blair's supposed guru, John Macmurray, showing that the version of communitarianism which has influenced New Labour is rather closer to Etzioni's. Stakeholding relates closely to SID, and communitarianism to MUD.

Chapters 6 and 7 deal directly with Labour Party policy and rhetoric under Blair's leadership. Chapter 6 shows how, in Labour's pursuit of a third way beyond left and right, stakeholding was taken up and dropped, or emptied of content; how questions of job security which were closely allied to the stakeholding agenda were recast in terms of employability; and how the idea of community was important to questions of social control, of parenting, and of voluntary work. This uneasy combination of elements created a contradiction at the core of Labour's policies. Chapter 6 also discusses New Labour's political positioning, demonstrating how the boundaries of political debate were redrawn so that what appeared and was presented as the 'centre-left' is in reality the centre right. The principal arena of debate is now bounded on one side by a synthesis of the free economy and the strong community – an apparently soft version of Thatcherism, but one whose antipathy to state intervention is particularly useful to the dismantling of the welfare state and the transfer of risk from the collective to the individual. On the other side, the extreme left is now defined by the Croslandite social democratic position of which Roy Hattersley has become the most vociferous exponent.

Chapter 7, which covers the period up to the end of 1997 when this book was completed, shows how New Labour's meaning of inclusion moved away from RED to draw on a combination of SID and MUD. It looks therefore at some of the debates and policy shifts taking place in the first months of the Blair Government, as the welfare to work programmes and the Social Exclusion Unit were put in place, and shows how New Labour arrived at a distinctive performative understanding of inclusion, drawing on both SID and MUD for a discursive reconstruction of the self. Inevitably, there will have been many political developments by the time this book is published, including the publication of the Green Paper on Welfare Reform, as well as the results of the Pensions Review and the setting of the minimum wage by the Low Pay Commission. The model of RED, SID and MUD is one way of examining the shifts and changes in political strategy. The 1998 Budget Statement was widely hailed as redistributive. Certainly increases in Child Benefit, although not immediately implemented, promised some eventual offsetting of the impending cuts in benefits to lone parents, and some improvement in the allowances for children in the poorest families. Such increases were clearly consistent with, and welcomed from, RED. But non-working adults, whether of working or pensionable age, were not helped at all. The Budget, built around the principle of 'making work pay', was clearly rooted primarily in SID, with the extension of in-work benefits through the planned Working Families Tax Credit. Gordon Brown's speech reiterated that 'the answer to social exclusion is economic opportunity'.

The centrality of child care in the Budget Statement, with the extension of child-care allowances (for approved forms of child care) for families in work illustrates the ambiguity of New Labour's treatment of unpaid work. The problem of valorizing unpaid work is used throughout the book to illuminate the differences between, and weaknesses of, the various interpretations of social inclusion – particularly the contradiction between Labour's emphasis on welfare to work and the importance attributed to parenting in maintaining social order. Chapter 8 asks how far New Labour might deliver the inclusion it prescribes. It is not concerned primarily with prediction, but with elaborating the criteria by which the success of Labour's policies might be assessed from the different standpoints of RED, SID and MUD. It also asks broader questions about the nature of social inclusion, and the policies which might bear on it – and thus the limits to the forms of inclusion Labour is likely to deliver.

The final chapter relates these limits to the underlying view of society which is implied by the third way. It compares this to the model of society set out by the French sociologist Emile Durkheim a hundred years ago. The language of social cohesion, social integration and solidarity is strongly Durkheimian, and Hilary Silver has shown the close and explicit connection between the French discourse of social exclusion and a Durkheimian understanding of society.[3] Although British discourses of exclusion differ from the French, and explicit references to Durkheim are very rare, contemporary political thinking implicitly reflects a strongly Durkheimian position. One feature of this is a tendency to repress conflicts. Any third way which does this is intrinsically likely to move rightward or leftward as such conflicts surface. I argue that the discourse of exclusion and inclusion can be seen as intimately linked to this repressive tendency, but that broader ideas of inclusion can also subvert it. In this sense, the discourse may lead beyond itself, into the very critique of capitalism which a Durkheimian perspective is unable to mount.

If political positioning is crucial to the third way, the political positioning of a commentator on it cannot be ignored. I am a socialist and feminist. I was a member of the Labour Party for some years from 1983. I am not writing from within RED, although my sympathies with this will be clear. I am deeply sceptical of the effects of discourses of exclusion and integration, which so easily obscure rather than illuminate patterns of inequality, and which do not question the nature of the society in which people are to be included. Yet this, as so much else, is ambiguous. I am still searching for a route to a just and sustainable future. And as part of this critical or even utopian project, the idea of an inclusive society might yet inform a further, more radical, discourse and even, eventually, a more radical politics.

1 Three Discourses of Social Exclusion

The term social exclusion is intrinsically problematic. It represents the primary significant division in society as one between an included majority and an excluded minority. This has implications for how both included and excluded groups are understood, and for the implicit model of society itself. Attention is drawn away from the inequalities and differences among the included. Notably, the very rich are discursively absorbed into the included majority, their power and privilege slipping out of focus if not wholly out of sight. At the same time, the poverty and disadvantage of the so-called excluded are discursively placed outside society. What results is an overly homogeneous and consensual image of society – a rosy view possible because the implicit model is one in which inequality and poverty are pathological and residual, rather than endemic. Exclusion appears as an essentially peripheral problem, existing at the boundary of society, rather than a feature of a society which characteristically delivers massive inequalities across the board and chronic deprivation for a large minority. The solution implied by a discourse of social exclusion is a minimalist one: a transition across the boundary to become an insider rather than an outsider in a society whose structural inequalities remain largely uninterrogated.

In practice, however, 'social exclusion' is embedded in different discourses which manifest these problems to varying extent. Three discourses are identified here: a redistributionist discourse (RED) developed in British critical social policy, whose prime concern is with poverty; a moral underclass discourse (MUD) which centres on the moral and behavioural delinquency of the excluded themselves; and a social integrationist discourse (SID) whose central focus is on paid work. They differ in how they characterize the boundary, and thus what defines people as insiders or outsiders, and how inclusion can be brought about. RED broadens out from its concern with poverty into a critique of inequality, and contrasts exclusion with a version of citizenship which calls for substantial redistribution of power and wealth. MUD is a gendered discourse with many forerunners, whose demons are criminally-inclined, unemployable young men and sexually and

7

socially irresponsible single mothers, for whom paid work is necessary as a means of social discipline, but whose (self-) exclusion, and thus potential inclusion, is moral and cultural. SID focuses more narrowly on unemployment and economic inactivity, pursuing social integration or social cohesion primarily through inclusion in paid work. The three discourses differ quite markedly in how they present the relationship between inclusion/exclusion and inequality, a theme which is central to the overall argument of this book.

The following discussion of RED, MUD, and SID also considers how the valorization of unpaid work plays through the different discourses. In October 1997 the Office of National Statistics (ONS) published the first estimates of the extent and value of unpaid work in the British economy. If a monetary value were put on such work, at 1995 values it would have been at least equivalent to £341 billion, or more than the whole UK manufacturing sector, and perhaps as much as £739 billion, 120 per cent of gross domestic product. Among the reasons for this statistical development was the insensitivity of conventional national accounts to the movement of activities between market and non-market sectors.[1] Yet despite this official endorsement, the dominant public and social-scientific understanding of 'work' remains paid work. Since the ONS figures confirmed that women do much more unpaid work than men, and that although men do more paid work, they also have more leisure, men's work is more acknowledged, as well as more highly rewarded, than women's work.[2] Following a well-established theme in feminist arguments, Miriam Glucksmann argues that work cannot be elided with those forms which happen to take place in a market setting: work refers to all 'activity necessary for the production and reproduction of economic relations and structures...irrespective of how and where it is carried out'. She describes the 'manner by which all the labour in a particular society is divided up and allocated to different structures, institutions and activities' as the total social organization of labour, and goes on to discuss historical changes in the gendered division of labour within and between household and market – shifts which the new satellite accounts are expressly developed to illuminate.[3] Both Glucksmann's perspective and the new official data raise another question. How is the recognition of not just the social but the economic value of currently unpaid work compatible with the distribution of the social product primarily through rewards for paid work? RED, MUD and SID have different capabilities for acknowledging, and thus for potentially addressing, this question.

RED: SOCIAL EXCLUSION AND CRITICAL SOCIAL POLICY

In 1979 Peter Townsend published a major study of poverty, analysing survey data from 1968–9. His purpose was to redefine poverty as an objective condition of relative deprivation. Rather than defining poverty, as earlier studies and official policy had done, in terms of levels of income necessary for subsistence, Townsend argued that the crucial issue was whether people had sufficient resources to participate in the customary life of society and to fulfil what was expected of them as members of it:

> Individuals, families and groups can be said to be in poverty when they lack the resources to obtain the types of diet, participate in the activities and have the living conditions and amenities which are customary, or at least are widely encouraged and approved, in the societies to which they belong. Their resources are so seriously below those commanded by the average individual or family that they are, in effect, excluded from ordinary living patterns, customs and activities.[4]

Expectations across society might differ in many respects, but Townsend claimed there was neverthless 'a loosely defined set of customs, material goods and social pleasures at any point in a nation's history which can be said to represent general amenities, or to which all or most people in that society are agreed to be entitled. Those who have few of these amenities can be said to be deprived'. Inequality might affect the style in which people participated in some social practices – the lavishness of holidays, or celebrations of birthdays and religious festivals. Poverty and deprivation went beyond this. There was a level of resources below which, rather than just a reduction in the scale of participation, there was a sudden withdrawal from the community's style of living: people 'drop out or are excluded'.[5]

Townsend was not the first to argue that poverty was a multi-faceted process rather than simply a matter of low income. But his was a sustained argument which widened the perspective from income to resources, and from consumption to participation. The analysis embraced housing, health and environmental pollution. It revealed disability as a particular factor in producing exclusion. It addressed deprivation at work, including hours of work, job security, and the working environment, and looked at the relationship between work, welfare and fringe benefits. The solution proposed was explicitly and broadly redistributive. Townsend recommended a decreased reliance on means-tested benefits, which he saw as a mechanism of social control as well as a rationing device: benefits should be paid as of right. He acknowledged a conflict between this approach and the principles and requirements of a capitalist market. Nevertheless, he argued that:

> National action to remedy poverty – through incomes policy, full employment, less specialization of work roles, higher social security benefits, new forms of allowances and rate support grants and a more redistributive tax structure – is implied.[6]

Poverty in the United Kingdom also included a chapter on one-parent families. This was a relatively new category in social thought. Townsend noted that there was no such term before 1964, when 'fatherless families' were collectively identified, and no national collation of statistics until 1967; 'motherless families' were incorporated later. Consistent with later trends in social science towards deconstructing rather than constructing categories, Duncan and Edwards have argued that lone-parent families should not be treated as a single group.[7] But Townsend was concerned about unmarried and separated mothers being pressed into employment despite their entitlement to benefit, and also concerned that lone fathers would continue to be subjected to improper pressure. Fathers only acquired the right to claim benefits as lone parents in 1975. This was one of a number of changes – including linking pension upratings to the higher of earnings or prices – brought in by the Wilson government, with Barbara Castle as Minister for Health and Social Security. Townsend attributed the poverty of one-parent families to a number of factors: the low earning-power of women; the absence of public child care; the practical restrictions that caring for children places on lone parents; attitudes to unmarried parents; the social expectation that women should be the primary carers; and the lack of income rights for women caring for children within marriage or outside it. The restructuring of the benefit system should incorporate larger maintenance allowances for children, allowances for the care of children, and an allowance for the upkeep of the family home in recognition of the unpaid work involved – all paid as of right, rather than means-tested.[8] These recommendations went some way towards recognizing the unpaid work of parenting.

The whole thrust of Townsend's argument was that poverty resulted in exclusion from social participation, but he did not use the term 'social exclusion'. Reflecting on this in 1997, he said that he had resisted the term for some time because he saw discrimination and exclusion as 'effects rather than causes', as 'by-products of . . . market manufactured class'; too much emphasis on social exclusion diverted attention from deprivation. However, he said 'I was wrong.... "social exclusion" directs attention to the marginalised and excluded and to the potential instruments of their exclusion'.[9] He argued once again for a redistributive strategy, not just through the tax and benefit systems and public services, but through the reduction of earnings differentials, a minimum wage, a minimum income for those unable to work, and financial recognition of unpaid work through at least a conditional participation income, if not an unconditional citizen's income.

The eighteen years between these statements were also the eighteen years of Conservative government, marked by dramatic increases in inequality, in unemployment, and in the numbers living in poverty, as well as more restrictive conditions for less generous social security benefits. The Tories had a redistributive strategy – but it was redistribution to the rich. Over this period, 'social exclusion' gained currency in critical social policy, especially in the discourse of the research and campaigning organization, Child Poverty Action Group (CPAG). CPAG marked the 1997 election with the publication of *Britain Divided: The growth of social exclusion in the 1980s and 1990s*.[10] Its three sections were subtitled 'creating poverty and social exclusion'; 'dimensions of poverty and social exclusion'; and 'combating poverty and social exclusion' – a formula which leaves open the relationship between the two terms. Walker, however, defined poverty in similar terms to Townsend: it is 'a lack of the material resources, especially income, necessary to participate in British society'. Social exclusion has a broader, more comprehensive, meaning: it 'refers to the dynamic process of being shut out, fully or partially, from any of the social, economic, political and cultural systems which determine the social integration of a person in society'.[11]

Contributors to the book were variously successful in maintaining this distinction. They emphasized that poverty does not necessarily lead to exclusion – a point made by Townsend in 1979, who noted that although poverty constituted a serious barrier to social participation, nevertheless stability of personal circumstances, length of residence, good health and frequent social contacts mitigated the effects of low material resources. The CPAG volume argued that social exclusion may be a cause, rather than just a result, of poverty. Homelessness, health, unemployment, food, utility disconnections were discussed, as well as (and in relation to) gender, ethnicity, the social security system and the overall distribution of income and wealth. The agenda was one of radical redistribution – although Townsend was one of a minority, together with Lisa Harker, who mentioned unpaid work. Harker, both here and elsewhere, called for universal child benefit, plus a benefit supporting child rearing.[12] This would be payable in addition to social insurance benefits, and calculated on an individual rather than household basis – thus reducing the personal economic dependency of women on men.

A concept of exclusion which refers to being shut out fully *or partially* is thereby extended to incorporate inequality, and its converse necessarily implies much greater equality. *Britain Divided* concluded on a cautiously optimistic note about the prospects for a redistributive agenda under Labour, citing Gordon Brown's John Smith Memorial Lecture where he argued that equality must be restored to its proper place in the trinity of socialist values, alongside liberty and community, and insisted that Labour would tackle poverty and inequality. Given Brown's later redefinition of equality as equality of opportunity (see Chapter 7 below), the caution may have been more appropriate than the optimism. But in the years of Thatcherite domination, direct defence of equality was difficult. It was assaulted as an immoral, even totalitarian, imposition of uniformity, and a brake on economic growth. Increasingly, the idea of citizenship was deployed in defence of welfare rights and welfare provision. Thus Walker argued that 'social exclusion may...be seen as the denial (or non-realisation) of the civil, political and social rights of citizenship'.[13] Peter Golding argued that poverty led to a reduction in participation tantamount to partial citizenship, as low income families were excluded from new information technologies, entertainment and leisure pursuits, as well as from financial institutions and from political life.[14] Ruth Lister's *The Exclusive Society* was subtitled 'citizenship and the poor', and traced the development of the broadening view of social exclusion as the antithesis of citizenship.[15]

Citizenship is, of course, another word which can embrace many meanings, and whose inflection to the individual or the social may vary considerably. Goodin argues that citizenship is a more egalitarian concept than inclusion.[16] Whereas inclusion focuses on the division between insiders and outsiders, and does not address the relationship between boundary and centre, citizenship focuses on the characteristics which are shared. However, models of citizenship differ in their scope, and thus in what respect citizens are to be deemed equal. The version used as an antonym to social exclusion drew heavily on T. H. Marshall's model, set out in 1950, which incorporated civil, political and social rights. Marshall too saw citizenship as implicitly egalitarian in relation to the rights and duties attaching to any particular definition. But he also argued that the twentieth century was characterized by the progressive extension of social rights: 'the whole range from the right to a modicum of economic welfare and security to the right to share to the full in the social heritage and to live the life of a civilised being according to the standards prevailing in the society'.[17] It was this emphasis on social citizenship rights, and the right to share *to the full* in the social heritage, which made this a useful language for egalitarians for it implied, as Marshall said, greater economic equality. On the other hand, he also observed that the move towards greater equality would be limited by the tension between the principle of social justice and the operation of the market. Moreover, citizenship could operate to legitimate inequalities, provided that they did not transgress equality of opportunity, did not cut too deep, and occurred 'within a population united in a single civilisation'.[18]

Marshall's framework was not adopted uncritically. He had addressed inequalities of class, but not those consequent on ethnicity and gender. Some argued that the concept of citizenship needed radical overhaul to avoid the problem of assimilating women to an essentially male model of the citizen.[19] Nevertheless, it formed the basis of an egalitarian, redistributive, broad understanding of social exclusion, inclusion and citizenship. Although social exclusion was, at the extreme, the product of poverty, citizenship was fundamentally affected by inequality. Lister's statement sums up the standpoint:

> It is not possible to divorce the rights and responsibilities which are supposed to unite citizens from the inequalities of power and resources that divide them. These inequalities – particularly of class, race and gender – run like fault-lines through our society and shape the contours of citizenship in the civil, political and social spheres. Poverty spells exclusion from the full rights of citizenship in each of these spheres and undermines people's ability to fulfil the private and public obligations of citizenship.[20]

Between 1979 and 1997, the social-democratic redistributive agenda was recast in this new language of exclusion and citizenship. Social exclusion was more clearly understood as a dynamic process, and a multi-faceted one, than poverty had generally been, and questions of gender and ethnicity had much higher profile; not only poverty, but the whole gamut of social inequalities were brought into the frame. Used in this discourse, RED, social exclusion mobilizes more than the concern with outcast poverty from which it started. It addresses the exclusionary processes in all areas of society which result in inequality itself. The characteristics of RED can be summarized as follows:

- It emphasizes poverty as a prime cause of social exclusion.
- It implies a reduction of poverty through increases in benefit levels.
- It is potentially able to valorize unpaid work.
- In positing citizenship as the obverse of exclusion, it goes beyond a minimalist model of inclusion.
- In addressing social, political and cultural, as well as economic, citizenship, it broadens out into a critique of inequality, which includes, but is not limited to, material inequality.
- It focuses on the processes which produce that inequality.
- It implies a radical reduction of inequalities, and a redistribution of resources and of power.

If Labour's understanding of social exclusion were consistent with RED, it would imply moving towards a more radically redistributive programme than that set out in the 1997 manifesto. However, other discourses, with different implications, are available.

MUD: THE UNDERCLASS AND THE CULTURE OF DEPENDENCY

The evolution of RED took place in a political context where social citizenship rights were under continued attack from the New Right. Unemployment and the numbers in poverty soared in the early 1980s to levels unprecedented in the post-war years, and social security spending rose with them. The government's response was to tighten eligibility for benefits and reduce their value, deny the existence of poverty, suppress and abolish some of the key indicators of its extent, and blame the poor for their own situation. References to the 'underclass' and to a 'culture of dependency' became embedded in a discourse concerned with social order and moral integration.

The New Right of the 1980s is now widely misunderstood as an exclusively neo-liberal project, aimed at the deregulation of the market and the reduction of state intervention. It was, however, made up of two apparently contradictory, but actually symbiotic, strands of neo-liberalism and neo-conservatism. Neo-liberal economics underpinned widespread privatization, and justified growing inequalities in the name of incentives. But neo-conservatism, which developed alongside neo-liberalism, was concerned with order rather than freedom, with family, nation and morality – and held no brief for a minimal state. This was not the last gasp of old conservatism struggling to survive. The 'free' economy needed a strong state to impose and uphold the conditions of its operations, especially in the restrictions on trade union resistance. The state also had to police the effects – most notably in the 1984–5 miners' strike, protests over the poll tax, and urban unrest, but also on a more routine basis. The strong state in turn relied on the market – and especially the ever-present threat of unemployment – as a potent source of social discipline.[21]

This dual character of the New Right is important to understanding the political realignments of the 1990s. It is also fundamental to understanding the discourses about poverty which RED was intended to rebut. Those reliant on benefit were always separated into the deserving and the undeserving poor – those who really needed help and those who were scroungers exploiting an overgenerous and insufficiently-policed system. At least for the deserving poor, benefits were generally seen as good for the individual recipients, if expensive for society as a whole. Echoing arguments from the United States, this changed. Economic dependence on 'welfare' was construed as 'dependency', a pathological moral and psychological condition created by the benefit system itself – and fostered by the libertarianism of the 1960s – in which the state was seen as a universal provider, sapping personal initiative, independence and self-respect. Benefits were bad for, rather than good for, their recipients. If this was true of individuals, it was even more true of the poor collectively: welfare spending gave rise to a 'culture of dependency'. This discourse inexorably took over the public domain. In a television documentary about poverty and unemployment, the political commentator John Cole described the 'giro culture' as 'an endemic culture of no work and reliance on benefits', characterized by a 'downward spiral of idleness, crime and erosion of the work ethic'.[22] The focus had shifted from the structural basis of poverty to the moral and cultural character of the poor themselves.

The idea of an 'underclass' was central to this shift. Townsend had himself used the term without any critical connotation to refer to different groups of the excluded poor: the elderly, disabled, chronically sick, long-term unemployed and one-parent families.

A large, and proportionately increasing, section of the population are neither part of the paid workforce nor members of the households of that workforce...The ways in which they have been denied access to paid employment, conceded incomes equivalent in value to bare subsistence, attracted specially defined low status as minority groups, and accommodated, as a result, within the social structure as a kind of modern 'underclass', need to be traced.[23]

This was a statement about the place of the poor in – and notably not outside – the overall social structure. It was free from claims about the lifestyles of the poor, and free from moral condemnation, except for the social processes which generated poverty.

In 1990, Frank Field's *Losing Out: The Emergence of Britain's Underclass* argued that the extension of citizenship rights heralded by Marshall had been reversed by the effects of Thatcherism, particularly by exclusion from work and increased reliance on means-tested benefits. Exclusion from citizenship was the mark of the underclass, which would not disappear without 'the implementation of a series of policies aimed at re-establishing full citizenship'.[24] He was critical of the growing tendency both to describe and to explain poverty in cultural terms and thus effectively blame the poor for their circumstances. He used an article by Ralf Dahrendorf as an example. Dahrendorf, like Field, had written about the underclass in terms of exclusion from citizenship: 'The existence of an underclass casts doubt on the social contract itself. It means that citizenship has become an exclusive rather than an inclusive status. Some are full citizens, some are not'.[25] But he also argued that the underclass was characterized by low educational attainment or functional illiteracy, that incomplete families were the norm rather than the exception, and that it was culturally distinct from the rest of society:

> It includes a lifestyle of laid-back sloppiness, association in changing groups and gangs, congregation around discos or the like, hostility to middle-class society, particular habits of dress, hairstyle, often drugs or at least alcohol – a style, in other words which has little in common with the values of the work society around.[26]

Field was at pains to emphasize the structural, rather than cultural, factors leading to the growth of an underclass. Unlike Dahrendorf, he insisted that the underclass remained committed to work, this being the 'cornerstone value of the whole system'; it was 'important not to lose sight of the fact that the main aim of this...group is to win a place back in society by gaining a job'.[27] But he did not deny that they were behaviourally distinct and a problem for the majority: 'the existence of an underclass tends to make our society a less civilised one in which to live', and 'it should come as little surprise that some of those who feel they have no stake in 'official' society should react in a way that demonstrates their exclusion'.[28] However, in discussing the characteristics of a system which tended to trap the poor on benefits, he did express concern about the moral consequences of benefit dependency and the erosion of initiative, and referred to the 'personal pathologies of many of the underclass, and the culture induced by poverty'.[29] Over the following years, Field moved to a much clearer view that state provision created dependency and eroded incentives to work and to save.[30]

The characterization of the underclass in cultural terms was consolidated by the intervention of the American commentator, Charles Murray. Murray's tract, *The Emerging British Underclass* was published both in the *Sunday Times*, which financed his visit to Britain in 1989, and by the right-wing think-tank, the Institute of Economic Affairs (IEA). He argued that an underclass had long existed in the United States, and was now developing in Britain. He described himself as 'a visitor from a plague area come to see if the disease is spreading'. He asked 'how contagious is the disease?'; 'is it going to spread indefinitely or is it self-containing?'. The 'disease' was cultural, spread by 'people...whose values are contaminating the life of entire neighbourhoods' – by rejecting both the work ethic and the family ethic which are central to the dominant culture.[31] Not all the poor were part of an underclass. Its existence could be diagnosed by three symptoms: 'illegitimacy, crime and drop-out from the labour force': and 'if illegitimate births are the leading indicator of an underclass and violent crime is a proxy measure of its development, the definitive proof that an underclass has arrived is that large numbers of young, healthy, low-income males choose not to take jobs'.[32]

These three factors, Murray argued, interact to produce pathological communities in which the socialization of children – especially boys – is inadequate: 'communities need families. Communities need fathers'.[33] Fathers are necessary as role models to civilize the young; but marriage and family responsibilities are necessary to civilize men, who are, without these constraints, driven to prove their masculinity in destructive ways. The benefit system feeds the growth of the underclass, by making it too easy for lone mothers to rear children, and removing the pressure on single mothers to marry. In a later account, Murray's emphasis shifted even further towards demonizing lone parenthood, and he proposed decreasing economic support for lone mothers and their children, while increasing the stigma attaching to them.[34] The policy implications were not the extension of citizenship rights, but their greater conditionality, reduction or removal.

This is, of course, exactly what happened in the United States. The Personal Responsibility and Work Opportunity Reconciliation Act of August 1996 abolished Aid to Families with Dependent Children (AFDC), replacing it with Temporary Assistance to Needy Families (TANF), in which there was no entitlement to benefits. It devolved welfare provision to individual states, but within a highly prescriptive framework underpinned by replacing federal matching funds with cash-limited block grants. Levels of grant would be cut if states failed to get people off welfare and into work: 25 per cent of all claimants should be in work by October 1997, and 50 per cent by 2002; for two-parent families, the targets were 75 per cent by 1997 and 90 per cent by 1999. For the first time since Roosevelt's New Deal, eligible claimants could be refused benefits if the cash ran out. A limit of five years was imposed on the total length of time a family could receive federal TANF funds. State plans were required to include a provision that if a family received benefit for more than two years, at least one adult in the family would have to participate in workfare-type activity. Discretion to waive this rule was permissible only where there were children under the age of one. States were required to refuse benefits to those refusing work or workfare programmes, and were to be penalized for not meeting target participation rates in work-related activities by TANF claimants. Teenage mothers would be ineligible for TANF unless attending school and living with their parents or guardians – thus seeking 'to discourage single parenthood and illegitimate births by denying entitlement to huge swathes of the US welfare system'.[35] Wisconsin was among the states which had pioneered experiments in workfare before the 1996 Act, under waiver of the federal rules. Over the ten years from 1987 to 1997, the number of claimants dropped by 60 per cent. In 1997, the Wisconsin Works or W–2 programme went state-wide. All claimants were now required to work – in unsubsidized or subsidized employment or in 'community service' jobs at below the minimum wage. Lone mothers were required to return to work when their youngest child was twelve weeks old. The Governor of Wisconsin, Tommy Thompson, who pioneered the reforms was questioned as to the morality and Christianity of a policy which separated very young babies from their mothers and led to an increased reliance on soup kitchens and emergency shelters. He replied that paying people not to work, not to get married and to have more children was unchristian, and encouraged irresponsible behaviour.[36]

Murray's description of the underclass cast it in cultural and moral terms. In the United States, the so-called underclass is largely black, so the discourse has an additional racial element. This is not so immediately present in Britain, where commentators are often at pains to point out that the victim-villains are poorly qualified white working class young people. But like earlier accounts of dangerous classes lurking at the margins of society,[37] including Marx's lumpenproletariat, it is a very clearly gendered picture. The delinquency of young men is directly criminal and anti-social, accompanied by wilful idleness and drug abuse. Young women's delinquency manifests itself in their sexual and reproductive behaviour, the imputed irresponsibility of lone parenthood. The two are connected through the assumption that lone parenting is inadequate parenting, with both forms of delinquency attributed to a failure of socialization, especially into the work ethic and a belief in marriage.

By 1992, when John Westergaard took the underclass as the subject of his presidential address to the British Sociological Association, it was clear that there were three different meanings attaching to the term: outcast poverty; the moral turpitude of the poor; and a less specific, rhetorical usage which had become common in the media. Westergaard argued, as Stuart Hall had done five years earlier,[38] that the term underclass implied a dichotomous view of society, and served to obscure inequalities among the majority:

> What the three have in common is, to start with, a postulate of the recent emergence of a significant minority of the population who are trapped, outside and below 'society at large' either by cultural depravity or economic deprivation, and an inference, whether expressed or implied, that the divide between this underclass and the great majority is increasingly *the* most salient and challenging line of division for the future, by contrast with the older divisions of class now said to be in eclipse.[39]

Westergaard went on to argue that this was exactly why the concept had such appeal. It allowed the recognition of the increasingly obvious persistence of poverty to co-exist with arguments or assumptions about the attrition of class divisions in society as a whole.

Critical social policy was more concerned to defend structural interpretations of poverty against cultural accounts which blamed the poor. The term 'underclass' became very unpopular because of its association with Murray's rhetoric of moral inferiority and social contagion. Despite its capacity to capture the ways in which aspects of poverty compound one another, it was rejected on three grounds: its imprecision; the lack of empirical evidence supporting its cultural claims; and its punitive rather than supportive policy implications.[40] Its ambiguity meant that those who used it as a description of the monstrously divisive consequences for the poor of Thatcherite policies unwittingly opened the door to a quite different discourse about the potential consequences of the poor for the comfortable majority, where redistribution gave way to retribution. The idea of the dependency culture, for whose existence there was little evidence,[41] also facilitated this switch from structural to cultural interpretations. Its central tenet was that groups of people excluded from society as a whole, and especially when dependent on benefit, would develop a distinctive set of morally undesirable attitudes and behaviours, characterized by various forms of parasitism, crime and immorality. Lister argued that 'those who invoke the development of an 'underclass' to make the case for the restoration of full citizenship rights to the poor are playing with fire'.[42] The contested meaning of the underclass gave way to a strong preference for talking about social exclusion instead: thus in RED, social exclusion is used to actively refuse the moral agenda of the underclass debate.

This has had little impact on the popular usage of the term 'underclass', especially in the media, where it continues to carry both structural and cultural meanings. Adonis and Pollard defend its use. It 'captures the essence of the class predicament for many at the bottom: a complete absence of ladders, whether basic skills, role models, education or a culture of work'.[43] It is characterized by 'unemployment and unemployability' as well as single motherhood and educational failure. The cultural interpretation wins out: 'there is no question that upbringing plays a big and probably growing role in transferring poverty and social inadequacy from one generation to the next'.[44] But as social exclusion entered public political discourse, it did so in conjunction with references to the underclass – with Blair himself repeatedly referring to an underclass excluded from the mainstream. Social exclusion is also an ambiguous term, capable of carrying both structural and cultural meanings. Thus Duffy defines social exclusion as 'a broader concept than poverty, encompassing not only low material means but the inability to participate effectively in economic, social, political and cultural life, and in some characterisations, alienation and distance from the mainstream society'.[45] Where it is used in conjunction with the underclass, social exclusion is at risk of co-option into a highly problematic discourse, MUD, whose main characteristics are these:

- It presents the underclass or socially excluded as culturally distinct from the 'mainstream'.
- It focuses on the behaviour of the poor rather than the structure of the whole society.
- It implies that benefits are bad, rather than good, for their recipients, and encourage 'dependency'.
- Inequalities among the rest of society are ignored.
- It is a gendered discourse, about idle, criminal young men and single mothers.
- Unpaid work is not acknowledged.
- Although dependency on the state is regarded as a problem, personal economic dependency – especially of women and children on men – is not. Indeed, it is seen as a civilizing influence on men.

SID: SOCIAL EXCLUSION, SOCIAL INTEGRATION AND EUROPE

The increasing public reference in Britain to social exclusion was not only the result of resistance to the underclass discourse, but the growing importance of the European Union. The origins of the European-wide emphasis on social exclusion lay in France, where the opposite of exclusion was insertion. Silver argues that social exclusion has a specific meaning in the French republican tradition, within a paradigm rooted in both Durkheimian sociology and Catholicism, and concerned with moral integration.[46] Exclusion is understood as the breakdown of the structural, cultural and moral ties which bind the individual to society, and family instability is a key concern. French discourses of exclusion, themselves contested, broadened out to a consideration of groups marginalized economically, socially, culturally and, in the case of outer suburbs, spatially; and to the fields of education, employment, housing and health. Although insertion, as the obverse of exclusion, acquired a similarly wide brief, a key measure was the introduction in 1988 of a residual benefit, the RMI (*Revenu Minimum d'Insertion*), stressing the reciprocal nature of solidarity. Recipients of RMI were required to sign a '*contrat d'insertion*' – in many cases focused on employment, but in some involving other forms of social participation negotiated with social workers, and addressing aspects of 'daily living, behaviour, and family relationships'.[47]

Silver sees moral integration as the distinctive characteristic of what she calls the 'solidarity' paradigm. Her reading of Durkheim, however, understates the extent to which he saw social integration as based in work (see Chapter 9). It also understates how far the moral integration of 'solidarity' is focused on work – with work itself perceived as having social as well as moral and economic functions. Conversely, she neglects the moral element in liberal underclass discourse (her 'specialization'), seeing the main source of integration as based in exchange. Spicker argues that although the language surrounding the RMI is more communitarian, the effect is similar to US workfare programmes – and similarly individualizes the problem of unemployment.[48]

As a result of its origins within French social policy, the concept of social exclusion at European level became, as Room put it, a curious amalgam of a liberal, Anglo-Saxon concern with poverty and a more conservative, continental concern with moral integration and social order.[49] But to suggest that there is a single discourse of social exclusion in Europe would be misleading. The multi-lingual character of the Union necessarily implies a variety of discourses, which will not map precisely on to each other, even when translated from the same documents. However, the differences run deeper than this, leading to a series of overlapping national discourses of exclusion, rather than a pan-European consensus.[50] Discursive variation is accompanied by national policy differences, as discourses of exclusion are deployed within distinct political settings – although these national policies are increasingly oriented to and implicated in contested interpretations of a European framework.

This book is not a comparative study of discourses of exclusion or of social policy across Europe, but an examination of a single national case. Its focus is the different discourses around exclusion available to New Labour, and the uses made of them. However, among those resources are the concepts of exclusion embedded in the documents and policy instruments of the European Union itself. The discourse of key European policy papers – in their English versions – reveals a much narrower understanding of exclusion than that implied by Silver's 'solidarity' model. This can be typified as a social integrationist discourse, SID, which stresses the integrative function of paid work. SID had a wider currency in British political discourse, and by using European documents as illustrative of it, I am not implying that this was the main source of the discourse, as will be clear from Chapters 3 and 4.

SID can be illustrated by the two European Commission White Papers on social and economic policy issued in 1994 – *European Social Policy* and *Growth, Competitiveness, Employment* [51] – which are widely supposed to epitomize the social, rather than purely economic, concerns of the Union. Despite the language of solidarity, these policy documents emphasize exclusion as exclusion from paid work rather than a broader view of exclusion from social participation, and prescribe integration through paid work. The terms cohesion, solidarity, integration and exclusion recur. The core concerns of both documents are economic efficiency and social cohesion: 'we are faced with the immense responsibility . . . of finding a new synthesis of the aims pursued by society (work as a factor of social integration, equality of opportunity) and the requirements of the economy (competitiveness and job creation)'.[52] The economic discussion is couched in terms of efficiency, deregulation, and the need for economic growth, while the 'social' discourse counterposes solidarity, integration and cohesion to unemployment, poverty and social exclusion. Sometimes exclusion is identified with poverty: 'with more than 52 million people in the Union living below the poverty line, social exclusion is an endemic phenomenon';[53] while the need for economic and social cohesion calls for 'solidarity . . . in the fight against social exclusion', to combat the 'poverty . . . which splits society in two'.[54] The processes of exclusion are described as 'dynamic and multi-dimensional', and linked 'not only to unemployment and/or low incomes, but also to housing conditions, levels of education and opportunities, health, discrimination, citizenship and integration in the local community'.[55] Yet although this list might appear to echo the factors identified in RED, it is notable that the terms social exclusion and exclusion from paid work are used virtually interchangeably, while a similar elision occurs between 'people' and 'workers'. A section headed 'the free movement of persons' goes on to discuss only the 'free movement of workers'. 'Promoting the Social Integration of Disabled People' discusses only training and assistance to enter the labour market. On the 'key issue of improved access to means of transport and public buildings', the Commission will 'press for the adoption of the proposed Directive on the travel conditions of *workers* with motor disabilities' (emphasis added).[56]

Since *Growth, Competitiveness, Employment* starts from a concern with unemployment, its focus on paid work is unsurprising. Few, in any case, would dispute that unemployment is a contributory factor to social exclusion, and work a factor in social integration. This, however, is not the same as treating them as synonymous – a slippage which makes difficult the exploration of their empirical connection. The assumption that social integration and participation in paid work are coterminous is particularly clear in a discussion of education and skills: 'The basic skills which are essential for *integration into society and working life* include a mastery of basic knowledge (linguistic, scientific and other knowledge), and skills of a highly technical and social nature, that is the ability to develop and act in a complex and highly technological environment, characterized, in particular, by the importance of information technologies' (emphasis added).[57] The emphasis on the importance of information technology skills is probably exaggerated even in terms of the skills needed for employment, but as a description of the skills needed for integration into society, it is an odd list. *Growth, Competitiveness, Employment* treats the absence of these skills as the cause of social exclusion – or what *European Social Policy* calls exclusion 'from the cycle of opportunities': 'The failure of education...is an increasingly important and increasingly widespread factor of marginalisation and economic and social exclusion. In the Community, 25 to 30% of young people...leave the education system without the preparation they need to become properly integrated into working life'.[58]

Working life means paid employment. Unpaid work makes only a brief appearance in these documents, and then with a view to bringing it into the market sector to create more jobs. In ruling out *ab initio* the possibility of 'a generalized reduction in working hours and job sharing' as economically inefficient, the economic White Paper says we need to 'think up new individual or collective needs which would provide new job opportunities'.[59] It proposes meeting old needs in new ways. 'Women's full integration in the labour market is expected to create jobs in the provision of services and goods not yet integrated into the market and currently being provided by either women's unpaid labour or paid informal women's labour'. Improving existing career opportunities for women will itself generate additional demand for child care. Where jobs are not created spontaneously, member states are exhorted to 'encourage growth in the employment intensive area of the care sector and of the provision of household services', and thus to 'enhance the perceived value, and therefore encourage increased skills in such sectors'.[60] The assumptions about skill and value embedded here include the view that unpaid work is unskilled. Greater recognition of unpaid work other than through market mechanisms is ruled out. The extent of unpaid work, its necessity to the maintenance of social life and human relationships, and the limits to potential marketization are underestimated, and the problems of low pay and gender segregation in the labour market ignored.[61]

In these documents, markets are not seen as benign. Markets have failings, produce unacceptable inequalities and embody short-termism, and thus require regulation, or at least management: 'only a properly managed interdependence can guarantee a positive outcome for everybody', and 'collective solidarity mechanisms' are essential to counter adverse effects.[62] This could be a prescription for a redistributive welfare state, which might therefore acknowledge and reward unpaid work, but it is not. The cost of welfare provision is seen as excessive: 'current levels of public expenditure, particularly in the social field, have become unsustainable and have used up resources which could have been channelled into productive investment'.[63] 'Solidarity' is a device for reducing the costs of social provision, not for redistribution. The forms of solidarity invoked are manifold: between those who have jobs and those who do not; between generations; between regions; between 'those who earn their income from work and those who earn their income from investments'; and between men and women, 'making it easier to reconcile family life and working life'. Notably, solidarity is not just a policy issue for member states, but a matter for individuals: it is 'the business of each citizen to practice "neighbourly solidarity"'.[64] Hutton described *Growth, Competitiveness, Employment* as the last gasp of social Europe before it was suffocated by the monetarist criteria agreed as the foundation of monetary union. But the tension between 'monetarist' and 'social' Europe, and the dominance of the former, are already apparent in the document itself. Further movement in that direction followed, as austerity measures were brought in by governments across Europe anxious to qualify for entry into the single currency – in many states provoking social unrest in response to cuts in welfare rights.

The emphasis on paid work is endemic in the financial and legal framework of the Union. As the term social exclusion gained currency in Europe, currency, in the form of European funding, attached to projects to combat it. But the rules governing the use of the Community's Structural Funds reinforce the understanding of social participation as labour market activity. The Social Fund, the main source of cash to combat exclusion, may only properly be used to fund measures directly related to the labour market, either through integration of marginal groups into it or through the promotion of equal opportunities. In practice, since funding goes to projects proposed by member states on the basis of additionality, many projects concerned with the welfare of marginal groups which are ostensibly directed to improving their labour market integration appear to have a wider brief.

The legal definition of citizenship within Europe is also biased towards paid work. Louise Ackers argues that the general emphasis on 'workers' rather than 'people' in European law produces a stratified system of citizenship in Europe.[65] Although the Maastricht Treaty declares nationals of all member states to be European citizens with the right to move and reside freely within the Union, this right does not confer equal access to social rights and benefits in the country of residence. Whereas paid workers, self-employed people and those exercizing their right to remain after ending paid employment have full social rights in their country of residence, members of their families have only derivative rights. This applies, of course, to women engaged in unpaid caring – for children or adults – who therefore do not have the same rights as paid workers. If family members and dependants can acquire social citizenship rights by proxy, non-employed persons not attached to a worker – students, disabled adults, retired people, for example – do not acquire them at all. Their right to move and reside freely within the Union is limited by the condition that they do not become a charge on the public purse of the host country. The essential point is that the emphasis on paid work as the primary means of social integration and the privileging of paid work over unpaid work has significant and gendered repercussions for citizenship status itself.

A discourse about social exclusion which focuses on integration through paid work tends to reduce the social to the economic, and simultaneously limits understanding of economic activity to market activity. If inclusion tends to shift the agenda away from equality, the focus on inclusion through paid work exacerbates this. SID thus has a number of features which distinguish it from RED and MUD:

- It narrows the definition of social exclusion/inclusion to participation in paid work.
- It squeezes out the question of why people who are not employed are consigned to poverty. Consequently, it does not, like RED, imply a reduction of poverty by an increase in benefit levels.
- It obscures the inequalities between paid workers.
- Since women are paid significantly less than men, and are far more likely to be in low-paid jobs, it obscures gender, as well as class, inequalities in the labour market.
- It erases from view the inequality between those owning the bulk of productive property and the working population.

- It is unable to address adequately the question of unpaid work in society.
- Because it ignores unpaid work and its gendered distribution, it implies an increase in women's total workload.
- It undermines the legitimacy of non-participation in paid work.

RED, SID and MUD are presented here as distinct discourses. They are, of course, ideal types. All of them posit paid work as a major factor in social integration; and all of them have a moral content. But they differ in what the excluded are seen as lacking. To oversimplify, in RED they have no money, in SID they have no work, in MUD they have no morals. In terms of Walker's broad definition of social exclusion as exclusion from social, economic, political or cultural systems, the discourses emphasize different elements – and posit different causal relationships between them. Thus both SID and MUD are narrower than RED, with SID reducing the social to the economic and substantially ignoring the political and cultural. MUD, on the other hand, emphasizes the cultural, with the economic deriving from this, while the social and political are sidelined. In reality, although there are examples which conform very closely to a particular model, much public discourse slides between them. That, indeed, is one of the reasons why a concept like social exclusion is so powerful. Not only does the multiplicity of meanings which attach to it give it wide acceptance, but it operates as a shifter between the different discourses. Like the 'underclass', 'social exclusion' can, almost unnoticed, mobilize a redistributive argument behind a cultural or integrationist one – or represent cultural or integrationist arguments as redistributive.

But there are also major differences between the discourses in their capacity to recognize, let alone valorize, unpaid work. Part of the point of Glucksmann's model of the total social organization of labour is that work, or economic activity, occurs not only within the market in the conventionally-defined economic sphere, but also outside it. To understand the shifting forms of work and the relationships within which they are embedded, the analysis cannot begin from a standpoint which privileges one particular form or site of work. Many of the problems with which politicians and policy makers now grapple can be seen in terms of the breakdown of a historical organization of labour in which men had primary responsibility for paid work and women primary responsibility for unpaid domestic work, albeit often combining this with some paid employment. SID barely acknowledges non-market work at all, or treats it as a residual form. The unpaid work of child care, for example, is either to be drawn into the market, or squeezed into the spaces around paid employment. Unpaid work is addressed solely from the standpoint of the market. This is slightly less true of MUD, which, while deploying the idea of 'dependency' in its refusal to valorize unpaid work, simultaneously complains of the consequences of inadequate parenting. Yet this contradiction is itself masked by the fact that parenting is not understood as work. In general, the emphasis on paid work as a vehicle of inclusion, and the construction of exclusion as non-employment, inherently privileges market activity: it does not address either work, or social integration, in terms of the total social organization of labour.

In the following chapters, I shall argue that the developing discourse of New Labour shifted it significantly away from RED towards an inconsistent combination of SID and MUD. The impossibility of adequately acknowledging unpaid labour from this standpoint produces deep contradictions between different elements of policy, most especially between the rediscovery of community and the attempt to draw everyone into paid work through the New Deal or welfare to work programmes. This contradiction can be resolved only by a rightward shift to a reformulation of the Thatcherite free economy-strong state dyad in terms of community, or by a leftward shift towards a RED agenda. A central political question for Labour's first term in office will be how it negotiates between the different available discourses of social exclusion, and how, especially through the Social Exclusion Unit, it translates them into policy. Their performance will be judged not only on whether they deliver 'social inclusion', but what kind of inclusion they deliver, for whom, and on what terms. The following chapters outline the emergence of the new political discourse, and their implications for delivering inclusion.

2 From Social Justice to Social Cohesion

NEW LABOUR, NEW THINK-TANKS

One of the less remarked privatizations of the 1980s was the privatization of policy-making. The Thatcher era was marked by an increasing reliance on think-tanks ostensibly independent of the Conservative Party, notably the Adam Smith Institute (founded in 1979), the Centre for Policy Studies (1974), the Social Affairs Unit (1980) as well as the longer-established Institute of Economic Affairs (1957). The growth of these nominally independent organizations, at least some of which had charitable status, was accompanied by the abolition of the government's own think-tank, the Central Policy Review Staffs (CPRS). The role of outside organizations was reinforced by cuts to the statistical and research base. The Royal Commission on the Distribution of Income and Wealth was abolished in 1979, and the Rayner Review of the Government Statistical Services in 1980 led to substantial staff losses. Much statistical work which might previously have been carried out by government statisticians was undertaken by policy-oriented research institutes inside and outside academia and by specialist pressure groups, aided by the spread of computer technology.

Opposition parties are necessarily dependent on outside bodies for investigating policy options since they do not have access to the civil service. Think-tanks and surrounding networks played a central role in the recasting of Labour's policies in the 1990s, with the Institute for Public Policy Research (IPPR), Demos and Nexus joining the Fabian Society as semi-detached organizations. They provided a resource for politicians in several senses. As Thompson and du Gay note, think-tanks play a key role in mediating between academic and political domains.[1] They also enable public response to policy options to be tested, without directly implicating – or at least without committing – the party itself. But the mediating role is also a gate-keeping one. The more think-tanks are central to the policy process, the more research and discussion must be channelled through them if it is to have an effect on policy. Moreover think-tanks and their staff are neither elected nor accountable, and Labour's think-tanks and the networks around them, while sometimes claiming openness, in fact had at their core a small, self-selected, largely metropolitan and disproportionately male elite. The concentration of influence was exacerbated by the increasing frequency of media-hyped publication launches and conferences, invariably London-based.

The four organizations most important to Labour in the run-up to the 1997 election were very different in character. The Fabian Society, founded in 1884, was involved in the original formation of the Labour Party and retains this constitutional link. It is one of the socialist societies (alongside the Christian Socialist Movement) with voting rights at the Party Conference and representation on the National Executive Committee. It has an individual membership structure (with 5000 members in 1997) as well as some local groups, runs discussions and conferences, and produces a quarterly magazine, *Fabian Review*, and a series of reports and pamphlets. Many pamphlets are written by Labour MPs and sometimes merely reproduce their speeches, such as Blair's *Socialism* and Mandelson's *Labour's next steps: tackling social exclusion*. A large proportion of Labour MPs are also members of the Fabian Society – 181 in May 1997, including 63 of the 88 Ministers and all but two of the 22 members of the Cabinet. But although the Society is clearly an old Labour institution, it became increasingly New Labour in style and content. Its publicity material declared it to be 'putting the new into new Labour', and its goal to 'take new Labour's modernization project into the new millennium'. Stephen Twigg was General Secretary for the year before he famously and unexpectedly defeated Michael Portillo in Enfield South. His valedictory contribution to *Fabian Review* noted that 'welfare reform' was a long-standing priority of the Society – but asked, in terms rather less consistent with this history, 'what policies should be adopted to fulfil our mission to reduce poverty without requiring further increases in public spending? A successful welfare to work programme holds the key to so much of what we are seeking to achieve'.[2]

Demos, in contrast, was created in 1993 by Geoff Mulgan and Martin Jacques. In part, this was a replacement of Jacques' 'New Times' project which developed out of his effective hijacking of *Marxism Today* from the Communist Party of Great Britain in the 1980s. Jacques remained on the advisory council of Demos alongside a range of prominent individuals from academia, the media and industry (including Douglas Hague, previously an adviser to Margaret Thatcher), but by 1996 Mulgan was sole Director. By 1997, Demos had grown from 'a charity with £5000 to a £600 000-a-year...policy production line',[3] while Mulgan had been co-opted to Blair's advisory team. Jacques, in contrast, was openly critical of New Labour. Unlike many prominent 'policy wonks' Mulgan did not stand for Parliament, but joined the ranks of unelected, unaccountable advisers to the Blair Government. Within days of the election he was working half-time in the Prime Minister's Office as an adviser on the welfare to work programme, and by the summer was acknowledged as the key intellectual influence behind the Social Exclusion Unit. Mulgan's own views are discussed below in Chapter 7. The output of Demos, including a journal, *Demos Quarterly*, and free-standing reports, is very variable both in topic and quality. Its professed intention to 'think the unthinkable' led to a certain amount of mockery, especially for a proposal for limited-term marriages, and mention of re-introducing the stocks, while one of the *New Statesman*'s weekly competitions invited wacky ideas worthy of Demos. Satirical dismissal, however, is no more appropriate in the case of Demos than it was with the Adam Smith Institute (ASI) in the early eighties. Many of the ideas emanating from the ASI which seemed absurd at the time found their way into Thatcher's policies. But while the ASI's radical policies were defined against collectivism and socialism, and thus primarily against Labour, for Demos the 'other' is not Thatcherism, but social democracy – manifest most clearly in John Gray's *After Social Democracy* (see Chapter 5) – and its unthinkable thoughts those unthinkable by the left.

Nexus was set up in May 1996 by David Halpern and Neal Lawson, Managing Editor of *Renewal*. *Renewal* was launched in 1993 as a journal of New Labour politics aimed at 'a modernising project for British society' that goes beyond 'dropping the burden of past policies'. Nexus was a loose network of individuals and groups, some jockeying for influence in the power structure of the emergent new era. The inaugural seminar in November 1996 was addressed by Tony Blair, and sponsored by the Deloitte and Touche Consulting Group. Five months later, a one-day conference at the London School of Economics, organized in conjunction with the *Guardian*, was attended by over a thousand people. It involved a range of organizations including the Fabian Society, Demos, the IPPR, Charter 88, the Liberal Democrat Party and the *New Statesman* – a magazine which, under the ownership of Geoffrey Robinson (subsequently appointed Paymaster General) and the editorial hand of Ian Hargreaves from May 1996, had become increasingly Blairite. Tony Giddens, in his new role as Director of LSE, welcomed the conference, as 'the largest and most inclusive of its kind'. Its title was 'Passing the Torch' – meaning, as Helena Kennedy explained, that as the New Right political project was at an end, it was time for them to hand over to the centre-left. This formulation emphasized the continuity of the Nexus project with the New Right as much as its difference from them. Among the plenary speakers were Tony Blair, John Gray and Roy Jenkins, whose apparent suggestion of a potential merger between Labour and the Liberal Democrats created a small stir in the media. Jenkins spoke of the need to heal the split in the centre-left which had existed since 1981, but made no apology for having caused it; and of the need to loosen the ties between parties and party funders, meaning Labour and the unions. Gray tried to assimilate the conference to his own position, asserting that 'we all reject the "levelling collectivism" of the old left' although the responses of audiences in smaller sessions during the day suggested a widespread commitment to the redistribution Gray rejected. Blair's enthusiasm for modernization and the possibilities of information technology led him to welcome Nexus as the first virtual think-tank: the Joseph Rowntree Reform Trust had funded the facilities for electronic debate, based on extensive web-site and e-mail conferencing. The 'inclusive' possibilities of this might overcome the metropolitan bias of other think-tanks, but introduced another division based on access to the new technology.

The IPPR was founded in 1988 at the instigation of Neil Kinnock, with the support of Clive Hollick who received a peerage in 1991. The professed aim of the IPPR was to 'provide an alternative to the free market think tanks' and to 'contribute to public understanding of social, economic and political questions through research, discussion and publication'. By 1996, its annual turnover was £1 326 438, most of which came from donations – from individuals, trade unions, charitable foundations and private sector corporations. Although formally separate, the IPPR was effectively an in-house policy unit, whose closeness to Labour is demonstrated by the careers of its key personnel. Patricia Hewitt, formerly Kinnock's Press Secretary and Policy Co-ordinator, and from 1997 MP for Leicester East, was Deputy Director until 1994; she was replaced by Anna Coote, who became special adviser to Harriet Harman in her role as Minister for Women. Hewitt remains on the board of trustees. *New Economy*, the IPPR's quarterly journal launched in 1993, was edited by their Senior Economist Dan Corry – head of the Labour Party economic secretariat from 1989–92, and appointed Special Adviser to Margaret Beckett in 1997. David Miliband, who acted as Secretary to the Commission on Social Justice, left the IPPR in 1994 to become Blair's Chief Adviser, and, in 1997, head of the No. 10 Policy Unit. Tessa Blackstone, formerly Chair of the IPPR's trustees became Minister of State for Education in 1997.

THE COMMISSION ON SOCIAL JUSTICE

The Commission on Social Justice, whose work was carried out through the IPPR, was initiated by John Smith after the 1992 election defeat. It was chaired by Sir Gordon Borrie QC, formerly Director General of the Office of Fair Trading, with Patricia Hewitt as Deputy Chair. The terms of reference of the Commission were: to consider the principles of social justice and their application to the economic well-being of individuals and the community; to examine the relationship between social justice and other goals, including economic competitiveness and prosperity; to probe the changes in social and economic life over the last fifty years, and the failure of public policy to reflect them adequately; and to survey the changes that are likely in the foreseeable future, and the demands they will place on government; to analyse public policies, particularly in the fields of employment, taxation and social welfare, which could enable every individual to live free from want and to enjoy the fullest possible social and economic opportunities; and to examine the contribution which such policies could make to the creation of a fairer and more just society. This was summarized by the *New Statesman* as the 'Herculean task of spring-cleaning the left-wing mind'.[4] Although the Commission was more broadly representative than much think-tank activity, public-service and trade-union representation was very thin.[5] Nor did it include or consult directly representatives of the poor or unemployed. The Transport and General Workers Union commissioned its own report, *In Place of Fear*, and a Citizens' Commission was set up, to articulate user views, reporting as *It's Our Welfare*.[6]

The final report, *Social Justice: Strategies for National Renewal*, was, like the output of Demos, significant not only for its substantive policy implications, but for its overt political positioning. It reiterated repeatedly the interdependence, rather than opposition, between economic efficiency and social cohesion or social justice. The insistence on this connection was part of the general characterization of New Labour as a 'third way' distanced both from the free market and socialism, or, increasingly, social democracy. *Social Justice* articulated this in terms of a three-fold classification of deregulators, levellers and investors, in which both deregulators and levellers were accused of misunderstanding the nature of modern capitalism and setting up a false choice between collective action and market dynamism. Deregulators espoused a free market, but pursued policies which resulted in political centralization and the destruction of intermediate institutions between individuals and the market or the state. Levellers were accused of being 'concerned with the distribution of wealth to the neglect of its production', ignoring the relationship between the two, and focusing primarily on the role and level of social security benefits. The castigation of the levellers' strategy for social justice as 'based primarily on redistributing wealth and incomes, *rather than* trying to increase opportunities and compete in world markets'[7] rests, like much else in the report and in later New Labour rhetoric, on a (deliberately) false antithesis. It is not only, as Townsend described it, a grotesque caricature of social democratic commitment to redistribution.[8] It is also the reverse of the truth about socialism: the connection between social relations of production and the distribution of the social product is fundamental to the case for social ownership, a connection ignored in arguments that ownership is unimportant. But the misrepresentation was a necessary foil to the construction of an alternative position, centred on equality of opportunity; Hewitt was explicit that its purpose was to distinguish New Labour from old Labour.[9] Investors, the good guys, believed in combining 'the ethics of community with the dynamics of a market economy', and that 'the extension of economic opportunity' was the basis of both economic prosperity and social justice.[10] They applied the key values of the postwar welfare state to the modern world. But in representing these values as opportunity, security and responsibility, *Social Justice* transformed the meaning of redistribution, and introduced another false antithesis on the way: 'Unlike the Deregulators, who would use insecurity as the spur to change, the Investors insist on security as the foundation of change; but unlike the Levellers, the Investors achieve security by redistributing opportunities rather than just redistributing income'.[11] This formula of redistributing opportunities, reiterated by Hewitt to the Commons Social Security Committee, became central to New Labour's ideology.

The character of the Borrie report underlines the point made forcibly by Paul Andersen and Nyta Mann that the making of New Labour substantially predated Blair's leadership, and that he only took up where Kinnock and Smith left off.[12] Themes and phrases which recur in subsequent rhetoric and policy run through the report: the interdependence of economic efficiency and social justice; the need for strong communities; insecurity of employment resulting from global-ization; the need for a welfare state to offer 'a hand-up, not just a hand-out'. Lifelong learning, individual learning accounts, and graduate repayment of tuition fees are floated, as are Citizens' Service, an environmental task force, and welfare to work. The Australian JET (Jobs, Education, Training) scheme for lone parents receives approval.[13] One commentator praised the report for 'putting social exclusion back at the centre of the political agenda', expressing enthusiasm for its treatment of unpaid work which, unlike the Rown-tree and Dahrendorf reports, thereby put women at the centre of its arguments.[14] The language of social exclusion, inclusion and cohesion does suffuse the report, in ways uncomfortably poised between RED and SID, while the treatment of unpaid work reveals the contradiction between the two. But the apparent emphasis on unpaid work, and the attempt to recognize its moral and economic worth, is undercut by the treatment of paid work as the primary and proper mode of social inclusion and integration.

Social exclusion is used in the broad, RED, sense of exclusion from economic, social and political participation as a result of poverty. Many of these references occur in the context of attacks on the levellers' commitment to redistribution: they are criticized for arguing that 'we cannot rely on paid work to haul the poor out of poverty' and that 'substantial resources will have to be redistributed to prevent a large minority of people being completely excluded from social parti-cipation'.[15] Other references commit the authors to the same inter-pretation. They complain that 'social and economic *exclusion* – from work, transport, politics, education, housing, leisure facilities – is an increasingly obvious and depressing feature of life in many parts of the UK'.[16] The case against exclusion is cast in terms of its consequences for the wider society: it undermines social cohesion, and in so doing, imposes an economic cost. It is a utilitarian, rather than a moral, argument. Thus 'social cohesion has economic value', and 'social division has economic cost', while 'the social exclusion of between a tenth and a third of citizens will impose long-term "clean-up" costs'.[17] The 'virtuous circle of social inclusion' is contrasted with the 'vicious circle of exclusion and division'. The 'vision of a more inclusive, productive and cohesive society' is one where 'rights carry responsib-ilities, and individuals have the chance to realise their potential'.[18]

There is little doubt that paid work is seen as the main vehicle of inclusion or integration. Reduction of long-term unemployment – or, oddly, a 'fair and efficient distribution of unemployment and employment' – is necessary for paid work to 'maintain its function as a mechanism of social integration'; and 'attachment to the labour market...is the key to breaking the vicious cycle of long-term unemployment and social exclusion'.[19] Of course, employment and full employment are important within the RED model; involuntary unemployment is a major cause of poverty. The argument here is much stronger. The importance of employment lies in an integrative function over and above the provision of an income. Discussions of Japan and Belgium underline this argument in different ways. Japan, the authors say, permits and encourages 'apparent overstaffing', using employment as 'a highly efficient means of social integration, because they know that nothing is more expensive than social disintegration'[20] – although it is doubtful whether they would use this argument to defend overstaffing in the old communist economies, where the practice was universally condemned by Western economists as inefficient. Conversely, a Belgian experiment with a version of Citizen's Income is interpreted by the Commission as causing social exclusion, as 'levels of participation in education and training may actually have fallen' following the introduction of an unconditional benefit for young people.[21] The (possible) drop in labour market participation, or preparation for it, is equated with a rise in social exclusion.

If everyone must be included, then everyone must work. The report argues (rightly) that official measures understate unemployment, and that many early-retired and disabled people would like to work. It also observes that most lone parents on income support would 'prefer employment now or in the future'.[22] (While even this ignores the range of choices within which such preferences were expressed, it is more accurate than the later claim by Harriet Harman that 'most lone parents want to work'.) An alternative category is used, of 'unemployment and economic inactivity', incorporating all those of working age who are not in paid work. This underpins proposals that an availability-for-work test should be applied to lone parents of school-aged children, and to the partners of unemployed men.

Where social integration is understood to mean labour market attachment, with those outside the paid workforce defined as socially excluded, unpaid work is thereby marginalized. Yet *Social Justice* stresses the importance of unpaid work. The Commission acknowledges that seven million people have caring responsibilities for ill or disabled relatives and neighbours, and recognizes the importance of parenting. Despite the definition of the non-employed as economically inactive, such work is argued to have economic, not merely social, worth: 'the economic and social value of good-quality parenting has been neglected for too long. At the heart of a secure family is the unpaid work of parents and other carers which needs to be recognised in family-friendly policies at the work place and in the organisation of the welfare state'. And since 'our society and our economy would not function without the unpaid work which millions of people do in their families and communities', this must in future be recognized within employment policy and a new social security system.[23] Such claims fit more easily with RED than with SID, for their implication is a redistribution of resources towards those engaged in work which is currently unpaid, and thus a weakening of the link between paid employment and economic resources. And there are some suggestions which point in this direction: that a 'carers' insurance' should be provided within the benefit system; that eligibility for carer's benefit should be independent of the benefit status of the recipient of care; that the level of the Invalid Care Allowance should be raised to the same level as Unemployment Benefit (since replaced by the Jobseeker's Allowance). The case for a Participation Income, conditional on 'active citizenship', as opposed to an unconditional Citizen's Income, is considered: this 'could go a long way towards eliminating means-testing, recognising the value of parents' and carers' unpaid work and encouraging people to take up employment, education or training'.[24] To finance this at an adequate level, however, would mean increases in taxation. But while the welfare state is seen on the one hand as an essentially redistributive mechanism through which unpaid work could be recognized, on the other hand, its job is to get people off welfare. In yet another false antithesis, it must be transformed 'from a safety net in times of trouble to a springboard for economic opportunity'. High social security spending is a 'sign of economic underperformance, not social success'.[25]

Recognizing the value of unpaid work, indeed, means not recognizing its full economic value, since its cheapness is its main recommendation. Thus, for example, 'as the need for long-term care increases, it will make good economic, as well as social, sense to acknowledge the value of carers' work within the social security system rather than trying to meet the full costs of professional care'.[26] There are also proposals to extend the amount of unpaid work in other areas, notably in schools – using volunteers who would 'not require the same level of either training or salary' as teachers or other workers. Volunteers might give one-to-one help to children having difficulty with basic reading and writing (those children whom, it might be thought, need most skilled and professional help), and contribute to care in the community, playgroups and holiday schemes or environmental work as well as 'mentoring in children's homes and residential long-term care homes, assisting in health service delivery, developing educational programmes for prisoners and making dangerous public places safer'. Where volunteers are not seconded by employers, they should receive a 'fair and realistic sum', perhaps £50 per week plus lunch and expenses; retired volunteers would need only expenses.[27] The argument that work is intrinsically integrating allows this mobilization of cheap or free labour to be presented as in the interests of the volunteers themselves. The danger of such schemes – beyond their intrinsically exploitative nature – is that they reduce the demand for labour in terms of proper jobs which can deliver not only inclusion through work, but inclusion through access to a living wage. The general emphasis in the report on supply-side factors as causes of unemployment serves to obscure this point.

The contradiction inherent in the treatment of paid and unpaid work in *Social Justice* can be understood in terms of a residual tension between SID and RED. The discussion of unpaid work is unsatisfactory, but it is there, and its presence reveals the weaknesses of the dominant argument, in which paid work and economic participation are seen as synonymous, and those outside the paid workforce are described as socially excluded. The persistence of RED is visible too in a continued concern with inequalities within and beyond the labour market – a concern which calls into question the assertion that paid employment necessarily results in social integration. The UK is described as 'a society corrupted by inequities of class, which intersect with those of gender, race and disability', even though 'the nature of those inequities, and their implications, are changing'.[28] Inequalities of income are reflected in inequalities of health, while inequalities in earnings in 1994 were greater than at any time since 1886. Occupational segregation persists (although men are seen as the 'real victims' of economic restructuring, and vigorous effort is recommended to 'pull down the barriers which keep men out of "women's jobs"').[29] Full-time workers in Britain work longer than elsewhere in the European Union, with (prior to the introduction of the Working Time directive under the auspices of European health and safety legislation in 1996) no restrictions on working hours. Many workers in the UK are 'forced by inadequate basic wages into long hours of overtime in order to maintain a decent income'.[30] The most effective way out of poverty for most two-parent families is to have two earners –

although such households are described as 'work-rich' rather than overworked.

The report has therefore to concede that attachment to the labour market under such conditions does not necessarily deliver *social* inclusion. The virtues of paid work are qualified: 'Paid work is – or should be – a route to an adequate income, social networks and personal fulfilment. Too often it is none of these things.'[31] Workers may find it difficult to sustain personal relationships and social contacts outside the workplace when 'some employers... demand hours of work which are not only damaging to health and safety but disastrous for family life'.[32] And 'if employment is divided between very highly-paid jobs for some, and very low-paid jobs for others, the problems of social division and exclusion will only be intensified'.[33] The Commission recommends the introduction of a minimum wage. It also endorses the importance of 'inclusive' companies, where the 'varying interests of employees, suppliers, shareholders and the local community' are 'given appropriate weight and consideration to the benefit of all concerned'.[34] Like most advocacy of stakeholding, this fudges the question of potential conflicts, rather than mere differences, of interest, and begs the question of who decides what is 'appropriate'.

Social Justice is consistent with RED in its recognition of unpaid work, and of the inequalities among paid workers and their consequences. These conflict with the more prominent emphasis on inclusion through paid work, more typical of SID, so that there is a gap between the diagnosis of the problem and the prescription for its solution. These contradictions are not resolved. However, the move towards their resolution depends on the reconstruction of redistribution as the redistribution of opportunities – and on a separation between just and unjust inequalities: 'although not all inequalities are unjust... unjust inequalities should be reduced and where possible eliminated'.[35] Inequality is chiefly a problem because, if too extreme, it is disruptive of social cohesion. Thus inclusion is given precedence over equality, and SID takes precedence over RED.

By the time the Borrie report was published on 24 October 1994 – with the obligatory launch event and resulting media coverage – Smith was dead and Blair was established as the new leader of the Labour Party. Blair's promotional statement on the back cover said it would 'inform Labour's policy making and provide the basis for a vital national debate about the future of work and welfare', and described it as 'essential reading for everyone who wants a new way forward for our country'. He also made clear the direction in which the residual tensions in the report would be resolved: 'Social Justice can be extended within existing levels of spending...A successful economic policy combined with effective modern welfare would mean a reduction in the benefit bill'. The RED response was given by Townsend: 'I did not dream that the Commission...would neglect the principles of equality, solidarity, minimum sufficiency, public service, public ownership, affordability and internationalism to the extent that it does'. A *Guardian* leader also complained that 'not nearly enough is done to reverse Britain's inequalities. Just because Labour wants to drop its tax and spend image is no reason for Borrie to ignore justice'. Frank Field, with distinct echoes of MUD, said that he hoped the party would be more radical than the Commission and would 'see that self-improvement has to be the cornerstone for any welfare reform'.[36] But public discussion of the report was short-lived. As a focus of discussion in the Party itself, it was sidelined by the debate over Clause IV, while as a castigation of the state of the nation, it was overtaken by the publication of the Rowntree report.

AN INQUIRY INTO INCOME AND WEALTH

The report of the Joseph Rowntree Foundation Inquiry into Income and Wealth, chaired by Sir Peter Barclay, was published in February 1995. The membership of the Inquiry Group included representatives of the voluntary and public sectors as well as business and academia, and was not confined to the diaspora of New Labour.[37] The remit of the Inquiry was twofold: to consider evidence on matters relating to living standards, income and personal wealth; and to make recommendations for changes in policy and practices where appropriate. Had Thatcher not abolished the Royal Commission on Income and Wealth, the first part of the investigation would not have been necessary, as the relevant information would already have been not only available in the public domain, but synthesized. In reality, the project drew on scattered official and unofficial sources, and on a special research programme established by the Foundation.

The report was in two parts. The first was a summary of findings, with policy recommendations; the second a more technical presentation of evidence, edited by John Hills – who in 1997 became Director of the Centre for the Analysis of Social Exclusion at LSE. The key findings were: that the income gap between rich and poor increased rapidly between 1977 and 1990; that this increase was exceptional internationally, and had multiple causes, in rising unemployment, widening wage differentials, decreasing benefits and a more regressive taxation system; that some geographical areas and some groups in the population – including ethnic minorities – were particularly adversely affected; and that inequalities in wealth had stopped declining. Rising inequality was argued to be damaging both to the social fabric and to economic efficiency. Proposals for change emphasized more active labour market measures, including direct employment, subsidies to employers, and some combination of a minimum wage and/or extended in-work benefits. Other recommendations were: increases in benefit levels, including pensions, and changes in the benefit regime in a more generous direction to ease the transition to work; future changes in the taxation system to favour those on lower earnings; increased housing subsidies and lower rents; and special measures to revitalize marginalized areas. There is, then, a redistributive agenda which, while aiming to tackle unemployment through a welfare to work strategy, also accepts the necessity for a more generous benefit system.

Widespread media attention gave the report influence far beyond its readership. Three aspects are particularly relevant to the present argument. First, although the rhetoric of inclusion and exclusion does not override the concern with inequality, this report is also concerned primarily with the dichotomous division between the bottom 20–30 per cent of the population and the rest. It is not inequality *per se* which is the target of criticism. Three principal aims of social policy are defined: meeting basic needs; preventing exclusion; and establishing opportunities and incentives so that people can make the greatest possible contribution to society. Even widening inequality might be justifiable, the report says, if its effects were to increase growth and make the poorest better off, but this has not happened. The bottom 20–30 per cent have become poorer, not just in relative terms, but in many cases absolutely. The report is unequivocal that 'the living standards and life opportunities of the poorest...are simply unacceptably low in a society as rich as ours',[38] and this becomes the central theme.

Secondly, the attempt to persuade the reader that inequality is an important issue is couched in terms of economic efficiency and social cohesion. A strong case can be made that the most morally offensive aspect of inequality is its consequences for the poorest, and that addressing the increased poverty that has resulted from Thatcherism should be the highest political priority. The Inquiry does not do this, but argues in more utilitarian terms: 'our prime concern is not with morality. Rather, we are concerned with ... overall *social* effects, which impact on the whole community ... and with the long-term *economic* costs of what has happened'.[39] Concern for vulnerable individuals is linked to the consequences for the non-poor: 'Our central concern is with the failure of the poorest 20–30 per cent of the population to benefit from recent economic growth – not just out of concern for those directly affected, but also because of the damage done to the overall social fabric, and to the economy when a substantial group has no stake in its performance.'[40] Despite calling for benefits to be increased by more than inflation, the report also argues that redistribution (or 'compensation' of those who are the losers from social and economic change) should not be such as to reduce levels of economic activity.

Again, the intrinsic link between social cohesion and economic performance is emphasized: 'increasing inequality, by damaging social solidarity, fostering the "them and us" mentality, and excluding some from the benefits of growth, damages the long-term health of the economy'.[41] The economic costs are both direct and indirect: lost production and benefit costs, but also costs of policing the consequences of unemployment and exclusion, crime and disorder. And although the bulk of the report is measured in tone and careful to demonstrate the various causes of poverty and the different groups affected, the real threat to social cohesion is portrayed as unemployed young men. In various forms of social disorder, 'the inflammable material has been the same: groups of disaffected young men with no ... stake in society or ... economy'.[42]

Thirdly, although the report purports to be about income and wealth, it deals almost exclusively with income. Wealth merits four lines in the seven-page summary, and roughly three per cent of the total text. The division between the top 1 per cent or 10 per cent of the population and everyone else is thoroughly obscured. Although the brief discussion points out that forms of wealth differ across the population, with cash most common for the least wealthy, residential property for the middle groups, and shares and land for the richest, the implications of this are ignored. Nor are figures given for the concentration of different forms of wealth, which would show that wealth in the form of land and productive property is concentrated in very few hands. The division between the very rich and the rest of society is not, apparently, seen as a threat to social cohesion, nor as implicated in the plight of the poorest.

THE DAHRENDORF REPORT

The Liberal Democrats' venture into the future was on a much smaller scale than either the Borrie Commission or the Rowntree Inquiry. The Commission on Wealth Creation and Social Cohesion was initiated by Paddy Ashdown and chaired by Ralf (by then Lord) Dahrendorf and reported in July 1995. It had only eight members, including David Marquand, Frank Field and Will Hutton; there was no representation from the public sector or from trade unions, and only one woman.[43] The report, which makes direct reference to both Borrie and Rowntree, as well as to *Growth, Competitiveness, Employment*, is explicit about its participation in the creation of a new political discourse centred around inclusion and exclusion. These are presented as matters for concern primarily because of their consequences for social order. The insistence on paid work as the means of inclusion and integration is unequivocal, and the neglect of unpaid work absolute. But there is a significant undertow of a broader idea of social exclusion, in which the counter-concept is citizenship. There are also elements which are more radical than RED, notably a more critical approach to what constitutes wealth. This is hardly a green document, since it does not eschew economic growth; but it does question the relationship between growth and cohesion, and insist that growth must be both ecologically and socially sustainable. Its political location is also reflected in its emphasis on the importance of liberty, and the dangers of repressive authoritarianism.

The self-conscious attempt to establish a 'vocabulary...for change' rests on the recognition that 'the language in which political debate ...is conducted both reflects and determines approaches to action'.[44] Social cohesion, inclusion and stakeholding are key terms. The definition of social cohesion rests both on economic integration – through 'opportunities' – and on moral consensus: a cohesive society is one 'which offers opportunities to all its members within a framework of accepted values and institutions'. It is the social equivalent of environmental sustainability. The alternative is a breakdown of the social order, again in both economic and moral terms, described as 'disarray' – an odd term, which conjures up images of untidiness rather than social collapse. But 'exclusion, disruptive inequalities, fracturing of ethnic, religious or other groups, and the threat of anomy, of a general dissipation of values and the consequent dissolution of structures, are all forms of disarray'.[45]

Inclusion describes the cohesive society. It is set in opposition to equality, and defined in terms of access to opportunities:

> The best concept which we have found to describe an economy and a society based on social cohesion is that of *inclusion*. An economy – a society – which excludes significant numbers from its opportunities may make some very rich but it cannot be called prosperous; it has failed to generate the kind of wealth which leads to general well-being. People who are or feel excluded detract from the wealth of the nation, both in the sense that they cannot contribute, and in that of absorbing unproductive social energies as well as welfare benefits. Our concern is not with inequality as such, but with privilege, and with lack of access to opportunities, to the labour market, to civil society, to political participation. Thus inclusion does not mean equality; it means citizenship.[46]

The use of citizenship as synonymous with inclusion and thus the opposite of exclusion recalls Marshall. But commitment to the social and economic rights of a Marshallian or RED model is withheld: this is 'a matter for debate', in a way that civil and political rights are not.[47] This formulation does not even demand equality of opportunity: merely that not all opportunity (to do what?) should be denied. It is implied, rather romantically, that greater equality of opportunity is something which previously existed and has been lost: 'people no longer live in the same universe of opportunity'.[48] Opposition to RED was confirmed by Dahrendorf's speech in the House of Lords, where he commented on the Borrie report that references to justice suggested redistribution. In contrast, this report 'accepts a wide range of inequality as long as every citizen is on board'. He went on:

> What matters is not equality but inclusion. The excluded – the underclass, many of the young, certain single mothers and some members of ethnic minorities – present us with a threatening problem. Their predicament is morally unacceptable. It also demonstrates that we are not living up to the professed values of a civilised society. Can we be surprised if more and more people do not take these values seriously and violate them at will?[49]

If 'inequality as such' is unimportant – to the extent that relevance of the conventional measure of overall economic inequality, the gini coefficient, is questioned – actually existing inequalities are an issue. A report appearing five months after Rowntree could hardly deny this. Rising inequality is a threat to cohesion, since 'widening income differentials result in a serious disjunction in the commitment of different groups to the values and institutions of society'.[50] This is true at both ends of society. Privilege, as well as exclusion, is a problem, and the two are related. If 'inequality...becomes relevant for a decent civilised society only if and when it affects people's citizenship rights', this occurs both when some are excluded from 'the universe of opportunity', and when some are so wealthy that they are able to deny others 'full economic, social and political participation'.[51] This focus on the exclusivity of a privileged elite, as well as the exclusion of the underprivileged, is characteristic of Will Hutton.

The issue of commitment, however, underlines the fact that social cohesion is seen as resting on common values. The problem of an excluded class is that it creates an 'insecure and fractured society with fewer and fewer shared values and common interests'. Again, the image of a more cohesive past is evoked. The nature of the values and interests which were, are or should be held in common is generally unspecified, although the values include trust, co-operation, reciprocity and an ethic of public service. In an inclusive society, commitment to values and institutions is demonstrated by individual members, who have both rights and obligations. Social cohesion requires that all citizens share 'a basic common status', but also 'a sense of belonging,...civic pride, and...participation in common concerns of a public nature'.[52] Inclusion is not merely a right or a status, but something which must be actively performed – although the problem of how the public, common concerns come to be accepted or imposed as such is not addressed. The idea of active citizenship – promoted by Douglas Hurd during the 1980s – is fundamental here, as in Borrie. In a stakeholder society, not only individuals, but 'companies, organizations and communities are linked to common purposes'.[53]

The emphasis on common values and civic commitment, a central communitarian theme discussed further in Chapter 5, is bound up with the fact that exclusion undermines order. The excluded are a problem because they impose costs on the whole of society: 'those who are marginalised have less of a stake in society and its values; their proclivity to criminal behaviour is almost bound to increase'.[54] In terms consistent with Field's earlier comments on the underclass, and with MUD, the report argues that 'a society which allows the exclusion of even a small section of its citizens...cannot be surprised if those who are excluded do not obey the law. Worse, such reactions are infectious'.[55] The group alluded to here is, of course, unemployed young men; women are merely invisible. The discourse is overtly gendered, since 'men between the ages of 16 and 25 are responsible for the bulk of violations of the law';[56] and this has consequences for the treatment of work.

The problem of exclusion is, in the end, construed in terms of male unemployment, and social integration effected by paid work. The statement that 'significant numbers of people lose their hold on the labour market, then on social and political participation in their community' does not overtly refer only to men. However, while the authors are concerned that 'one in four adult men are either unemployed or economically inactive',[57] there is no corresponding discussion of female unemployment, nor of the different ways in which women might negotiate inclusion or suffer exclusion. The decline of full-time, tenured work is seen as a central problem, with no comment on the fact that full-time paid employment has only been typical for men, and tenured work largely for middle-class men. 'Work' means paid work, and is integrative: 'Work and activity provide the crucial link between the needs of a competitive economy in a globalising market and the requirements of individual and social well-being. Work is not only a source of income, and thus of the ability to save and to spend, but also of self-respect, and more, of the integration of individuals into society.'[58] The firm is therefore a crucial institution in maintaining social cohesion, as well as in wealth creation. A form of Citizen's Income is recommended for those in employment, while Income Support, for all those capable of work should, after six months, become dependent on participation in community work, education or training.

Unpaid work is invisible here. The failure to address caring, parenting and the interrupted employment careers – and lower pay – of women feeds into the recommendation not to restore the link between earnings and the basic pension, but to insist on second pension funds whose value would be determined by lifetime earned income. Such activities belong firmly in the private sphere, which is perceived not as an alternative site of economic activity, but as a qualitatively different social space from either the market or the public domain, all being defined by the different values which dominate them. The private sphere is based on love, friendship, kindness; the market on incentives; the public domain, where active citizenship is practised, on service to the community. Activity in the private sphere is, therefore, not economic activity, and not subject to an economic calculus.

The Dahrendorf report is firmly situated within SID, but also draws on MUD, in spite of liberal antipathy to coercive and authoritarian measures. But there is a contradiction between the stress on employment and substantive neglect of unpaid work, and the unusually broad concept of wealth. The report argues that wealth cannot be measured in terms of GDP or GNP, but must include indicators of the social and political economy – the kind of wealth which leads to general well-being. It proposes that a regular wealth audit be conducted by the Central Statistical Office (CSO) – now the Office of National Statistics (ONS) – which would include, besides the conventional measures, an employment audit, as well as indicators of social condition, social opportunities, social cohesion and political freedom. Notably, these do not explicitly include general indicators of equality. Ironically, however, one of the criticisms levelled at GNP is its failure to measure 'non-marketed activities such as domestic work and child-rearing'.[59] This recognition, although not integrated into the rest of the discussion, has potentially radical implications.

CONCLUSION

The output of the think-tanks and the three major reports focused on in this chapter demonstrate the nature of the emerging 'centre-left consensus' which New Labour both exploited and sought to create. It is a discourse which progressively undermines a redistributive agenda, and in the process redefines the idea of social inclusion in narrower terms. This is undercut by attempts to address the question of unpaid work. Activities like parenting are perceived, as in earlier discussions,[60] as socially necessary and time-consuming, and thus as necessitating more flexible employment, principally, but not only, for women. But unpaid work is never quite seen as work, as economically productive or as contributing to wealth, so that (re)distribution of the social product is tied to the (re)distribution of paid work. Thus despite the relatively high profile of unpaid work in Borrie, the focus on inequality in Rowntree, and the potentially radical criticisms of conventional economic measures in Dahrendorf, all of them are pulled towards SID. It is a discourse about the interdependence of social cohesion and economic growth, in which paid employment is the central means of social integration and social control, and unemployment the overriding element in social exclusion. The insistence on the integrative role of employment, especially for men, and the perceived need to hold down spending on social security benefits, push the concept of social exclusion away from the broad idea of social participation characteristic of critical social policy. This trend is even more pronounced in the ideas of an inclusive society which emerge from the stakeholding literature, to which the discussion now turns.

3 The Optimism of Will

Will Hutton's book *The State We're In*, published in January 1995, advocated stakeholding as an antidote to the divisive effects of unfettered markets, and the recipe for social cohesion and inclusion. It far outsold the Borrie and Rowntree Reports. By 1997, *Social Justice* had sold 12 400 copies, and Rowntree just over 3000. Sales of *The State We're In* stood at 235 000. The softback edition was number 77 in a ranking of books first published in paperback in 1996; no other work of politics, economics, sociology or social policy was in the top hundred. In that year alone, its sales neared 140 000. The sequel, *The State To Come*, a much shorter book published at the start of the election campaign, sold over 35 000 copies in four months. Anger, optimism about the possibility of diagnosis and cure within capitalism, and accessibility of style helped Hutton capture and shape the mood of the mid 1990s. His previous influence as a journalist and broadcaster, and from 1996 as Editor of the *Observer*, increased dramatically. Even the rock band Radiohead claimed Hutton's inspiration for their 1997 release *OK Computer*. The Tory ideologue David Willetts described him as 'today's most influential and widely quoted radical thinker'.[1] David Marquand and Anthony Seldon suggested that Hutton's 'influence on the next fifty years may yet prove to be as seminal as that of Keynes and Beveridge on the last fifty'.[2] Marquand described stakeholding as the third paradigm of post-war thought in Britain, succeeding both Keynesian social democracy which dominated from the late 1940s to mid 1970s, and the New Right which dominated the next twenty years.

Although the terminology of stakeholding quickly permeated political discourse, its meaning was more elusive. The concept had been present in management literature for decades, and some of its new versions involved little more than the transference of business ethics to the management of society. Its sudden popularity arose from the particular political conditions of the 1990s. On the one hand, there was the collapse of actually existing 'socialism', the delegitimation by the New Right of all forms of collectivism, regulation and corporatism, and from 1995 New Labour's abandoning of all commitment to common ownership in the ditching of Clause IV. On the other hand, the very privatizations set in train by the New Right, especially of the public utilities, suffered their own legitimation crisis, partly as a result of poorer services but largely because of public anger at excessive profits and huge rises in executive pay. The anger was partly because the utilities were perceived as dealing in, and now profiting from, basic necessities – although so, of course, do supermarkets. It reflected a residual feeling that the utilities still properly belonged, in some sense, to the public and should operate in the public interest. Rising inequality also strained the legitimacy of the free market. Thus Hutton said that 'neither old Left nor new Right policy frameworks offer any way forward – and the search is on for a "third" way'.[3] Stakeholding is an attempt to address obvious economic and social problems within this political straitjacket. It condemns some of the effects of the free market, but seeks to accommodate or resolve differences of interest between shareholders, directors, workers, customers and the wider community, without recourse to public ownership, and with varying amounts of regulation.

Hutton's argument operates within these same constraints. He attacks the consequences of eighteen years of Tory misrule. They delivered rising inequality, social disintegration, the erosion of intermediate institutions, the collapse of social cohesion. The progressive deregulation of markets undermined social stability, while the 'promotion of uncertainty, risk and insecurity... made the... economy as a *system* less efficient'.[4] Markets have a tendency to monopoly, to inequality and to instability, and 'throw up a distribution of income and of risk that challenge[s] any conception of fairness or justice':[5] 'the operation of the unchecked market, whatever its success in sending effective measures about what is scarce and what is abundant, has an inherent tendency to produce unreasonable inequality, economic instability and immense concentrations of private, unaccountable power'.[6]

This is not, however, a general critique of capitalism, which Hutton defends on pragmatic grounds, and on the principled grounds both of its own merit and the demerits of socialism. Pragmatically, capitalism has 'triumphed for the moment in the great battle with socialism', and any political project must accept this if it is to have any hope of implementation.[7] Hutton is also reluctant to criticize capitalism in general. He argues (like Marx) that it is enormously creative, that the price mechanism is 'a superb way of allocating resources', and that markets have an important benefit of decentralizing decision-making. The solution, therefore, is 'not to call for the socialisation of capitalism, big government or a new corporatism'.[8] Hutton refers to Labour's old Clause IV as 'the infamous clause that celebrates public ownership of the means of production'; its defenders wrongly supported social ownership despite the fact that 'nationalisation...promoted neither efficiency nor the common good'.[9] Public ownership and 'collectivism' are neither desirable nor necessary. It may be true that markets, left to themselves, have negative tendencies, but markets never are left to themselves. They are always embedded in societies, in networks of values and institutions, which temper both their effects and their efficiency. There are, in short, different kinds of capitalism. Thus while Hutton is outraged at rising inequality, poverty and insecurity, these problems are attributed not to capitalism in itself, but to the particularly inefficient and inequitable form of capitalism which Britain is heir to, which he calls gentlemanly capitalism.

The origins of the relative decline of the British economy, in this as in other accounts, lie in the accommodation reached in the nineteenth century between the rising bourgeoisie and the aristocracy. Aristocratic values consequently dominated the ruling class, and the bourgeoisie sought to emulate the lifestyle of the aristocracy – to the long-term detriment of investment and industrial development. Gentlemanly capitalism is characterized by a value system which is intrinsically 'favourable to finance, commerce and administration – but not to industry'.[10] It 'places particularly high status on the less risky, invisible sources of income generated in trading and financial activity rather than production'.[11] This value system has structural consequences. Shareholders, particularly large institutional shareholders, have no interest in the companies in which they invest other than the extraction of dividends. Companies, therefore, are expected to generate high short-term profits for investors chiefly interested in a fast buck. The problem is compounded by the whole complex of legal, financial and political institutions, which have developed in ways which reinforce this short-termism. Hutton contrasts Britain with other capitalist economies, in Europe and in Asia, which are characterized by more cross share-holding, more long-term commitment by shareholders, and greater trust. Alternative versions of capitalism are embedded in different value systems and social structures. Those characterized by long-termism, trust and stability are more efficient; they are also more socially cohesive.

The values of gentlemanly capitalism, deeply entrenched in the British elite, and the institutions developed on the basis of them, are ultimately responsible for the deep inequalities and social divisions of contemporary Britain. The consequences are both morally reprehensible and economically inefficient:

what binds together the disorders of the British system is a fundamental amorality. It is amoral to run a society founded on the exclusion of so many people from decent living standards and opportunities; it is amoral to run an economy in which the only admissible objective is the maximisation of shareholder value; it is amoral to run a political system in which power is held exclusively and exercised in such discretionary, authoritarian fashion. These exclusions, while beneficial in the short-term to those inside the circle of privilege, are in the long run inefficient and ultimately undermine the wealth-generating process.[12]

Hutton's concern with exclusion focuses, therefore, not just on the bottom 30 per cent shut out from the mainstream of society and from 'proper citizenship',[13] but also on a small elite at the top. This elite is best understood as characterized by exclusivity rather than exclusion, both in terms of access to wealth and exercise of power. The public school system is the central mechanism of its reproduction, both in terms of establishing essential social networks, and in terms of transmitting the rotten values of British capitalism.

The result is what Hutton calls the '30/30/40 society' – a description which is widely known but frequently misunderstood. Blair got it wrong in his 1996 Conference speech: '30 per cent do very well. 30 per cent just getting by and 40 per cent struggling or worse'. This reverses the proportions of Hutton's hierarchy, since the 40 per cent are at the top; and it misrepresents the principle on which the model rests. It is a classification of adults of working age, according to employment status, with security of employment as the key variable – not, like Rowntree, a classification of the household population by income. Thus although there is considerable overlap, the bottom 30 per cent is not the group conventionally perceived as the excluded poor, which includes both pensioners and working poor. Rather, it refers to potential workers who are not in paid work, and who may be either unemployed (8 per cent), 'economically inactive' (21 per cent), or on training schemes (1 per cent).[14] Hutton does not discuss the composition of the group in detail, but we can infer from its definition that not all are poor. A very few will be very rich. Some (principally men) will be early-retired with reasonable pensions. Some (principally women) will be partners of those in the top 40 per cent or the middle band – although they are properly treated as insecure since they are only a separation or divorce away from poverty. Some will be forced into inactivity by the combination of a partner's unemployment and the structure of the benefit system, ratcheting up the number of households with no earner. The majority, Hutton argues, risk poverty and marginalization turning to 'complete social and economic exclusion'.[15] If poverty and unemployment are permanent only for a small minority, there is a more widespread problem of 'churning', as a larger group move 'from unemployment and inactivity to semi-employment and back again – representing a de-skilled underclass which cannot fully participate in the economy and society'.[16] They suffer hardship, but also, he says, cause problems: 'crime, family breakdown, a growing army of only partly socialised young men and vast social security spending... are the results'.[17]

The middle 30 per cent is in employment, but afflicted by (growing) insecurity and/or low pay. They are workers in full-time jobs for less than two years, or in part-time jobs for less than five; self-employed for two years or less; on short-term contracts; or earning less than half median earnings. Some would fall in the bottom 30 per cent on Rowntree's criteria – but Hutton sees them as less marginal because their labour market participation is higher, if unstable. Thus the 30 per cent usually referred to as the excluded poor cuts across Hutton's two lower groups and includes the pensioner poor, who lie outside this analysis altogether. An important feature of the experience of the middle group is increased risk – not just the increased danger of job loss, but the increased penalties which attach to it.

The 40 per cent at the top are those in relatively – but only relatively – secure employment. These workers have been in their full-time job, or self-employed, for over two years, or in their part-time job for more than five years, and earn at least half the median wage. In so far as the very rich work, or hold directorships which are technically classified as work, they are absorbed into this 40 per cent. Other inequalities are also masked: the group covers a wide income range, from 'fat cats' and newspaper editors to nurses and bus drivers, while women are more likely to work part-time, and less likely to occupy the best-paid positions. Hutton's central thesis is that this group is shrinking: 'by the year 2000, full-time tenured employment, around which stable family life has been constructed along with the capacity to service 25 year mortgages, will be a minority form of work'.[18] As this process has continued, and social protection has been simultaneously eroded, risks have increasingly been born individually rather than collectively, raising levels of anxiety and undermining social cohesion. And although those in the top group are relatively privileged, they are not immune to risk. Their access to occupational pension schemes, sickness benefit, paid holidays, their employment rights, and their general security of employment makes them qualitatively different from the middle group, but they are not necessarily highly paid, and many are dependent on a wide range of public provision. Increased insecurity in the labour market is mirrored by marketization in society, in pensions, housing, healthcare, education, transport, television and the privatization of space itself, creating a collapse of the public sphere and an 'increase in anxiety, dread of the future and communal breakdown'.[19] 'Risk has grown, but the protections have shrunk',[20] while 'social cohesion is deteriorating year by year'.[21]

Stakeholding, for Hutton, is a shorthand term for an attempt to construct an alternative form of capitalism:

> Part of the process of ideological self-definition is finding a word to describe the variety of capitalism one is championing, and stakeholding is an attractive choice. The idea has long been deployed in management literature and various firms have described themselves as stakeholder companies. The best types of overseas forms of capitalism have been achieved by striking the right balance between commitment and flexibility. Stakeholding is a neat way of encapsulating just that.[22]

Hutton's goal is an efficient and socially cohesive capitalism and he does not see this combination as intrinsically contradictory. Social exclusion is economically expensive as well as morally indefensible: 'Social inclusion, a well-functioning democracy and a high-investing business sector supported by a long-termist financial sector are not optional extras; they are interdependent and fundamental necessities'.[23] 'The dynamism of capitalism is to be harnessed to the common good',[24] in order to 'build a just society and moral community that is congruent with private property, the pursuit of the profit motive and decentralised decision-making in markets'[25] – one where rather than market principles being allowed to rip through society to its destruction, the market itself is tempered by the values of the moral community. Stakeholder capitalism is distinguished from the deregulated market by its value system which is reflected in its vocabulary: 'social inclusion, membership, trust, co-operation, long-termism, equality of opportunity, participation, active citizenship, rights and obligations' rather than 'opting out, privatisation, the primacy of individual choice, maximisation of shareholder value and the burden of social costs'.[26]

For Hutton, the irresponsible exercise of property rights is at the heart of the problem of gentlemanly capital: 'the eccentric aspect of British capitalism is how poorly its owners discharge their responsibilities'.[27] The first task for exponents of stakeholding therefore is 'to design a system of property rights in which obligations to the wider community are built into the core idea of property, so that ... firms are obliged to take into account the interests of wider stakeholders in their decisions'.[28] The issues which differentiate versions of stakeholding include who are defined as the 'wider stakeholders'; how their interests are represented; and whether firms are legally or morally obliged to 'take them into account'.

Hutton is committed to regulation. There needs, he says, to be a substantial body of legislative change covering five areas: 'the workplace, the welfare state, the firm and the City, the constitution, and economic policy more generally'.[29] Beyond these, globalization, though an overstated problem, means that the move towards stakeholder capitalism necessitates the reform of international economic organizations. The central focus is on questions of corporate governance and on strategies for limiting the abuse of rights attaching to property. Hutton proposes 'changes to the rules governing company takeovers, the composition of company boards, insolvency, banking law and accounting practice'.[30] He is extremely critical of the status quo, both as regards the structures of corporate governance and the behaviour of managers. The interests of workers, customers and the general public as stakeholders in companies are not represented either formally or informally. 'Firms do not have to establish supervisory boards.... There is no formal incorporation of key stakeholders – trade unions and banks – in the constitution of the firm. There is no obligation to establish works councils or to recognise trade unions as partners in the enterprise. The public cannot easily obtain company information.'[31] The recommendations of the Cadbury Committee on corporate governance and the Greenbury Committee on executive pay are seen by Hutton as inadequate because they are voluntary and based on self-regulation, although they have the merit of upholding elements of the stakeholder notion. Greenbury, indeed, he sees as 'reminding us, if reminder was needed, of the gap between the rhetoric about leading British managers maintaining high ethical standards and the grubby reality'.[32] He also argues for a minimum wage, together with increased rates of tax on high incomes. Constitutional changes are necessary to protect against the arbitrary abuse of power, including an elected second chamber, fixed-term parliaments, a more proportional voting system, devolution, decentralization, freedom of information and a code of rights. There should be strong measures to enforce the new rules: 'Laws are made to be complied with – as much by those at the top of our society as at the bottom.'[33]

Hutton is however, a reluctant and ambivalent regulator, and there is a tension between his scepticism about the efficacy of ethical constraints and his emphasis on values as the core problem of British capitalism and therefore the key to change. He also argues that the task is to get institutions voluntarily to act in a socially responsible manner; that 'obligations should not be too prescriptive'; and that government should 'design incentives, make laws and create new innovative institutions...while trying as far as possible not to intervene directly as a market actor itself although that may be necessary'.[34] He is also ambivalent about whether there are real, structural conflicts of interest between stakeholders, or whether apparent conflicts are the product of unhelpful and irresponsible attitudes – an ambivalence which emerges most clearly in his attitude to trade unions.

Hutton is concerned about 'the collapse of trade union power behind the new labour market',[35] and recognizes the central role of organized labour in progressively improving social conditions within and beyond the workplace. He argues that 'responsible' trade unions are one of the guardians of social inclusion. But 'responsible' is the operative word, and in *The State We're In*, Hutton apparently subscribes to the myth that the unions used to have 'too much power'. Although *The State to Come* suggests the case against unions has been overstated, it also says that by the 1970s they had 'collapsed into lobbies for ever higher wages, and...unjustifiable working practices without the acceptance of any parallel obligations'.[36] Since in 'co-operative capitalism, management needs employee organisations with which to co-operate' unions must abandon their adversarial ethos.[37] He therefore welcomes the fact that Tory legislation has so 'enfeebled' the old role of trade unions that a change in culture has been precipitated, and argues that this should be rewarded and institutionalized:

Trade unions...have started to redefine themselves as social partners in the management of capitalism. They can still serve the *individual* interests of their members – ensuring proper pension rights and employment contracts – but within the framework of a capitalist economy. The withdrawal of labour in a strike, although a fundamental human right, is less and less seen as the principal objective or weapon of trade unionism.

These trends should be entrenched by arming trade unions with proper constitutions and constitutional entitlements. Union recognition should be mandatory where a majority of workers freely wish it. Consultation with unions and representation of unions on company boards should be compulsory. Unions themselves should accept reciprocal responsibilities, building upon the existing reforms and exposing companies to the risk of being sued for breach of contract. Social partners have rights; they also have responsibilities [emphasis added].[38]

The suggestion that trade unionists have conventionally regarded strike action as their principal weapon, let alone objective, rather than a last resort, is a myth largely based upon media reporting of industrial relations issues.[39] Strikers incur heavy costs, usually even where successful, and certainly where unsuccessful as in the 1984–5 miners' strike. Most industrial action is not taken because trade unions are seen by either members or officials as 'the shock troops of the working class in building a socialist Jerusalem'.[40]

Hutton's avowal of support for trade unionism sits uneasily alongside his portrayal of what unions are for and what responsible unions might do. If 'stakeholding simultaneously endorses the market economy while attempting to achieve some proper balance between capital and labour' it is quite opposed to reviving 'the failures of British corporatism'.[41] Corporatism here means formal tripartite consultation between employer organizations, trade unions and government. This rested on the assumption that trade unions existed to represent the interests of workers collectively, and that such collective interests were meaningful, real and legitimate. In stakeholding, the negotiation between the two sides of industry occurs at the level of the firm, where mandatory union representation on company boards would 'force the two sides of industry into a partnership'.[42] But an important element in this representation is the assumption that workers have interests only as individuals, not as a collectivity, and it is these individual interests which unions exist to defend. Workers, as individual members of firms, should be treated well, because this fosters trust and commitment; they should be encouraged to upgrade their skills. Firms wishing to retain skilled and committed workers will pay them more than the minimum market price. Although Hutton sees this as treating workers as people rather than commodities, it can also be seen as simply acknowledging that some workers are worth more as commodities than has hitherto been acknowledged. Workers, individually, should be encouraged to own shares in the firms they work for. Employment rights should be strengthened and extended to those in part-time work and on short-term contracts. Trade unions then have an important and legitimate role in defending those rights. They can police 'the range of health, pensions and safety-at-work issues which concern workers';[43] this, together with individual case work, has always formed a large part of the work of trade union representatives. They can 'express individual workers' desire for fairer contracts between employer and worker';[44] the question, of course, is whether they are effectively able to secure fairer contracts. Workers are entitled to 'representation, consultation and prior notification of major events', including forthcoming redundancies or new investment.[45] Unions provide an 'institutional conduit for trading off more job security and continuity of employment... for lower pay increases', and to ensure that 'if compulsory redundancy cannot be avoided, then at least employers... [offer] generous redundancy terms' thus 'making sure that the costs of flexible labour markets are more equally shared between worker and employer'.[46] There can be few trade unionists who would see this as an adequate representation of workers' interests, although many might see it as the best that can be achieved in current circumstances, because the balance of power between capital and labour has – as Hutton acknowledges – so fundamentally shifted.

INTEGRATION THROUGH WORK

The principles of the stakeholder society go beyond the confines of the stakeholder firm. They are that 'open economies and democratic societies are the basis for wealth creation'; 'we must all be *included* in the workings of the economy and society'; 'ownership confers obligations – including paying tax'; 'the good economy is the one where you do the right thing without being policed'; 'businesses are social institutions, not creatures of the stock market'; 'good businesses are bound to make healthy profits but they must share their prosperity'; 'successful market economies rely on a host of intermediate organisations'.[47] Nevertheless, much of the argument concerns the nature of stakeholder firms. This is partly because 'the basic actor in a market economy is the firm';[48] and it is partly because work is the primary means of social integration for individuals. This assumption is embodied in Hutton's description of the 30/30/40 society, based on attachment to the labour market, and is explicit in Hutton's assertion that 'the ultimate stake for most adults is a job'.[49] Employment is 'the most effective instrument for...bringing the marginalised back into the fold'.[50] Participation in paid work delivers inclusion and defines the individual's place in society:

> Above all, work offers a sense of place in a hierarchy of social relations, both within the organisation and beyond it, and men and women are after all, social beings. Inevitably, some work is demeaning and poorly paid, but the same need is there. Those who work belong; those who do not are excluded...The firm is not only at the heart of the economy; it is at the heart of society. It is where people work and define their lives; it delivers wages, occupation and status.[51]

Paid work is also the defining element in identity: 'to work is to be'.[52] It is ' to acquire skills, to win friends, to gain status, to assert your very existence'. This means that although 'the fulcrum around which the good society turns is an equitable distribution of work and income',[53] it is work itself, as much as the income which it generates, which is important. As in Borrie's contrast between work-rich and work-poor households, work is an asset rather than a liability – or, in the language of classical economics, a utility rather than a disutility. Hutton is insistent that this is so, even for those whose wages and conditions are poor – although he is adamantly opposed to workfare. This insistence leads him to see work, rather than labour or labour power, as the good which is traded in the market: 'the commodity that new right economists and politicians want us to buy and sell with so little hindrance is not any commodity; it is that most precious resource, work, of central importance to our very humanity'.[54] Robert Tressell's central character in *The Ragged-Trousered Philanthropists* had grave difficulty in explaining to his fellow workers that employers were not doing them a favour in providing them with work, and that it was their labour rather than the opportunity to work which was the commodity at issue. In that case too, the risk of involuntary unemployment and consequent poverty led to a confusion between purchasers, providers and product.

Hutton is right, of course, that work can have non-pecuniary benefits, and that it is an important element in social identity. It is hard to disagree that paid work can contribute to self-esteem, both through the earned income and through the opportunity to exercise skills; or that it may impose a structure on otherwise unstructured time, and be a place of much-needed social interaction.[55] It is equally important to recognize that employment does not necessarily do all or any of these

– and that the non-pecuniary benefits may be as skewed as the financial rewards. Hutton does not, for example, consider whether work which is 'demeaning' can simultaneously deliver self-esteem. Teleworking offers neither structure nor social interaction. Some forms of work may inhibit other kinds of social participation. People who spend long or asocial hours in boring – and sometimes isolating – work may thereby be excluded from the wider life of the 'community', not least their own families. Hutton recognizes that long working hours impinge on parenting, and also on 'the capacity to sustain friendships outside work, to become a member of local clubs and societies, to play a part in the local neighbourhood';[56] but this, it seems, is not social exclusion. Even in supposedly skilled and rewarding professions, the non-pecuniary benefits of work may be overrated. It is salutary to remember that some of the early-retired in Hutton's bottom 30 per cent are teachers, who in the mid 1990s were leaving the profession in such numbers that the Conservative government legislated to prevent them. Work may be 'a supremely social act', but it is not necessarily 'a means of acting and interacting with the world that fulfils an individual's humanity'.[57] Socialists have long argued that work could and should be just this, but can only generally be so under relations of production more radically transformed than is suggested by stakeholding.

The main problem with Hutton's arguments about the importance of work to identity and integration is not that they are wrong, but that they are one-sided. They overestimate the benefits and understate the negative aspects of work, and the extent to which it is carried out under economic compulsion; they underestimate the importance of other possible sources of identity and integration; and they are heavily, but in the main covertly, gendered. The negative social effects of unemployment, and the positive integrative role of work, are overtly extrapolated from the perceived consequences for men. Hutton observes that rising insecurity in the labour market means that 'the capacity of *men* to take on the long-term commitment of a 25-year mortgage is progressively deteriorating'(emphasis added).[58] Reporting on a visit to Australia, he describes the consequences *for men* of unemployment and divorce:

> Instead of the systematic and regular patterns of social interaction that accompany regular paid employment and which are the foundations of community, interaction has become sporadic and intermittent. Worse, for those caught up in low-paid jobs accompanied by spells of unemployment, the new structures reinforce a downward

spiral not so much into poverty but solitude and desperation. In a market society, people take a more hard-headed approach to their relationships, trading them in when they consider them unsuccessful; women, for example, leave their unemployed or poorly paid husbands with rising aggression.[59]

The result is a new phenomenon: 'the marginalised, divorced middle-aged man, living alone, without the old structures which might have re-integrated him into society'. True to Durkheim, Hutton adds that 'male suicide rates...are...growing fast'.[60] Not only suicide, but murder may result, for such lack of integration produces 'deranged people who 'are disconnected from, and incapable of, empathising' with potential victims.[61] Writing about Thomas Hamilton and the Dunblane massacre, Hutton argued that integration of men was essential to social control:

> Individuals – especially the growing number of marginalised men living alone – need to be integrated better into the networks of mutuality and reciprocity on which a well-functioning society rests. Then...there may be some chance of making the deviant recognise the consequence of breaking basic human rules on such a scale – and of embedding him in human relations that can act as a constraint.[62]

GENDER, UNPAID WORK AND ECONOMIC INACTIVITY

Hutton's main preoccupation is with changes in the labour market which mean that 'men in particular are having a much tougher time'.[63] He claims, with some exaggeration, that men are losing their dominance in the world of work, and recycles the old nimble fingers argument. Women are progressively advantaged in the labour market because the service sector 'favours female abilities rather than male'. Now, 'work that demanded brawn and muscle is giving way to work requiring dexterity and skill, where communication and teamwork are more important than force'.[64] He argues that the question of women's work is becoming more clearly political than ever; but he means women's participation in the labour market. There is almost no consideration of informal, voluntary, or domestic work.

This neglect is present in the 30/30/40 classification itself, in which the bottom group consists of those unemployed and 'economically inactive'. The point that official figures understate real unemployment is not in dispute, but the official categories of employment/

unemployment/ economic inactivity themselves fail to acknowledge unpaid work.[65] Hutton argues that those 'economically inactive' used to consist mainly of women 'voluntarily withdrawing from the labour market to bring up children', and that economic inactivity among women is still typically chosen. His concern is with the increased representation of men in this category, so that it is now 'largely peopled by men of working age and single parents'.[66] Rather more carefully, he says that 'men are nearly as numerous in the bottom 30 per cent as women – a transformation of their position'.[67] Of course, this actually means that women are more numerous, just as they are more numerous among the low paid in the middle 30 per cent – and less so in the top 40 per cent, especially in the more highly-paid positions. This means that involuntary idleness – actual exclusion from work – is constructed as a principally male problem. It also means that the unpaid work of parenting and caring, whether done on a full-time or part-time basis, is construed both as chosen and as leisure, rather than as work. Long hours of paid work 'necessarily reduce the leisure that parents can spend with their children';[68] and 'historically many women have chosen part-time work because they want to strike a balance between work and family life – the kind of trade-off many men now wish they could make'.[69]

Where Hutton does address unpaid work, it is not on the basis of decades of feminist academic research, but in terms of an 'economy of regard', a term taken from Avner Offer. This economy is the 'essential glue both to a well-performing capitalism and the good society', and the key social unit in which it operates is the family. 'Parental care is a crucial, unmeasured gifted ingredient in the formulation of human capital – and one reciprocated by children when their turn comes to care for their ageing parents'. Hutton notes that one in seven British adults (actually mostly women) is 'providing unpaid care to a family member, friend or neighbour'; and also notes the financial cost to women of giving up paid work to care for children. But rather than developing this acknowledgement of unpaid work and considering its implications for the stakeholding argument, he reiterates that 'reciprocity, trust and giving without calculation underpin our sociability', and that the economy of regard thus properly extends beyond the family.[70] Pressed on this point, Hutton concedes that most unpaid work falls on women, and that the failure to pay for it could be seen to devalue women's role in society. But he insists that to place a market value on women's unpaid work, and thus to commodify caring and parenting, is to debase them.[71]

The focus on the world of work familiar to (employed) men means that while stakeholding implies everything must change, that 'everything' as Maureen Freely pointed out, means the firm, the City, macroeconomic policy, the welfare state, education and technology; it does not involve the home, which is a place of work for most women. 'The growing army of wives and mothers entering the workforce do so at a terrible disadvantage' because the unpaid work is still there to be done. The problems of reconciling full-time caring with full-time work – for all parents, but especially for lone parents and other lone carers – are profound. Failure to address this is a major weakness of the stakeholding argument:

> If the great stakeholder debate doesn't put the home, or the home/ work dilemma, or the reorganisation of work right up there on the chart next to the City and the firm, the welfare state, education, technology and all the other key issues, then the only women it has anything to offer are childfree women, and the only men it serves are the ones who have wives who are willing to make sacrifices to put their children first. The citizens with the biggest stakes and the biggest say will continue to be those who have been able to delegate most domestic responsibility.[72]

In other words, stakeholding, although it purports to address the whole political economy, fails to do so; it does not address the total social organization of labour.

INCLUSION AND INEQUALITY

Inclusion is the core, even the defining, value of stakeholding: 'a stakeholder society and a stakeholder economy exist where there is a mutuality of rights and obligations constructed around the notion of economic, social and political inclusion'.[73] With the exception of his discussion of responsible trade unionism, Hutton's use of a rights and obligations framework and his emphasis on responsibility are directed primarily at those who own and control capital, or more broadly at the rich. He is explicitly opposed to their more frequent use to stress the obligations of the poor while leaving the rights of the rich untouched – and in an otherwise rather kind review, criticizes Mandelson and Liddle's *The Blair Revolution* for this tendency.[74] He does not believe that 'the poor and single parents alike need to be incentivised not to live off the state, and so take responsibility for their own lives'.[75] He describes workfare schemes as 'noxious', 'morally repugnant and ineffective' and as 'an exercise in economic futility whose sole purpose is to reassure the advantaged that the approach to the unemployed is punitive'.[76] The much greater moral problem is that the 'better-off...deny their...reciprocal moral responsibility to the community of which they are part – and which allows them freely to exercise their wealth'.[77]

Hutton's view of the relationship between inclusion and equality is a shifting one. *The State We're In* and other 1996 writing presents a clear case that they are alternatives: 'Equality of provision needs to be surrendered before the larger necessity of universal inclusion;...some measure of inequality has to be traded off against universality of membership'.[78] While it is necessary to stabilize and reverse trends towards rising inequality, the broader goal of promoting social cohesion, moral order and inclusion is more important. The distinctive feature of this discussion, however, is that it is not focused primarily on the bottom 30 per cent – who need inclusion through paid work and a less punitive benefit system – but on the inclusion of 'the top third of our society into a system that embodies a morality of citizenship'.[79] As privatization has ripped through society, those who can afford to do so have increasingly opted out of public provision of all kinds, from health and education to transport. Rowntree warned of a 'drawbridge society'. For Hutton too, the spectre is of the affluent opting out, of a 'middle class [which] has deserted ordinary people'.[80] Binding them back into society, both in terms of their participation in shared provision, and in terms their commitment to underwriting social expenditure on those who need it, is an urgent priority.

However, if inclusion is recognized as the prime need, it will be necessary to make 'significant concessions to the interests of the middle class in order to enlist their willing participation in the creation of a stakeholder society, and above all of its new value system'.[81] He proposes that people should be able to buy better treatment within the state systems of insurance, health and education. The gains of this 'nationalisation of inequality' outweigh the losses:

> By incorporating inequality into the public domain at least it is contained and managed, with increased resources placed at the disposal of all. And, most importantly, the middle class is given a vested interest in the effectiveness of the entire system;...To import the class divisions of the private sphere may seem a surrender to middle-class aspirations and values, but this is surely better than

condemning public institutions to the second-class status that a middle-class exodus from them implies. In any case the aim is to imbue the middle class with a sense of their common citizenship, whilst recognising their impulse for self-advancement.[82]

Private education is crucial to the reproduction of gentlemanly capitalism. Hutton says that 'the dominance of the public school system is a long-standing offence to any notion of democracy or meritocracy in our society',[83] so that it is more important to address this division between the elite and the majority than to insist on a comprehensive system in the state sector. He struggles to find a solution which will not infringe the right of rich parents to educate their children privately, but which offends less against the principle of equal opportunities. Subsidies and tax incentives should stop, and their charitable status should be removed unless they take a high proportion of non-fee-paying students. In this way, as in others, the middle class would be prevented from separating off into an elite indifferent to the institutions suffered by everyone else. This is not so much a question of overcoming the social exclusion of those who wish to be included, but forcing inclusion on those who wish to retain exclusivity. The price of that inclusion is the tolerance of a high degree of inequality.

There remains a redistributive core to Hutton's argument. Social security provision needs to be increased rather than decreased, to offer 'reasonable living standards both for those permanently dependent on it and the millions...who use it...temporarily'.[84] He supports the restoration of the link between the state pensions and earnings: 'a reasonable state pension for all is an affordable, rational and democratic right in any society'.[85] Hutton disputes the idea that high unemployment benefits encourage unemployment. The rate of benefit withdrawal should be reduced to help the unemployed back into work. Very high expenditure is necessary to close income inequality, raise skill levels and lower unemployment, and this will take a long time. The principal means of addressing inequality is not redistribution, but 'empowering the disadvantaged with skills' through training, which can only be delivered if the public sector is 'rooted in the values of inclusion and citizenship'.[86] But it is not just a matter of raising skill levels; Hutton cites research which suggests that only about 20 per cent of the problem of unemployment is caused by poor education and training, and is concerned that too much emphasis on these rather than on raising investment is a diversion. Such spending, together with the financing of public services, mean an increase in the tax yield – from the corporate sector, high earners, inheritance tax and capital gains tax. Taxation is not a moral disaster, but a necessary element in social cohesion. It is the foundation of collective, rather than individual, protection against risk, which is both more efficient and more equitable. And there is a moral case for increasing inheritance tax on the wealthy:

> They depend upon the wider society's acknowledgement of their property rights if they are to enjoy them; indeed, without social order their rights are meaningless – and they have a greater stake in the social order holding together than the rest. A down payment, by way of inheritance tax at the time of assuming ownership of wealth, is that contribution.[87]

The State to Come is more overtly hostile to inequality, which by then Hutton called 'the single most salient fact in contemporary British society':

> Inequality helps to make the economy more unstable and the distribution of incomes more unfair, but that is only the beginning. It is inequality that fuels short-termism as the quest for ever higher incomes becomes more intense and feverish. It is inequality that feeds the new insecurity as the penalty in lost income for any move down the job hierarchy grows more severe. It is inequality that makes those at the bottom feel ever more desperate about their condition as the prospects of joining even those on average incomes seem ever more remote. And it is that which leads them to turn in on themselves, to take more and more dangerous drugs, thereby helping to drive the rise in crime.[88]

The attack is on excessive inequality and unjust inequality, not inequality itself: 'The great rewards in our society should fall to those who have genuinely earned them through the risks they have run and the judgement they have exercised – not because they were born to the right parents, move in the right circles or can take percentages from deals.'[89] But inequality undermines the work ethic, because rewards are wildly disproportionate to effort; and it feeds economic instability, short-termism, insecurity in the middle of society and desperation at the bottom. The difference between the arguments in *The State We're In* and *The State to Come* lies partly in their target audience. One purpose of the first book was to challenge conventional thinking on the left; the attack on inequality in *The State to Come* is sharper because it is primarily directed at the right-wing critics of stakeholding.

But it also represents a substantive shift. By July 1997, Hutton could pose the question about the relationship between inclusion and equality thus: 'Is the good society a more equal society and therefore inclusive or is the good society an inclusive society which could contain current levels of inequality?'. His answer was that 'more equality is the...necessary but insufficient precondition for an inclusive society'. Inequality must be reduced to 'some point society is comfortable with' – which raises the question of who constitutes 'society'. And it returns us to the problem of the moral responsibility of the rich: for you cannot, says Hutton, construct a solid welfare state based on an effective progressive taxation system in a polity where potential higher rate tax payers do not accept its legitimacy, and seek to avoid or evade payment.[90]

THE STAKEHOLDER'S DILEMMA

The essence of Hutton's argument is that one cannot talk about capitalism, only capitalisms. Capitalism is the only game in town; there is no alternative. Any way forward must be within a capitalist framework, and if capitalism itself is blamed, there are no grounds for hope, let alone optimism. Hutton launches a relentless indictment of the social desolation created by unfettered markets. But he rejects two major elements of the old social democratic project, social ownership and corporatism – while retaining a commitment to progressive taxation and redistribution. The constraints he sets on possible alternatives may be seen as real, or as at least in part ideological. Within these constraints, what then becomes important is to identify the pathological features of the British model, contrasted with the more socially cohesive varieties available elsewhere. Hutton may be overly impressed by some of these examples. Perkin's rigorous comparison of different systems of capitalism, while accepting the basic argument that economic relations are embedded in social relations and fundamentally dependent on trust, is more sceptical. He argues that the Japanese system depends on trust in the sense that the elites who profit from the system have been relatively successful in persuading the rest of society that their greater rewards are merited. It is 'a system that promises prosperity and security to all, but delivers only to the few' and is an economy 'underpinned by the underpaid and unpaid work of women'.[91] Meanwhile, capitalist economies across Europe, including Germany which Hutton so often cited as exemplars, reduced the social protection offered to their citizens to meet the criteria for monetary union.

The consequences of the constraints are that Hutton's diagnosis of the problem is more radical than his proposed cure, while the limitations of the solution also restrict the possibilities of diagnosis. This disjunction between diagnosis and prescription is most apparent in his ambivalence towards property rights and the owning class, and the oscillation between emphasizing material relations and values. The model of the 30/30/40 society is based, as we have seen, on security in the labour market, not on property ownership. Hutton knows that property ownership is a problem: a central element of the stakeholder agenda is that shareholder interests must be qualified by those of workers, customers and the wider community. He is critical of the generally celebratory attitude to inward investment, recognizing that this has chiefly been the product of foreign take-overs, and means the outflow of profits. He believes regulation will be necessary to bring about even the limited consideration of the interests of other groups that stakeholding requires. Thus far, he recognizes that there is an inbuilt conflict of interests between property-owners and others. It is exacerbated by the structural integration of the elite, based on networks established through the public school system (an observation long made about the British ruling class), and by their values, fostered in the same forum. Some coercion may be necessary – to increase taxes, to enforce ethical standards on businesses, to moderate the exclusivity of public schools. But if the public schools are so central to the maintenance of all that is corrupt and decadent in British capitalism, why not abolish them altogether? Because to do so would be politically impossible: it would be a fundamental challenge to power and privilege in a way that stakeholding is not.

For the rich are to be persuaded towards 'inclusion', through the argument that it enhances economic efficiency. We will all be better off, but the rich, as he points out, have more invested in the stability of the system than the rest of us. What is principally called for is a transformation in values, to enhance trust, commitment and long-termism. Adversarial relations between managers and unions are a matter of attitudes in need of transformation, not a structural reality; workers are entitled to 'decent working and living conditions' – the absence of which are in any case 'indissolubly linked with the rise of crime, drugs and violence'.[92] They are entitled to consultation and information. They are not entitled to challenge managerial decisions or the essential property rights of capital; that way lies 'irresponsibility'. And inclusion means accepting the fundamental inequalities of a capitalist system. At root, whatever the merits of Hutton's reformist proposals, this is still a recipe for managing capitalism better, and thus in one sense a prescription for the relegitimation of capitalist relations.

And yet Hutton is much more radical than most political commentators, particularly in his insistence that the primary problem lies with the rich. He is also more radical than many other advocates of stakeholding, in insisting on the necessity of regulation as well as cultural change. When stakeholding was hailed as New Labour's big idea after Blair's Singapore speech in January 1996, and then rapidly abandoned, John Plender blamed 'Huttonomics' for this retreat.[93] As New Labour moved rightwards, Hutton – who if anything was moving the other way – saw himself as excluded from the circle of influence around Blair.[94] By the autumn of 1997 he was openly critical of the new Government: 'What we need is a political party prepared to challenge and reform the structure of British capitalism even if it damages the incomes and interests of those at the top. But no such party exists any more'.[95]

4 Staking Claims

By 1996, the term stakeholding had become ubiquitous in political discourse but had a wide range of meanings as well as a general rhetorical use. The population at large were exhorted to become 'stakeholders in the Millennium celebrations'.[1] Even after Blair's retreat, the term lingered in Labour Party literature, and in plans for stakeholder pensions. The Party's General Secretary, Tom Sawyer, defended the constitutional changes at the 1997 Conference in terms of building a stakeholder party. The TUC produced a report on stakeholding at work. Others attacked stakeholding as corporatism under another name, or as pure managerial ideology. The Tory ideologue David Willetts declared it either a banal 'cliché in corporate strategy' or a 'dangerous piece of industrial interventionism'.[2] Ron Brown suggested that stakeholding meant tying the working class to the stake of big business,[3] while Arthur Scargill reportedly said that there was only one thing to do with a stake, and that was to drive it through the heart of capitalism.[4]

Kelly *et al.* have attempted to summarize the key themes of stakeholding, and the issues which separate its various exponents. In general, they regard stakeholding as 'a powerful organising concept' closely linked to questions of inclusion and governance, which has the potential to 'combine an individualist agenda with an active state' and which 'contains the seeds of a post-Thatcher, post-Labourist project' – in other words, which constitutes a third way.[5] At the heart of stakeholding is the 'tension . . . between the need for membership and inclusion, and the need for personal autonomy' but these are resolved in very different ways. There are 'major disagreements over whether a stakeholding agenda is best achieved by moral persuasion . . . or whether it also needs legislative and administrative action'.[6] Some versions of stakeholding are primarily individualist, concerned with the development of human capital and the individual possession of marketable skills, together with a cultural shift towards greater co-operation. Others emphasize rights, obligations and membership, or, like Hutton, structures and institutions, and place a greater emphasis on regulation to limit the negative effects of markets.

John Lloyd used the term 'soft stakeholding' for that version which is little more than the elaboration of business ethics. This emphasizes the importance of 'good behaviour' by owners, employers and managers, in the interests of both efficiency and legitimacy. Companies should not be run simply in the interests of making maximum short-term profits for shareholders: the interests of other stakeholders, such as workers and customers, should also be taken into account, if only because this is in the interests of the long-term economic efficiency of the firm. Although possibly endorsing some limited changes in corporate governance, this view generally eschews regulation. Essentially, 'soft stakeholding' is 'the view that company directors and managers should take explicit account of the voices of workers, suppliers, consumers and councils in the localities in which they operate, but that this should be a matter of good practice, not of legislation'.[7] Of the two most important theorists behind the stakeholding debate, Hutton is the harder. John Kay, although by no means the softest of stakeholders, is less sympathetic to regulation. More radical versions of stakeholding have been put forward by the TUC and the Green Party, illustrating the extreme flexibility of the concept.

JOHN KAY: STAKEHOLDING AND CORPORATE SUCCESS

In 1993, Kay published *The Foundations of Corporate Success*. Its object was to identify the features of a successful firm. He concluded that no general rule could be given, and that the attempt to do so would be self-defeating. What makes a firm – and a national economy – successful in a competitive market is the identification and exploitation of distinctive capabilities, not the pursuit of a copycat strategy. The principal aspects of distinctive capability are innovation, reputation and architecture, the last referring to the network of internal relationships of the firm and the external relationships in which it is embedded and which allow it to create organizational knowledge, to exchange information and to respond flexibly to change.

The concept of stakeholding is introduced almost incidentally. Kay defines a firm as a set of relationships between different groups of stakeholders. These stakeholders are variously listed: they always include shareholders, employees, customers, and sometimes investors and/or suppliers. The state is described as a stakeholder, partly but not wholly because of its interest in deriving revenue from the firm through taxation. The firm also has identifiable relationships with the community in general. The key measure of corporate success is added value, a concept broader than that of profit understood as returns to investors or shareholders; and this added value may be appropriated by different groups of stakeholders. The division of added value is influenced both by the contribution made by different groups, and by their bargaining power. This might conjure up a picture of squabbling over the spoils, but Kay's picture of the world is more benign. He argues that especially where competitive advantage derives primarily from architecture or reputation rather than from innovation, 'the profit-oriented firm will often want to share the added value it creates with other stakeholders, because doing so is good business'.[8] Shareholders, however, do have a special place among stakeholders. They are the residual claimants on added value, and the capacity to generate added value for shareholders is, says Kay, a measuring rod of success in all capitalist economies, despite the important variations between capitalisms in the extent to which this is true.

Classical and Relational Contracts

Kay discusses the nature of the relationships between stakeholders, and the different forms these may take. They may be classical and contractual, with detailed, precise specification of the duties of the parties to the contract, which can be legally enforced. Such contracts may be one-off, short-term agreements (spot contracts), or complex, long-term agreements. They are contrasted with relational contracts, which are long-term, implicit contracts based on trust whose 'provisions are often only partly specified' and which are 'enforced, not by legal process, but by the need the parties have to go on doing business with each other'.[9] Because there are often short-term gains to be made by breaking the trust inherent in relationship contracts, they are harder to make in a business environment where changes of control are common. But 'modern corporations have both classical and relational contracts between themselves and the communities in which they operate, and...business behaviour is governed by the terms of both types of contract'.[10] These contracts exist not only between the obvious stakeholders of employees, shareholders, customers and suppliers, but with government and 'the community'.

Relational contracts are, of course, not really contracts at all in the conventional sense, although they recall Durkheim's observation that not everything in the contract is contractual. What makes a relationship contractual is precisely that it is legally enforceable. The informal relationships Kay describes are not subject to formal regulation – and indeed Kay is adamant that they should not be. There is no necessary relationship between adding value for shareholders or other stakeholders and adding value for society. Nevertheless, especially where the added value derives from reputation or architecture 'there is a broad identity between the private and social value of corporate activity'. And 'firms which are typified by strong architecture are also associated with an emphasis on good working conditions, high levels of employee benefits and strong community involvement'.[11] Particularly where the added value derives from innovation, there may be less coincidence of interest. In some circumstances, markets 'fail', and externalities, information problems or monopoly enable firms to appropriate value they don't create, raising ethical questions about social responsibility. 'The community' is entitled to expect firms to behave responsibly, for example in showing concern for the health and safety of employees, customers and the general public. But this is properly a matter of business ethics, not regulation; firms should behave responsibly, and 'society' should exert only a 'light regulatory rein'. Safety, for example, is 'achieved by attitudes and behaviour rather than by close attention to rules'.[12] The same is true of training, employment of disadvantaged groups, and the control of transfer pricing: such matters should be dealt with by 'relational' rather than 'classical' contracts, the content of which must vary with the context and culture. Thus although Kay identifies a range of groups as stakeholders in the sense of having a legitimate interest in the operation of a corporation, duties to these stakeholders are a matter for the ethical conduct of managers. They are not interests which Kay sees as properly enshrined in legal rights over added value, or in regulation of the firms operations.

A collection of essays written over the following three years develops some of these themes, first in relation to firms and then in relation to the wider society.[13] Three important issues arise from these discussions: questions of ownership and its significance; which stakeholders' interests are given priority by Kay; and the repeated endorsement of the merits of market competition and the evils of regulation. These underlie his discussion of what he terms 'the inclusive society'.

Kay claims that the implication of understanding firms as sets of relationships is that they cannot be owned by anyone: 'You cannot own a structure of relationships between people, or own their shared knowledge, or own the routines and modes of behaviour they have established'. Perhaps 'a large corporation is not owned by anybody at

all'.[14] He argues that the supposition that companies are owned by
their shareholders is not legally true, since the company is in law a
distinct entity different from the sum of its individual shareholders.
Nor is it useful in understanding how corporations operate. Rather,
the behaviour of corporations is best understood through an organic
model imputing to them 'life' independently of their shareholders and
stakeholders. This time stakeholders are listed as 'investors, employees, suppliers, customers and managers'.[15] It is important that the
various rights and obligations of stakeholders be stated, and that there
be mechanisms for resolving disputed claims. But 'if a company is not
"owned" by its shareholders, and the shareholders are simply one of a
number of stakeholder groups, all of whom enjoy claims against it,
then there is no reason to think that the interests of shareholders do or
should enjoy priority over the interests of these other stakeholders'.[16]
Kay posits a model of corporate governance in which managers act not
as agents for shareholders, but as trustees who 'balance the conflicting
interests of current stakeholders and additionally weigh the interests
of present and future stakeholders'. Indeed, he argues that the purpose of a large company is not to maximize its profits but to 'develop
its business, in the interests of customers, employees, suppliers,
investors and the wider community'.[17] This, together with a conception
of the company as a set of relationships, skills and activities rather than
a set of financial claims, serves to foster long-term rather than short-
term decision-making.

There are some strange elisions here between what is and what
should be, and between what model best explains corporate behaviour
and what best characterizes the place of the company in the wider
society. But the claim that ownership is unimportant, that it does not
matter who owns the firm, and that no-one really does, is more than a
quirky observation. Its effect is that the marked social division between
those who own the bulk of productive wealth and those who do not
mysteriously disappears. If there is no ownership, there is no ownership class either. Capitalism is a set of relationships; but the very relationship which characterizes it is obliterated from view.

If owners are removed from view in one essay, in the next the
employees disappear as well. Generally speaking, Kay claims that the
discipline of a competitive market is such that 'the interests of shareholders can only be achieved by meeting the interests of customers'.[18]
There is no conflict of interest. In a monopoly situation, however, this
discipline cannot fully operate, and in the case of the privatized utilities, does not do so, even though 'putting customers first is the natural

instinct of the vast majority of managers of privatized utilities'.[19] Kay is adamantly in favour of privatization, which he claims delivered significant gains in efficiency, and revealed the dangers of structures of accountability. Principal among these gains has been the reduction in 'overmanning' even if this has been 'to replace disguised unemployment by actual unemployment'.[20] But although utilities have become more customer-focused, a new framework is needed which 'encourages and allows' managers of utilities to '[focus] unambiguously on the interests of customers'; the alternative will be more regulation and an 'erosion of management autonomy'.[21] The proposal is for a mechanism to distribute profits between shareholders and customers, to make the link explicit and thus increase the legitimacy of the privatized utilities, through their reconstitution as 'customer corporations', removing the 'apparent' divergence of interest between companies and the public. In this discussion, the visible stakeholders become customers and shareholders only. There is no mention of the extremely large salaries paid to senior managers. Employees disappear, except as obstacles to managers' good intentions towards customers: 'Many...managers [of privatized utilities] will volunteer that the opportunity to give priority to customer interests, with greater freedom from union influence and political restriction, has been the principal benefit of privatization'.[22]

If the state and the wider community, not to mention 'customers', are stakeholders in these companies, a central question is how these stakeholders interests are articulated. In theory, this could be through regulation or through representation on management boards. The discussion of accountability and regulation which accompanies Kay's proposals for customer corporations proposes the effective removal of regulation. The intention, he says, is 'to replace a regime based on a battle between managers representing shareholders and a regulator representing customers with one in which a customer-oriented management makes the trade-offs for itself'.[23] The board of a customer corporation should be 'widely representative of the community'. On the other hand, the board must be 'united in purpose and objective', and the customer interest is deemed to be better served by professional managers than by 'representatives of consumers' who are 'rendered unrepresentative by their very willingness to undertake the task'.[24] If the interests of employees as stakeholders are entirely ignored, those of customers, ostensibly given such priority, are not to be represented by customers themselves, but by professional managers committed to customer service.

Inclusive Economy, Inclusive Society?

The Business of Economics reproduces in edited form an essay which first appeared in *Prospect* in May 1996.[25] Here, Kay uses the term 'inclusive economies' as a label for 'non-individualistic market economies' exemplified by such countries as Japan, Norway, Singapore and Switzerland, noting that the implications of the term are similar to those of social markets or stakeholding or communitarian societies. The foil for this argument is the New Right. It is, says Kay, 'possible to believe that competitive markets are an effective and efficient system of organization and yet to reject the value system of the New Right, which applauds selfishness and glorifies private property'.[26] 'Economic efficiency, market forces, selfishness, insecurity and progress' do not 'go hand in hand'; 'uncertainty, homelessness and growing inequality' are not 'the price we have to pay for high and rising output'.[27] Inclusion is the term which differentiates Kay's position from that of the New Right:

> This term captures best the essential differences between the New Right philosophy and its alternatives. The New Right stresses autonomy – the right of the individual to pursue freely his or her own interests and objectives. The alternative is to emphasize inclusion – the right, and also the requirement, to be part of a community. The injustice that most concerns the New Right is coercion – a term which is used to cover taxation and economic regulation as well as more direct restrictions on personal freedom. But another injustice is that of exclusion – the inability of some to participate in an economy and a society which they would dearly love to join. In practice, autonomy is often a synonym for poverty. In inclusive economies there is no incompatibility between the functioning of markets and fairness, shared values, collective activity and institutions, and broadly accepted concepts of fairness.... These things are of central importance in making markets work.[28]

There are several points to note about this passage. Firstly, the identification of the New Right solely with its neo-liberal wing is erroneous. There was (and is) also a neo-conservative strand in New Right thought. The Health and Welfare Unit of the Institute of Economic Affairs exemplifies this both in terms of content and in terms of its intimate relationship with free market policies. Kay himself notes the increasing rather than decreasing role of the state necessitated by neo-liberal economic policies.[29] But in failing to recognize that the New

Right was essentially characterized by a symbiotic combination of free market and strong state, Kay both falls for the New Right's own rhetoric and overstates his own distance from it. Secondly, inclusion is cast in terms of 'community', whereas exclusion is described in terms of non-participation in economy and society, and of poverty; exclusion is primarily read as economic, while inclusion is broader, and is both a right and an obligation. Thirdly, it is the nature of social values, and the institutional consequences of these, not regulation, which is claimed to temper the ill effects of unfettered markets, while these same values – happily – serve to make markets function better. The claim is that there is not a trade-off between economic efficiency and social decency. The two go hand in hand. But the institutionalization of appropriate values means there can be less regulation rather than more, and the business community can be largely left to police itself.

Kay is adamant that this is not simply a matter of relying on altruism and high ideals. Markets are social institutions, and 'inappropriate or unacceptable behaviour' results in sanctions which mean 'you simply are not very successful'. The sanctions are informal, commercial and social, rather than legal, and Kay sees this as subtle but entirely necessary coercion, despite the fact that 'some people find it oppressive'. It is striking that Kay does not identify the agents of this coercion – indeed, it is characteristic of informal controls, preferred also by Etzioni, that this is particularly difficult to do. Control is exerted by the generalized 'inclusive economy',[30] operating through values rather than rules. This of course means that accountability is problematic. But Kay is not a great advocate of accountability, which in another context he argues 'undermine[s] the responsibility of...managers...for the consequences of their actions'.[31] Structures of accountability for any aspect of business behaviour receive as little attention as accountability for the operation of sanctions within the business community. Kay claims that 'the most effective means of accountability is the measurement of managerial or organizational performance relative to others engaged in similar activities' and that 'competitive markets are often...sufficient answers to questions of accountability and legitimacy'.[32] As with the New Right, which also emphasized accountability, the essential question is accountability to whom?

The opposition to regulation and structures of accountability is the means by which Kay differentiates what he means by inclusion from corporatism. Corporatists, he claims, use the language of inclusion in pursuit of opposite goals, because they seek central direction of the economy. For Kay, it is essential that 'the values of an inclusive economy are emergent rather than directed'.[33] He argues for the necessity of intermediate institutions between individuals and government, and for the virtue of 'fuzzy' structures of power which make it difficult for interest groups to identify and attempt to grasp levers of power. Kay does not clearly distinguish between the inclusive economy and the inclusive society, but both are essentially characterized by the values which they generate. Inclusive societies produce co-operation, trust and confidence, and provide security. These, as argued in Kay's earlier work, have positive economic consequences in encouraging long-term behaviour as well as in reducing the need for regulation.

Just as Barratt Brown and Coates have argued that the key question about corporatism is who is incorporated, the key question about inclusion is who is included, and on what terms.[34] Kay gives little attention to this question. Inclusion here simply means the embedding of market institutions in a social context which supports them. The 'inclusive' economy refers only to market institutions, and does not include the informal, voluntary or domestic economies, nor does it address the unequal terms on which people participate in market institutions although it differentiates their status in terms of stake-holding groups. Socially, the discussion is even more vague, basing inclusion on membership of that notoriously elusive entity 'community', and stressing the importance of the inclusion of 'potentially disaffected' groups as 'the only long-term solution to crime'.[35] He emphasizes the importance of security as an aspect of the inclusive society, but rates security in the sense of the stability of the business environment as more important than social security in the conventional sense.

Kay's analysis quite explicitly moves from the level of the firm, which he regards as the most fruitful and revealing level of economic analysis, to the level of the national and global economy, and national – and occasionally global – society. There is a great deal of slippage between levels. Not only is the analogy between firms and national economy tendentious and unexamined, but there is no consideration at all of the difference between economy and society. As with the New Right, society is collapsed into the market or into a moral and institutional framework for the efficient operation of the market. The idea of stake-holding or the inclusive society seems little more than a justification for replacing regulation and formal structures of control, responsibility and accountability with nebulous and flexible values. Clearly, however, it is seen in some quarters as a threat. The CBI criticized stakeholding, arguing that 'putting the interests of shareholders first should continue to be the goal for boards of directors and the measure against which they are held to account',[36] while the Institute of Directors described Kay's position as 'wet, woolly and vacuous'.[37]

THE IPPR: PROMOTING PROSPERITY

In January 1997, the Commission on Public Policy and British Business published *Promoting Prosperity: A Business Agenda for Britain*. It was launched with the endorsement of Blair and other representatives of New Labour. Additional publicity was attracted by Michael Heseltine, then Deputy Prime Minister, who extracted an invitation to the proceedings, occupied the seat intended for Margaret Beckett, and publicly insulted the members of the Commission;[38] they then wrote to the *Financial Times* in protest.[39] New Labour was closely identified with the 'soft stakeholding' of this report, which Blair said 'sets the business policy agenda for the next decade'. Lloyd also reported that Kay, who was a member of the Commission, 'pushed for a harder version but was outvoted by the businessmen'.[40] Like the Commission on Social Justice which produced the Borrie report, the Commission on Public Policy was set up by the IPPR. Both were clearly close to Labour Party policy, and intended to influence the formation of that policy. The gap between the publication of the two reports was two years and three months. The gap between their main themes is illustrative of the shift in the Party's preoccupations. The Borrie report, with all its shortcomings, can be seen as the last gasp of Labour's traditional redistributive agenda: *Promoting Prosperity* consolidated the Party's alliance with business.

Promoting Prosperity identifies four linked problems which undermine the performance of the UK economy: a 'tail' of inefficient and poorly run companies; too many underachieving people; too little investment; and too many shifts in government policy. Its prescriptions focus on four themes: promoting competition and co-operation; fostering long-termism and farsighted companies; raising standards in education, training and skills; and maintaining stability in the business environment. It places strong emphasis on the importance of education and training, implying that poor education is responsible for unemployment and thus for benefit dependency which is 'an economic drag anchor on the rest of society'.[41] It endorses the introduction of a minimum wage, but set through consultation with employers, and at a level which will not threaten employment levels. It also endorses the social chapter, and entry into EMU, in both cases to ensure Britain's active participation in relevant discussions; the potential costs of staying outside these are seen as higher than those of participation.

A distinction is made between shareholder and stakeholder models of corporate governance. In the former, shareholder interests are supreme, and mechanisms of corporate governance are directed at ensuring that management behaviour reflects the interests of shareholders. The stakeholder model sees the company as 'an organic entity whose interests are not identical with those of the shareholders...but an entity of which managers are the trustees, balancing the interests of all the groups crucial to its long-term success'.[42] In this model 'corporate governance is thus the system whereby managers are ultimately held accountable to all stakeholders for their stewardship'.[43] However, it is notable that stakeholders are not all those affected by the decisions of the firm, but those groups involved in its successful functioning, the 'people whose "investment" in a company in cash or commitment is essential to its success'.[44] They include 'at least some employees, management, shareholders, customers, creditors and suppliers'; and as suppliers are only counted as stakeholders where there is a need for 'high-trust, co-operative relationships', one may presume that the same is true of employees.[45]

Certainly there is no sense that the management are accountable to the employees. True, the report proposes the 'extension of statutory employee rights to information and consultation'. The first meaning of 'extension' might well benefit workers. At present, such rights only cover collective redundancy, take-overs and health and safety, and the Commission suggests that they should also cover 'timely provision of management proposals involving significant changes in employment numbers, working conditions, corporate strategy, financial matters and restructuring' – adding that such information should already be provided through company reports. However, the other sense of 'extension' is more problematic. In so far as rights to consultation currently exist, they are rights which rest with recognized trade unions. The proposal that all workers, whether members of trade unions or not, should be included in such rights is double-edged, especially given the rider of 'employees and management being left free to determine the form consultation should take'.[46] In non-unionized work-places, it would clearly be an advance; in others, it could undermine and bypass unions. Indeed, as with Hutton, the stress on individual employment rights rather than collective representation signals both a hostility to trade unions and a more profound denial of the legitimacy of collective interests and collective action, despite the general assertion of the importance of intermediate institutions. Mandelson and Liddle argue that 'the concept of a stakeholder economy addresses the needs and aspirations of individuals, not interest groups acting for them'.[47] The delegitimation of the collective subject has been one of the most far-reaching achievements of the New Right.

There is no implication that any power should pass to 'stakeholders'. Management should seek to make 'key stakeholders, in particular the employees, feel involved in the company's fortunes'.[48] But the Commission comes down firmly in favour of management's right to manage:

> A good management team will consult stakeholders because they are an important source of information and feedback about the business. It will also take account of their interests in order to elicit their co-operation and enthusiasm. Someone in the firm has to take decisions, however, and in making that decision they must balance different interests and take responsibility for doing so. That is the right and duty of the manager.[49]

Indeed, only high levels of unemployment make even the very soft stakeholding advocated here permissible. Up to the late 1970s, it is said, unemployment was so low that companies indulged in the 'short-termist' practice of 'overmanning to avoid expensive industrial conflict and to maintain a reserve of labour for any expansion. ... In that world, to emphasise stakeholder interests would be to accentuate a bias that already existed'. In the context of the new global economy, a more flexible labour market, and above all high male unemployment, this is no longer so: 'Yielding to short-termism now more often means paying out higher dividends and neglecting the development of the business and a skilled workforce. In this world, it is no longer dangerous to emphasise that in a good company the interests of the various stakeholders should be considered by management'.[50] Indeed, this is so much a matter of good management strategy that it may be difficult to tell whether the managers of a company favour the shareholder or the stakeholder model.[51] 'Fostering stakeholding' means 'to improve the information flow and relationships between management and institutional shareholders in order to mitigate short-termism', and to encourage a broader view of directors' responsibilities and remove impediments to the development of long-term relationships by businesses'.[52]

There is no move away from maximization of profits as the key indicator of business success. Although present company law should be recast so that directors' duties more clearly enable them to take into account factors other than shareholders' interests, this implies merely that 'firms should seek to maximize profits, and thereby further shareholder – and other stakeholder – interests over a longer time horizon'.[53] Stakeholder interests do not, on this interpretation, include the interests of the wider community or future generations, in the environmental impact of business activities. If the scope of company reports might be extended, 'businesses should be free to consult and determine what is most useful to disclose',[54] begging the question of most useful to whom.

The Commission has as its goal 'a more prosperous but also more inclusive society, with a higher quality of life for all its citizens'.[55] The terms exclusion and inclusion are used only a handful of times, but exclusion, not surprisingly, means exclusion from work. It is not simply a proxy for unemployment. Like Hutton, the Commission refers to 'unemployment, economic inactivity and high levels of welfare dependency'.[56] It is primarily concerned with the direct costs of unemployment, in welfare benefits, and the indirect costs in social disorder and rising crime. These costs are primarily linked to 'the social exclusion of prime-age men who would ordinarily be expected to participate in the labour market'.[57] Again, paid work is seen as the prime means of social integration – especially for men, for again it is men who are seen as constituting a social problem when unemployed. The Commission recommends a fundamental change in the benefit regime. After a year, there should be no option of remaining on benefit. Benefits should be transferred into employment subsidies. Employers would be given a 'substantial financial rebate' for six months to take on those out of work for a year; others would be employed part-time in local authority job-creation projects. They do not say whether this policy would be extended to lone parents. In-work benefits should be extended to those without families, and a low-level minimum wage set to prevent irresponsible employers exploiting the benefit system. To raise skill levels, more resources should be put into education and training, with government-funded nursery education, the reduction of all primary class sizes to thirty or less, and a transfer of funding away from higher education (which should be increasingly funded by the individuals who benefit) to schools, and to mandatory traineeships for those who leave school early. In dealing with unemployment, the emphasis is clearly on the supply-side factor of education and training, and the objective equally clearly a mixture of improved economic efficiency, reducing 'the fiscal burden on British business',[58] and social control.

Ian Lang, writing as Trade Secretary some three weeks after the IPPR report was published, still claimed New Labour's policy was dangerously interventionist: 'Stakeholding is a dangerous dogma. It seeks to achieve by stealth what New Labour cannot take by direct assault, namely the state direction of the affairs of business...To be lured by the siren voices of New Labour's stakeholding...would be to dash the prospects of everyone whom stakeholding purports to help. Choice, not state direction, is their protector'. Lang's argument could however be seen as an endorsement of 'soft stakeholding' in contrast to what he calls 'statutory stakeholding'. He also said that 'It is self-evidently the case that consumers, employees and suppliers help to determine the success of any business. Most businesses will choose to keep these parties happy. But what could be a sensible approach to management in many companies, becomes a dangerously interventionist agenda when imposed by government'.[59] Lang was expounding a predictable free market position. Yet this response, and the differences among the dominant advocates of stakeholding, illustrate that in one sense he was right. Stakeholding is primarily an attempt to find a third way, but the issues remain the same: how much regulation of the market by the state, what kind of regulation, and in whose interests? The last, and fundamental, question is inadequately addressed because of the refusal, in the accounts considered so far, to accept that any fundamental conflict of interests actually exists.

RADICAL STAKEHOLDING?

More radical accounts of stakeholding are available, but they receive little publicity. The TUC has endorsed stakeholding, and indeed John Monks, the General Secretary of the TUC, was a member of the Commission on Public Policy. The TUC report on stakeholding demonstrates the difficulty of participating in the dominant discussions while respecting the established trade union recognition that the interests of owners, managers and workers are frequently opposed.

Your Stake at Work: TUC proposals for a stakeholding economy has three distinct strands running through it. The first of these is the by now familiar theme of the need for long-term financing and long-term planning and for changes in corporate governance, coupled with an acceptance of the assumption that all stakeholders in a company – 'employees, customers, suppliers and the community, as well as the shareholders' – have a common interest in 'long term economic growth, high quality employment and environmental standards'.[60] The view that long-termism and trust are central to company success is reiterated:

> The argument for stakeholding goes beyond the fact that companies have moral responsibilities towards stakeholders. The development of stakeholder relationships can make a positive contribution to company success. There are two main reasons for this. Firstly, in a context of committed relationships based on mutual respect and trust, workers and other stakeholders are far more likely to be prepared to be flexible and apply new ideas. Secondly, workers and suppliers in particular have a very direct interest in the long-term success of a company – more so, in an immediate sense, than shareholders. Stakeholding allows companies to reap this inherent motivation. So, stakeholding is rooted in arguments both for competitiveness and for social inclusion. It is about allowing all those involved in a company fully to participate in and contribute to its success.[61]

The second strand, however, is far more suspicious about the consensual assumptions of this discourse, and explicitly uses stakeholding as a new term for old principles. These include much more information and consultation, increased power for workers' representatives (that is, trade unions) on company boards as a check on corporate power, investment in training, better employment rights, and, most centrally, an end to insecurity at work. It is tackling job insecurity which is the issue at the heart of stakeholding for the TUC: 'A company cannot be called a stakeholding company if it does not make the employment security of its workers a priority, and increased employment security is one of the most significant benefits that stakeholding would offer to employees'.[62] Rising insecurity cannot be blamed on globalization; it results from a hire and fire attitude on the part of management underpinned by the short-termism of financial institutions. And while the report chiefly concerns stakeholding in companies, there is 'the wider issue of giving people a stake in society'. Here, the principal issues are unemployment, a minimum wage, a fairer tax and benefit system, and ending discrimination on the basis of gender, race, sexual orientation or physical impairment: 'a stakeholding society is based on participation by the many, not privileges for the few'.[63]

Hutton's insistence on the importance of employment rights and job security brings his position closer to that of the TUC than is Kay's – despite the fact that Kay is repeatedly referred to in the TUC document, while Hutton receives only a single footnote.

The report distinguishes far more clearly than does Kay between how companies should, and how they actually do, operate. There is much talk about partnership, but it is about establishing the conditions under which partnership would be possible. In tackling corporate greed, full disclosure of the remuneration packages of directors is called for; but it is also argued that this will only be effective if stakeholders have some power. Otherwise those who benefit may be quite happy to face out disapproval and embarrassment as long as they can keep the money. Considerable changes in company and employment law are proposed on this and other matters, and there is no illusion here that appeals to ethics and voluntary codes will suffice: 'too many companies will choose to do nothing at all unless they are required to do so by law'.[64] Cultural change is seen as necessary, but riding on the back of legislation. A key change would be the legal definition of the interests of the company which directors are bound to pursue. There is some dispute over whether the present law defines shareholder interests as paramount. Kay argues that the company is an entity separate from the shareholders, and thus the interests of the company and shareholders are not identical; others disagree. The TUC proposal would clarify this by establishing that the interests of the company include not only the payment of sufficient returns to investors to secure investment, but 'the development of the skills and capabilities of employees and suppliers of the company; the achievement of stability and security in the company's employment and trading relationships; the provision of goods and services of good quality to the company's customers at fair prices'.[65]

While the interests of the company defined here include shareholders, workers, suppliers and customers as stakeholders, there is no mention of responsibilities to the wider community. There is a third strand in the report, however, which can be slotted into neither the business ethics version of stakeholding nor a traditional trade union one. This concerns the preparation of company accounts which are social and environmental, rather than purely financial; and the TUC suggests that in the medium term, once an appropriate methodology has been developed, these should be obligatory. The specific reference is to a process of social accounting, pioneered by Traidcraft with the help of the New Economics Foundation, which looks at environmental impact and at four stakeholder groups: shareholders, producer partners, staff and volunteers, and consumers and the wider public. A crucial point is that the stakeholders themselves define appropriate indicators for measuring social performance, and that this involves qualitative as well as quantitative data. Superficially similar ideas were developed by the Centre for Tomorrow's Company, which proposed a new format for annual reports measuring social as well as financial performance. The involvement of the Institute of Public Relations and the admission that this was about 'new ways of communicating' suggested a less radical agenda, notwithstanding the Centre's campaign for the recognition of the wider responsibilities of company directors.[66] Hutton, indeed, was scathing about 'the compromised attempts by the professional accounting bodies to devise more sophisticated accounting codes', both because they depend on self-regulation and because of the 'wider constitutional vacuum' in which they operate.[67]

The New Economics Foundation is more strongly influenced by green principles than is the TUC. NEF was established in 1986 and its publicity material describes its aims as 'to raise awareness about new economic approaches which put people and the environment first', putting quality of life above economic growth and profit. Their development of accounts which take seriously the social and environmental impact of business is close to a Green Party orientation to stakeholding. The Green Party also wishes to see a shift of emphasis away from shareholders' interests, with the ultimate goal of having capital provided either by those who work in the organization, or by the immediate community: 'the main stakeholders will become the workers, other businesses, shareholders, the local community and the environment'. While workers should have greater representation within companies, this is part of a 'process of moving towards the involvement of all the stakeholders'.[68] Greater accountability would be brought about by having smaller companies which are more 'open to community regulation, ensuring that greater care is taken both of the people who work in them and the needs of the local community and the environment'. Stakeholders include 'the shareholders, the workers, consumers, the local community and advocates for the local environment. New legal and institutional structures would be created to enable these stakeholders to have a voice in the running of companies and other relevant organisations'.[69] Thus the question of the wider social responsibility of companies is made more central. But it is notable that Green Party policy diverges from that of Kay, Hutton, the TUC and the Labour Party in three other significant ways. Firstly, it is opposed to the presumption of economic growth as good, favouring a stock economy; secondly, it defines as work 'all the activities people undertake to support themselves, their families and communities';[70] and thirdly, when it stresses the social duty of providing basic material security for all, it proposes the introduction of a basic income. Basic income and the ending of discrimination is seen as essential to 'partnership' in the workplace. The social inclusion of stakeholders necessitates reforming corporate governance, but also requires a radical transformation of the whole economic and social structure. When *The State We're In* was first published in 1995, Hutton was criticized for his failure to address environmental issues, and for his overriding assumption that the pursuit of economic growth is unproblematic. He accepted that 'environmental costs deserve to be ranked alongside social exclusion as a criticism of the current order', and that 'environmentalists correctly complain that conventional measurements of wealth dangerously neglect the sustainability of the natural environment'.[71] But he appeared to see the problem as one of widening the argument to show how stakeholder capitalism can be deployed to meet these concerns, not as calling into question the sustainability of capitalism itself.

CONCLUSION

The essence of stakeholding is the denial that there is fundamental conflict of interest between owners, managers, workers, and the common good. Except for the marginalized, radical versions, proponents of both soft and statutory stakeholding similarly eschew state regulation, or the 'incorporation' of trade unions as the collective representatives of workers. Stakeholders may have different interests, but they are not so different that they cannot be 'balanced' by responsible managers. The liberal-pluralist model of the state was that it 'balanced' and reconciled the different and occasionally somewhat conflicting interests of different groups in society. The consensual supposition was that all had an interest in the maintenance of the stability of the system. Similarly, in the new global economy, it is assumed that we are all, to quote Blair's 1996 Conference speech, on the same side and in the same team. But the responsibility for reconciling those interests has, in the stakeholder model, passed from the state to business, and to the ethical conduct of managers at that. Stakeholding is an attempt to reject the negative effects of the free market, without challenging the delegitimation of state intervention achieved by the proponents of the free market in the 1980s. But in trying to steer a narrow path between rejecting the market and rejecting the state, it has very little room for manoeuvre, and such space as it has is all to the advantage of employers rather than citizens who might potentially be stakeholders in a genuinely inclusive society.

5 Community Rules

Stakeholders make repeated reference to a world beyond the market: the community. Ferdinand Tönnies contrasted *gemeinschaft* (community) and *gesellschaft* (society or association) in terms of different forms of interaction: community is typified by dense, direct interaction in which people know one another in a variety of roles; association is characterized by much looser instrumental networks.[1] The general usage of 'community' in both lay and academic discourses lacks this clarity. While its resonance in political discourse increased in the 1990s, partly in reaction to the Thatcherite insistence that there is no such thing as society, its imprecision remains a problem. 'Community' may refer to neighbourhoods, while being prescriptive rather than simply descriptive of the forms of relationship within them. It may mean regional or national communities; the UK as a whole; the European community, which usually means those European countries within the European Union rather than Europe as a whole; or the world community. At each level of remove from localities, the reference becomes increasingly one of a commonality of interest, rather than a description of a form of interaction, while at local level, the coincidence of interest and residence is presumed. And community is also used to describe putative interest groups which are not geographically based at all, as in 'the black community', or the 'gay community'.

'Community' has enjoyed a resurgence in academic literature too, most notably in the liberal-communitarian debate in political philosophy.[2] Two writers, Amitai Etzioni and John Gray, have bridged the academic and popular debates, lending some intellectual credibility to the new political interest in community. Both have been regular newspaper columnists, and have written for influential think-tanks. Etzioni's *The Parenting Deficit*, a chapter of *The Spirit of Community*, was published separately by Demos, echoing similar ideas to be found in IPPR publications.[3] Gray is famous for transferring his support from the New Right to New Labour, a move reflected in the think-tanks publishing his work. The first three (of four) parts of *Beyond the New Right* were originally published by the Institute of Economic Affairs and the Centre for Policy Studies. Parts of *Enlightenment's Wake* were published by the Social Market Foundation, while *After Social Democracy*, reprinted in *Endgames*, was first published by Demos.

89

The third writer discussed in this chapter, John Macmurray, was a Scottish philosopher of religion born in 1891 and writing and broadcasting from the 1930s to the 1960s. Blair claims him as a key influence on his political thought, and he is included here for that reason. But his work also serves as an indication of the different inflections which can be given to communitarianism, in this case by a Christian socialist. Macmurray's views are strikingly different from those of Etzioni and Gray, whose preoccupations, especially the central emphasis on rights and responsibilities and the pursuit of a third way, are much closer to those of New Labour.

RESPONSIVE COMMUNITARIANISM: AMITAI ETZIONI

The Spirit of Community is a campaigning book for the communitarian movement in the USA.[4] *The New Golden Rule* is ostensibly more analytical, engaging to some extent with the related academic literature, and claiming legitimacy from social science.[5] Its arguments, however, differ little. Etzioni describes himself as a 'responsive communitarian' thereby distancing himself from conservative communitarians, and from libertarians, liberals and radical individualists. *The Spirit of Community* criticizes liberal arguments which place individual rights, freedoms and autonomy above the need for social order, but eschews an extreme authoritarian position, rejecting the puritanism of the 'moral majority'. *The New Golden Rule* argues that communitarianism offers a third way between anarchic individualism and repressive conformity: it 'leapfrogs the old debate between left-wing and right-wing thinking and suggests a third social philosophy'.[6] The communitarian paradigm is the 'new golden rule' which combines individual autonomy and the common good. It 'entails a profound commitment to moral order that is basically voluntary, and to a social order that is well balanced with socially secured autonomy'.[7]

To be in favour of a balance between individual autonomy and the common good is to be against sin. The identification of the common good with moral and social order, however, is to be rather more precise about sin and virtue, and shows Etzioni's position to be deeply conservative, despite his protestations. His definition of community rests not only on a particular form of social interaction, but on the function of this interaction in maintaining social control:

> Communities are social webs of people who know one another as persons and have a moral voice. Communities draw on interpersonal

bonds to encourage members to abide by shared values.... Communities gently chastise those who violate shared moral norms and express approbation for those who abide by them.[8]

This makes clear that the agenda is the remoralization of social life. In the 1950s 'core values...were relatively widely shared and strongly endorsed'. The 1960s undid traditional values, institutions and respect for authority but put nothing in their place; the counterculture 'weakened the country's values of hard work and thrift, as well as compliance with most rules of conduct, from dress codes to table manners, from established tastes in music to cuisine'.[9] The eighties compounded this 'moral confusion and social anarchy' with the celebration of individualism, selfishness and greed.[10] 'The moral order was hollowed out or weakened' by 'a rising sense of entitlement and a growing tendency to shirk social responsibilities'.[11] Increasing autonomy is not the problem: 'bounded autonomy', or 'a range of legitimate options within an affirmed normative framework' is a good thing; social anarchy, or 'the absence of order, regulation and normative guidance' is not. The slide towards anarchy is evident in the danger of crime in public spaces, the character of children's television, political corruption, sweatshop conditions at work, and above all in 'the waning of sexual mores'.[12] We need, he says, to 'concern ourselves with shoring up the social foundations of morality, so that communities can again raise their moral voices, families can educate their youngsters, and schools can graduate individuals who will become upstanding members of their communities'. The question is 'the ability to articulate and sustain any set of values in a social world that has largely lost this capacity'.[13] A central need is to correct the current imbalance between rights and responsibilities – although Etzioni would prefer not to talk about rights at all, since this language, he says, makes it difficult to 'achieve compromises and to reach consensus'. Rather, 'a return to a language of social virtues, interests, and above all social responsibilities will reduce contentiousness and enhance social co-operation'.[14]

Etzioni's argument is underpinned by a concept of human nature also presented as a third way between the overly 'sanguine' liberal model which presumes human nature to be largely good, and the overly 'dour' authoritarian model which presumes it to be irretrievably flawed. In contrast, the communitarian model is dynamic and developmental, stressing the importance of socialization. Etzioni argues that 'infants are the true barbarians at the gate', in need of both psychological and cognitive socialization.[15] Children must develop character, 'the psychological muscles that allow a person to control impulses and defer gratification, which is essential for achievement, performance and moral conduct'. They also need to learn the core values of society which 'contain moral substances that those with the proper basic personality can learn to appreciate, adapt and integrate into their lives: hard work pays, even in an unfair world; treat others with the same basic dignity with which you wish to be treated (or face the consequences); you feel better when you do what is right than when you evade your moral precepts'.[16] The basic elements of character and core values need to be internalized, rather than constantly externally imposed, since compliance without internalization causes alienation. Internalization takes place best in affect-laden relationships, so parenting is crucial. A 'moral deficit among the young' is largely attributable to a 'parenting deficit' created when both parents vacate the home for paid work elsewhere, leaving children either to inadequate day-care centres or to their own devices. 'Decades of widespread neglect of children' and lack of effective parenting are a major cause of crime, gang warfare, drug abuse, 'a poorly committed workforce,...a strong sense of entitlement and weak sense of responsibility'.[17] Parenting is labour intensive, so two parents are better than one. Lone-parent families and divorce are therefore to be frowned upon. Besides making divorce 'less lucrative' by pursuing absentee parents (chiefly fathers) for child support, and returning to the ritual of a daily family meal, 'a change of heart' is needed: 'people need to enter marriage more responsibly and be more committed to making it work'.[18]

Parents have a duty to attend to the moral education of their children, or they will not become civil members of the community. In the first two years at least, this cannot be safely delegated, so parents must spend more time with their children, either directly supervising them at home, or working (as volunteers) in the day care centres which the children attend. Parents should work at home, work different shifts, arrange for one parent to work full-time and the other part-time, work flexitime, or job-share. *The Spirit of Community* suggests that corporations should provide six months of paid parental leave, with the costs shared between the employers of the father and mother. A further eighteen months of unpaid leave should include six months support from public funds, with the cost of the rest 'absorbed by the family'.[19] *The New Golden Rule* proposes paid family leave for one year and a requirement that the employer keep a job for a parent for two additional years. Hutton's discussion of rising insecurity of employment suggests that such provision is unlikely to be negotiated in contemporary 'flexible' labour markets.

Schools may have to step in where parents fail to socialize their children adequately. In *The Spirit of Community*, Etzioni suggests that the role of schools should ideally be to impart information, on the basis of previous or ongoing socialization by parents. Later, he argues that all education transmits values, so schools are allotted an extended role: they 'will be better able to develop character if they are in session for more hours during school days, more days a week, and more months a year'.[20] English should be promoted as a common language, with a core curriculum common to all state schools, transmitting the shared values of the community:

> All public schools [in the USA] will dedicate some time to the teaching of civics, American history, and American literature. And ... these will be taught in ways that are respectful of basic American institutions and history... The underlying principle that needs to guide schools and colleges is that it is necessary that those who graduate will have some shared heroes, respect some shared symbols, and relate to some shared narratives, all reflecting the core of shared values.[21]

Even where initial socialization is satisfactory, 'the incontestable fact about human nature is that the good and virtuous character of those who have acquired it tends to degrade'. Constant social control through the informal mechanisms of communities is essential. Public shaming and humiliation are also effective means of social control, especially – but not exclusively – for those who infringe the law. Moreover, human nature is quite intractable, and even heavy socialization 'cannot expunge anti-social urges (such as aggression and inappropriate sexual inclinations)', so informal controls – backed up by legal sanctions in some cases – remain necessary throughout life.[22]

But what is socialization for? In one sense, it is simply to maintain social order, as far as possible through informal rather than formal mechanisms. However, the communitarian model is not neutral about the content of that order. A key goal is to produce a compliant workforce: 'if we are to maintain our edge in an increasingly competitive world, workers will have to come to their jobs drug free and sober, stay sober all the time they are on the job, and give a day's work for a decent day's pay'.[23] In order to do this they need to learn self-discipline:

Workers need...self-control so that they can stick to their tasks rather than saunter into work late and turn out slapdash products, becoming able to observe a work routine that is often not very satisfying by itself. Citizens and community members need self-control so that they will not demand ever more services and handouts while being unwilling to pay taxes and make contributions to the commons, a form of citizen infantilism.[24]

Etzioni's insistence that this form of communitarianism is not authoritarian or conservative rests on two claims: a commitment to gender equality, and the reliance on non-coercive methods of social control. Both claims therefore need careful consideration.

The solutions to the parenting deficit, besides making one-parent families less socially acceptable, all require an increase in unpaid work. Not only are parents to devote more time to their children, but other unpaid work, notably elder care, is already extensive. In addition, Etzioni wishes to 'return' a whole range of services to local communities, many to be carried out on a voluntary basis, thus producing a service 'more tailored to individual needs, more humane, and less subject to false claims' while cutting costs and reversing the situation in which the welfare state has weakened communities.[25] His list includes fire fighting, public safety (that is, crime control), mutual aid, credit co-operatives, block parties, local chamber music, jazz groups, development of parks and support for schools. The reduction of state provision is supported by the argument that voluntary associations and the institutions of civil society are the 'third leg' of society – the other two being the state and the market – and should be strengthened by being given a greater role. When Etzioni says that 'we' ought to assume more 'responsibilities for our children, elderly, neighbors, environment and communities',[26] the obvious question is who are 'we'? Who is expected to subordinate their individual interests to the common good and carry out the unpaid work on which communities depend?

Etzioni overtly intends no return to traditional communities in which women were routinely subordinated. Despite his general resistance to claims about rights, women 'are obviously entitled to all the same rights men are, including the pursuit of greed'.[27] He argues in favour of 'peer marriage' in which both partners have the same rights and obligations, and that the sexual division of labour between parents is a matter for private negotiation. But he also says that two-parent families are better than one-parent families, not just because parenting is highly labour-intensive, but because 'parenting works best when there is an emotional division of labor. One parent may be more supportive, the source of emotional security... The other parent may be more achievement-oriented, pushing children to extend themselves'.[28] The claim of gender neutrality is not wholly convincing. In reality the bulk of unpaid work in society, including parenting, and especially emotional work, is done by women. This situation is underpinned both ideologically, through beliefs that women are naturally nurturing, and economically, through gender segregation in the labour market and the financial dependence of women on men. The suggestion that in two-parent households parental leave might be taken by either parent serves as an example. Swedish experience supports the hypothesis that social convention and labour market conditions – particularly men's higher pay – combine to ensure that mothers, not fathers, are the ones who stay home. The economic and power relationships which actually prevail make the equal sharing of the increased burden of unpaid work unlikely, and an increased dependence on the invisible and unrewarded work of women a more likely consequence of Etzioni's proposals.

Etzioni's second point is that communitarianism is not coercive because it rests on informal social control. Morality is not upheld by force, other than in the last instance. Law, however, does back up morality. Communitarian law should always reinforce, not override, shared values. It is thus expressive of those values while helping to maintain social order by dealing with those who disregard moral pressure. As Etzioni puts it, 'law and morality, at their best, move like a person's two legs: they are never far apart'.[29] However, a strong moral order reduces the need for legal sanctions. Etzioni refers approvingly to stakeholding, and the virtue of making corporations more socially responsible by moral pressure rather than legislation. Morality is sustained by 'the gentle prodding of kin, friends, neighbors, and other community members'.[30] People may or may not be invited over for coffee, others may refuse to chat over the back fence, in the store or bar, but this constitutes 'mild social pressure' rather than coercion.[31] True, 'gentle snide comments' may give way to 'some that are not so gentle'.[32] But this is of little consequence: people who don't conform can join other communities, or 'put up with the fact that many people in a given community will avoid social contact with them'.[33] To argue that social pressure of this kind, including ostracism, is not coercive actually undermines Etzioni's own argument. If communities are to rely on moral pressures to maintain social order, they can do so only if these pressures have some coercive effects over potential dissidents. This then raises the question of who has the power to impose their standards, as well as the difficulties of ensuring just, equitable and accountable implementation through informal mechanisms. Etzioni recognizes that the questions of whose values are to be upheld, and how these are to be arrived at, are real ones. He argues, however, that what he proposes is not, like conservative communitarianism, a monolithic set of values and an imposed order, but an order which rests on a smaller set of shared, consensual, core values, arrived at by moral dialogue. This moral dialogue, described also as a megalogue or multilogue, and including public hearings and citizens' commissions as well as general public discourse, must be a genuine one. An 'inclusive community' requires an 'inclusive moral dialogue'.[34] 'Responsive communitarians seek to build communities based on open participation, dialogue and truly shared values'. To be sure, the reason for this is pragmatic as much as principled: 'if some members of the society are excluded from the moral dialogue, or manipulated into abiding by it, or their true needs ignored, they will eventually react to this lack of responsiveness in an antisocial manner'.[35] Such a dialogue is necessary at the level of the local community, the national community, and the global community.

Etzioni differentiates his position from that of liberals whom he sees as having a purely proceduralist orientation to dialogue and democracy. Although the dialogic process is an important factor in legitimizing the decisions which emerge from it, for Etzioni this is not enough. Legitimacy rests also on the substantive content of the emergent consensus. In the end, Etzioni can do little more than claim that certain substantive shared values are self-evident – that is, both self-evidently shared, and self-evidently legitimate: 'certain concepts present themselves as compelling in and of themselves'.[36] Arguments which rest legitimacy entirely upon procedural claims are open to the criticism that they ignore the realities of power relationships in the real world. The inclusive dialogue in which no-one has the power to impose their views or manipulate an emergent consensus in their favour is a chimera. Indeed, it has often been argued that consensual decision-making is dangerously repressive of dissent and disagreement. To couple the weaknesses of procedural claims to legitimacy with a claim to the obvious rightness of some substantive positions compounds the problem.

Equally unsatisfactory is his neglect of socio-economic questions, both in their own right, and as they affect the operation of moral constraints. He argues that such questions are outside the scope of a book about moral order, a claim which hardly stands up to scrutiny. The economic constraints on parents are, for example, fundamental to his argument about the parenting deficit. The few remarks that he makes on economic questions reveal him to be far from radical. Although he argues that a 'high degree of inequality is incompatible with a good society', and refers to the importance of social justice, meeting basic needs, progressive income tax and inheritance tax, he argues that equality is not a basic virtue.[37] Indeed, the intractability of human nature is used to argue against a redistributive society: 'Good societies, precisely because they need to base their order largely on voluntary commitments and to preserve a relatively high level of autonomy, are particularly limited in the extent to which they can foster "heroic" moral agendas, those that put heavy demands on their members – "heavy" because of their incompatibility with human nature.' This is Etzioni's answer to the question he calls the 'liberal cliché': 'why the "richest of nations" cannot use its assets to take care of the poor and sick, especially children, in other countries or even our own society'.[38]

COMMUNITARIAN LIBERALISM: JOHN GRAY

Etzioni calls for moral reintegration to repair the damage to the social fabric caused by moral decay. Although Gray also addresses problems of social disintegration and describes himself as a communitarian liberal, his starting point is very different. For Gray, 'the idea of community has acquired a powerful resonance in public discourse' because of the spread of economic insecurity; it is a 'potent symbol of the cultural losses of the eighties'.[39] But he is critical of much communitarian discourse, in Britain and America, and explicitly of Etzioni, for focusing too much on family breakdown as a moral question, and failing to address the real threats to communities which, for Gray, derive from free market policies at both national and global levels. He sees communitarianism as part of a fundamentalist agenda, which fails to recognize either the reality of a pluralist society or the value of autonomy. Gray argues that 'the pursuit of a delusive organic community distracts from the humbler but indispensable task of filling out that thinner common culture of respect for civil society'.[40]

Over a period of ten years, Gray evolved his distinctive position in a progressive public recantation of his former adherence to the New Right.[41] The Thatcherite ideologue had by 1997 become sufficiently prominent in the intellectual circle around New Labour to be a keynote speaker at the pre-election Nexus conference. The nature and limits of the change in Gray's thinking bear directly on the question of New Labour's political positioning. For although he has undoubtedly altered his position, the change is less radical than he suggests. Paradoxically, his increasingly critical view of markets – which does not translate into a criticism of capitalism – involves a shift from MUD towards SID. And in 1997, he was still committed to redefining the boundaries of political debate to exclude social democracy, in which RED is firmly rooted.

The main change in Gray's position lies in a switch from unequivocal support of the neo-liberal New Right to a more critical view of the social effects of unfettered markets. He examined the philosophical foundations of liberal thought, and found them wanting, while still insisting that the central institutions of liberal civil society have been important to the promotion of human well-being. He went on to attack the New Right for its 'fundamentalist conception of market institutions and its hubristic neglect of the human need for a common life'.[42] From a perspective which he then described as conservative individualism, he argued that while the New Right correctly recognized the benefits of markets and the dangers of government, it failed to understand that market institutions are social artefacts, embedded in wider social structures. It 'neglected . . . the dependency of civil society and its institutions on the resources of common culture' and 'did not grasp that market institutions fail insofar as they are not underpinned by trust, integrity and the other virtues of fair dealing'.[43] Embeddedness contributes to both the effective operation of the market, and human well-being. The support of the institutions of civil society is a proper concern of government; but they cannot be invented, or imported from elsewhere. A fundamental conservative insight which the New Right suppresses is the dependence of civil society on 'the soundness and vitality of cultural traditions'.[44]

Over the nineties, this critical attitude intensified. Unconstrained markets 'undermine social and political stability, particularly as they impose on the population unprecedented levels of economic insecurity with all the resultant dislocations of life in families and communities'.[45] The mobility of labour required by market forces is profoundly disruptive. 'The desolation of communities by unfettered market forces and the spectre of jobless growth produce[s] an ever larger, and increasingly estranged, underclass.'[46] The resultant destruction of informal social controls produces rising crime. Markets lead to anomie and social breakdown. Gray argues therefore that markets may need to be constrained or channelled, to meet the needs of communities. As for Etzioni, social control is high among these needs. But Gray disclaims the conservative position in which, he says, communities are seen as adjuncts to markets, for 'market institutions are stable and enduring only in so far as they are embedded in the common culture of those whose needs they exist to serve'[47] – begging the question of the purpose of capitalist markets.

Endgames, where Gray adopts the label 'communitarian liberal', says little about communities, but asserts the 'dependency of individual autonomy on a strong network of reciprocal obligations' embedded in concrete forms of life.[48] Communitarian liberalism is distinguished from liberalism by its rejection of individual choice as the ultimate virtue and by its denial of the moral supremacy of market institutions; such institutions are means, not ends. Five years earlier, Gray had argued that the justification of market institutions lay not in their efficiency, but in their contribution to autonomy; they were therefore more moral than socialist or social democratic alternatives.[49] Communitarian liberalism differs from social democracy in rejecting egalitarianism, while its recognition of autonomy and pluralism separate it from conservative and neo-traditionalist communitarianism. Pluralism means that a common culture unified by a single world-view is now impossible: 'We cannot recapture a 'thick' common culture grounded in a deep consensus on morality and history; but we must...strengthen and develop a thinner, yet durable and resilient, common culture of shared understandings of fairness and tolerance'.[50] However, Gray does not withdraw his earlier claim that the 'common culture may be reinforced by laws and policies which resist pluralism when pluralism threatens the norms of civil society itself'.[51]

For communitarian liberalism, 'individual human flourishing presupposes strong and deep forms of common life', or 'a strong public culture in which choice and responsibility go together'. This means that individual autonomy 'is realizable only as a common good', and that 'the conflict between autonomy and community is superficial'.[52] Market competition must be limited if it restricts, rather than enhances, autonomy, and should be excluded from areas like the public provision of health and education, where it violates common social understandings of fairness. In policy terms, this is a marked shift, for Gray had previously suggested that the market should be extended into these areas.[53] In philosophical terms, it illustrates his claim that autonomy and fairness cannot be understood or defined as applications of abstract, universal principles, but only as 'shared understandings arising from common forms of life'.[54] Like Etzioni, Gray neglects the question of the power relationships within those forms of common life, and thus the differential power to define what constitutes autonomy or fairness.

The appeal to a common culture suggests that Gray, like Etzioni, understands social inclusion primarily as moral inclusion, and his discussions of exclusion and the (re)integration of the excluded, bear this out. *Beyond the New Right* contains a programme for an 'enabling welfare state' which should intervene only when the resources of civil society are exhausted or inadequate. This implies greater reliance on welfare provision by families, neighbourhoods, churches and friends, more 'self-provision' and more charity. But state schemes are appropriate 'to return to the productive economy people who... have fallen out of it, but who possess or can acquire the skills and capacities to become active, self-reliant participants in the market economy' and 'to promote the autonomy of members of underclass groups by returning them to and reintegrating them into the market economy'.[55] Such schemes should always carry obligations, or else they constitute a moral hazard and feed dependency. Gray's criticism of the welfare state in 1990s Britain is that it fails to reintegrate the underclass into civil life, but 'imprisons it in ghettos of dependency'.[56]

The reference to civil life might suggest a broad notion of social inclusion; the emphasis on market integration tells against that. So too does his definition of the underclass as 'that section of society, comprising several millions of households, which is effectively outside of the market economy, or only peripherally involved in it'.[57] Gray's attribution of the causes of poverty, however, as well as his emphasis on the moral hazards of welfare provision, suggest that it is moral inclusion that most concerns him. 'Most modern poverty', he says, 'is a cultural rather than merely economic phenomenon'.[58] It is caused above all by family breakdown, as well as by poor education, 'lack of human skills', the 'depletion of human skills across generations and the emergence of a dependency culture'.[59] The underclass is also a threat to social order: 'Those who lack property and are denied the opportunity to acquire it may reasonably be expected to lack the dispositions appropriate to civil life and may well become its enemies'.[60] Somewhere, too, there is a fifth column waiting to recruit them: 'a society with a substantial propertyless underclass cannot reasonably be expected to be stable when the resentments of those with nothing are open to exploitation by radical movements'.[61]

Gray's later work appears to show a shift from MUD to SID. Despite describing the term 'underclass' as 'American' and as 'fashionable but deeply misconceived', he continues to use it.[62] But he attributes the development of an underclass to unemployment, resulting from jobless growth, and the emphasis shifts to the question of exclusion. The number of workless households constitutes an 'expanding "underclass" of families excluded from the common life of society'.[63] This 'exclusion from the productive economy' is blamed on New Right policies.[64] Social exclusion is to be prevented by 'enabling all to participate in the productive economy'.[65] But the shift to SID is at best partial, and may be a change of language rather than substance – illustrating the very flexibility of concepts of exclusion and inclusion. Gray still refers to 'forms of unemployment and poverty whose roots are in deskilling and family breakdown', and argues that 'the principal causes of most modern poverty are cultural and are not removed by the provision of income'.[66]

Gray's discussion connects economic and moral integration through the role of paid employment in conferring identity and self-esteem. 'In all modern western societies jobs have long been experienced not merely as means of acquiring income but as the principal source of our social identity.'[67] He argues that social policy must, among other things, assist those without paid work, including lone parents, into 'productive work, participation in which is, for us, the pre-condition of self-esteem and independence'.[68] Yet his concern with jobless growth, which he sees as a consequence of globalization, suggests that the market can no longer be relied on to perform this integrative function. He argues against SID that we need to detach self-esteem from paid work, so that 'our sense of personal identity and self-esteem depend as much upon our contribution to the larger informal economy of family and community as on the possession of a permanent job',[69] thus requiring civil society and intermediate institutions to carry out the morally integrative role in which the market has failed.

Gray's departure from SID rightly recognizes the problems which result from the discursive construction of identity on the basis of paid employment. But his argument has three weaknesses. He fails to recognize that the relationship between self-esteem and employment is already gendered – just as he fails to recognize the extent of unpaid work and its gendered distribution. And while he suggests separating self-esteem from employment, he does not suggest separating the distribution of the social product from paid work. He rejects basic income schemes as themselves exclusionary on three grounds. Firstly, they attach an extra significance to citizenship, and exclude non-citizens. Secondly, they reduce the 'political incentive to reintegrate the excluded'. Thirdly, and most importantly, they are morally objectionable because they breach the principle of reciprocity: they give rights without corresponding obligations. Therefore, 'In regard to the so-called underclass, they reinforce the denial of agency and the lack of mutuality and of a sense of membership which are the most disabling features of the culture of dependency'.[70] Gray's attack on social democracy, in which RED is rooted, and which might provide the material basis for separating self-esteem from paid employment, was in 1997 as forceful as ever, although its grounds were somewhat changed.

In *Beyond the New Right* Gray argued that central planning, market socialism and all commitment to egalitarianism must be struck from the political agenda in favour of a new consensus based on acceptance of the free market and private property in the means of production. As part of this new consensus, social democrats needed to shed 'disabling illusions of egalitarianism'. Legitimate political disagreement would then focus on a narrower range of difference: 'The real space for public discourse is...in the area of detailed debate about the scope and content of public goods, the depth and limits of the common culture, the relative costs of government failure and market failure, and the content and levels of provision of basic needs'.[71] This discourse should reject the language of rights, which is universalistic, monolithic and antithetical to compromise, in favour of 'fairness' and autonomy: 'If rights are eliminated from political discourse, then a settlement can sometimes be reached...which is stable because it is perceived as fair.... The effect of rights-discourse is to render political conflicts non-negotiable'.[72]

After Social Democracy also seeks to redefine the legitimate boundaries of political debate.[73] Its central thesis is that social democracy is a spent force, and that attempts to return to it are anachronistic. The demise of the Soviet Union not only removed socialism 'from the agenda of history'. The end of the cold war was accompanied by global mobility of capital and a concomitant reduction of the powers of national governments. Globalization – although sometimes recognized by Gray as a project rather than simply an external force – renders social democracy impossible. What remains is simply a competition between different forms of capitalism. While this is not a moral attack on social democracy, it is an argument intended to delegitimize it. Social democracy, says Gray, was centrally about equality and redistribution, and based on full employment engineered if necessary by government intervention. Its animating ideal was 'a form of society-wide egalitarian community of which the workplace was conceived to be the germ'.[74] Full employment cannot be implemented; and egalitarianism once more comes under attack.

Gray argues that market freedoms operate against social cohesion, social solidarity and common citizenship. The New Right misunderstood welfare institutions, seeing them as 'mechanisms for income transfer or poverty relief, rather than devices for security against common risks and the dangers of exclusion' and 'promoting social solidarity and common citizenship'.[75] Preventing exclusion, however, only necessitates meeting 'satiable human needs' (including autonomy). Equality may be defended only in so far as it is 'demanded as a safeguard against exclusion', not, as in social democracy, on the grounds of social justice.[76] For equality itself has no moral basis, although high levels of inequality may be of concern because they threaten stability or cohesion, where they breach local understandings of fairness.

The ideological distance Gray has travelled is not as great as it at first appears. His characterization of the New Right as coterminous with neo-liberalism leads him to misunderstand his own position as a move away from the New Right, when it is perhaps more accurately assessed as a change of position within it. Whereas the views that there is no such thing as society (Thatcher) or that society is the benign but unintended outcome of market processes (Hayek) are typically neo-liberal, neo-conservatism always emphasized the importance of the state, of government, and of traditional institutions – importantly including the family and the church. However, although Gray uses families and churches as examples of institutions of civil society, he distances himself from neo-conservatives like Roger Scruton. Firstly, he sees the emphasis on the strong state as a pragmatic response by the New Right to the effects of the untrammelled market. Secondly, he regards the attempt to re-impose the traditional family as both illiberal and impossible. A commitment to autonomy and a pragmatic acceptance of pluralism make this inappropriate. We must, he argues, accept the variety of family forms as a fact – although his earlier qualification of this renders his position ambiguous:

A liberal state ... has the vital responsibility of tending and sheltering the social matrix of responsible choosers, the family. It cannot shirk the formulation of a family policy. In this, though it ought to eschew the spurious liberal ideal of neutrality with regard to all forms of family life, it is bound to respect the legitimate variety of forms of family life in society today. In other words, although policy should aim to discourage forms of family life, such as that of single-parenthood, where it is demonstrably injurious to children, it cannot engage in projects of social engineering aiming to revive a vanished form of family life.[77]

His position can be seen as a new 'soft' synthesis of liberal and conservative positions, in which the negative effects of markets are policed, partly (still) by a visibly authoritarian state, but more effectively by the morally constraining mechanisms of civil society. The market is still central: 'Today we can see that robust and adaptable market institutions are an indispensable instrument for enhancing the well-being of the great majority'.[78] Gray characterizes the political task of the age as 'reconciling the subversive dynamism of market institutions with the human need for local rootedness and strong and deep forms of common life'.[79] His sustained attacks on social democracy make it quite clear that the third way which he seeks is not between state and market, or between socialism and laissez-faire capitalism, but between social democracy and laissez-faire capitalism. The enemy on the left is now social democracy, which is to be undermined by appeals to globalization, just as the old, socialist left was attacked for its failure to understand the realities (and virtues) of the market. The territory of legitimate political debate is simultaneously narrowed and shifted to the right. Rather than being a centre-left position, this can only be interpreted as the centre right (Figure 5.1). The significant shift is from thinking that this 'soft' synthesis can be promoted within the

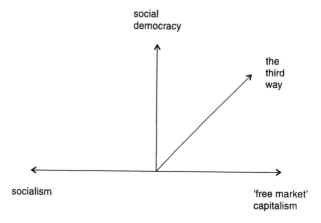

Figure 5.1   The Third Way: Centre-Left or Centre-Right

Conservative Party to a recognition that it may be more effectively pursued elsewhere. Thus he argues that 'Labour's likely turn is towards an attempted fusion of the individualist economic culture of liberal capitalism with communitarian concerns about fairness and community'.[80] Conservatism is, at least temporarily, dead: 'The genuine understanding of enduring human needs which conservative thought once possessed – needs for membership in strong forms of common life, and for security and stability in economic life – has now passed to other modes of thinking, such as ... New Labour'.[81]

CHRISTIAN COMMUNITARIANISM: JOHN MACMURRAY

Blair claims that his sympathy for communitarian themes lies in the influence of the Christian socialist John Macmurray. When contemporary politicians claim to be Christian socialists, this tells us little about their beliefs, for Christian socialism has a very varied history. That many do so raises uncomfortable questions about their reinforcement of the cultural hegemony of a minority religion in a multicultural, multifaith and largely secular society. The Christian Socialist Movement includes several members of Blair's first Government besides Blair himself, notably Gordon Brown, Tessa Jowell, Jack Straw, Derry Irvine and Calum MacDonald, who was promoted to Malcolm Chisholm's post at the Scottish Office when Chisholm resigned over cuts to lone parents' benefits. The purpose of adopting the label of Christian or ethical socialism is often to signal a distance from egalitarian or 'economic' socialism and especially from Marxism, and to set ethical and economic socialism in opposition to one another. Socialism based on a moral imperative is falsely contrasted with socialism as the outcome of an economically-determined historical process; a shift is then made to defining 'economic' socialism as somehow unethical, while 'ethical' socialism no longer rests on or requires economic change, and is curiously compatible with capitalism.[82]

Macmurray's position was the antithesis of this. Samuel Brittan argues that Macmurray can hardly be seen as a communitarian at all in the sense that this is now understood, being far more liberal.[83] But he is also more critical of capitalism and more committed to equality than either Etzioni or Gray; and his writings do not support the idea that the primary role of community is to maintain social order. The themes of community and responsibility and the centrality of education are there; but so too are the themes of freedom, of integrity, and the grounding of these in material equality. Although Macmurray was committed to the goal of an inclusive community, his understanding of this was very different. And there are passages which read as ironic comment on Blair's political practice: 'The tremendous idea of creating the community of all mankind as the fulfilment of the Divine purpose, does not lead [Jesus] to an effort to secure the support of the cultured or ruling classes...he draws the conclusion that he must choose the band of disciples who are to help him create the Kingdom from the common folk...and must resolutely turn his face away from the rich and the ruling classes'; 'those who are important because of privileges of wealth and social position are of no use for his purpose'.[84] If the primary good is open and equal communication between persons, what passes for fellowship is often nothing of the sort: 'We slap one another on the back and call one another by our Christian names to pretend that we are really in touch with one another'.[85]

In what might appear an endorsement of a recognizably communitarian position, Macmurray wrote:

Each of us is born into a society and our lives are bound up with the community to which we belong. Human goodness is a common goodness, a social goodness. Life has been transmitted to us by our parents and all our capacities are inherited capacities. Society gives us nourishment and education and the opportunities of self-development. We owe all we have and all we are to the community to which we belong. The community is our real environment, and we live only in it and through it. Therefore the purpose which ought to control our lives is not our own selfish purpose, but the social purpose. We are part of a community of social life, and the goodness of our individual lives depends on our devoting them to the common good. Each of us has a place and a function in society....The good man is the man who serves his country, serves his generation, identifies himself with the good of the community, and devotes his life to the accomplishment of a social purpose.[86]

However, the purpose of this passage is to argue that this view of morality and community is wrong. True morality is personal morality, that is, it lies in being persons, in being fully ourselves, and in meeting others in their free and full personhood. This means that you cannot test freedom by whether it conforms to morality; the question is whether morality conforms to freedom, and the idea of a moral law is 'an absurdity'. Consequently, 'there is no place in good human behaviour for the idea of obedience'.[87] Obedience throws the responsibility for our actions on to something or someone else, while to seek obedience from others is to refuse to trust them. Morality lies in sincerity of self, but the minimum requirement of morality in both direct and indirect relations is justice. In the direct relations of small communities, this can be achieved by common consent to a set of reciprocal rights and obligations, supported by trust – and, in the abnormal situation of breaches of trust, by the sanction of public opinion. But the idea of community as a moral policeman was anathema to Macmurray. He stressed the positive forces of trust and the habit of co-operation, rather than the negative force of sanctions, which call up a Hobbesian view of society. In indirect relations, characteristic of larger societies, justice can only be discharged through law.

Macmurray's starting point was not the need for order, but what it is to be human. Our human nature is, he said, 'our capacity to think really and feel really for ourselves, and to act accordingly'.[88] Consistent with this, in his 1950s Gifford Lectures he argued that the self is agent rather than subject, acting rather than contemplative; but the individual self is an embedded self, an abstraction having no reality outside of a community of persons in relation.[89] Macmurray was claiming more than that human life is essentially social: the intentionality of relations is the distinguishing human characteristic. We are therefore most distinctively human 'in communion' with others – not as I, but as 'you and I' in a mutual relationship of recognition of the other, who is not treated as a means to an end. Only in such a pure relationship, which assumes agency, responsibility and choice on the part of self and other, is a genuine meeting of persons possible. A community is a group within which such relationships prevail, and in which they are conscious and intended. It should be an inclusive group. Exclusion of anyone involves a closing off of the self – generally through fear – and thus a diminishing of one's own humanity. Citizenship was, for Macmurray an exclusionary device: ultimately, to be inclusive, community must be universal.

The central referent of the term community is thus a quality of personal relationship. Communities are bonded by direct personal relationships, by fellowship, and by conscious acknowledgement of this connection. Macmurray's insistence on intentionality did not imply voluntarism, for he was equally concerned with the material conditions which would make such relationships possible – which include both economic interdependence and material equality. Conversely, economic factors cannot of themselves produce community; without the 'positive and direct impulse to community' which 'makes economic

co-operation possible', and in the absence of the solidarity of community, class struggle will result.[90] Although economic relations are
embedded in relations of community, community does not exist to
provide the stable conditions for economic efficiency. The relationship
is reversed. Production should 'not only supply material needs but 'in
addition ... and as the full purpose of this ... provide the conditions for
free mutual relationships'.[91] Nor did Macmurray see participation
in paid work as essential to self-esteem or as the proper vehicle for
determining a share of the social product. Human dignity and freedom
begin where necessity ends: leisure, not work, is where people may be
fully human. The work ethic gets short shrift: 'The gospel of work and
of the dignity of labour is not a true one.... Work is a necessity, and so
far as we are under the constraint of necessity our human dignity has
no opportunity to unfold and express itself in reality'.[92]

Although Macmurray said that Jesus's concept of equality is an
equality of human worth he was unequivocal about the importance
of material equality. Equality of worth is in practice undermined by
inequality. Charity is not – as Gray argues – virtuous. It disrupts
equality, places the giver in a superior position and destroys mutuality.
By extension, this must also apply to personal economic dependency,
which is of course institutionalized in the family, both in relationships
between women and men, and between parents and children. Macmurray differs from most communitarians on this topic too. His claim that
the family is the original human community, sustained by affection
rather than by force or duty, romanticizes the family; and his discussion of the early socialization of babies paints a very rosy view of
motherhood. But he is adamant that men and women should have
'complete freedom to enter into personal relations on a basis of
absolute equality', and that the social conditions for this did not, in
fact, exist – and should be established.[93] He also recognizes that the
sexual division of labour which developed historically left women
responsible for the maintenance of community, while men were
encouraged to specialize. 'The social unity ... must be maintained', he
said, 'but it can no longer be maintained through the differentiation of
the social functions of the sexes'.[94] He was opposed to trying to
maintain marriage and the family, which are merely institutions, since
to do this is to place a functional relationship above the requirement of
personal integrity. It is emotional sincerity, and that alone, which
makes a relationship (sexual or otherwise) moral. In so far as the
family was failing, it was because it was being called on to 'bear a
burden of responsibility it cannot possibly carry'.[95]

Freedom is also dependent on material equality: 'real freedom is always proportionate in a society to the equality between its members' and 'the condition of a democratic culture [is]...something like an equal distribution of the common wealth'.[96] Without this, and expressly in society divided by class, the forms of democracy may be not only a sham but a means of preventing the achievement of the conditions of real democracy. The extent to which a society is declared to be committed to democracy or to individual freedom is beside the point. What matters is the extent to which these values are embodied in its structure and institutions. Thus 'a communion which consists in the idea and the sentiment of being members of one body, however strongly thought and felt, still remains illusory...so long as it does not express itself in the provision by all for the material needs of each'.[97] A society can be said to value individuals only when its organization is designed and judged in terms of 'personal life as the ultimate and determining value', which necessitates meeting the actual and substantial needs of its members.[98] Macmurray went on to say quite categorically that 'a capitalist society does not organise its social activity in this way',[99] but rather values individuals in terms of their contribution to social organization, a fact made particularly clear in the treatment of the unemployed. Since the standard of judgement in economic life is efficiency, its demands may be destructive of community, as for example in the requirement of mobility of labour.[100]

Although pure relationships cannot be artificially created, the conditions under which they become possible include both material equality and an emotional literacy and self-knowledge which would now be described as reflexivity. The development of these qualities has implications for education, the primary instrument for developing human nature. Macmurray did not see children as barbarians, but thought it radically false to see them as 'little animals who acquire the characteristics of rational humanity through education'.[101] Their sole adaptation to the world at birth is their impulse to communication, not just for the satisfaction of biological needs, but for personal connection. All other purposive behaviour is learnt, through reciprocal communication, initially with the 'mother' (who need not, he pointed out, be the biological mother, and might be a man; parenting is learnt too), and subsequently through a widening network of relationships.

Just as the economy must be subordinate to the more genuinely human need of community, so 'the main function of education is to train men and women for freedom, not for work'. We cannot avoid the 'necessity of training children for their future functions as citizens of

an industrial community'.[102] But rapid change makes habits of passive
obedience inappropriate, and the necessity for lifelong learning means
that we should avoid putting children off learning by trying to teach
them too much: 'a child should learn what he wants when he wants to
learn it'.[103] Training distorts education, and it is further perverted by
examinations and the competition for qualifications. Examinations
should be abolished. The shortcomings of the education system should
not be blamed on teachers, who know that training for work runs
counter to true education. There should be less focus upon the
intellect, which produces an instrumental attitude to life, and more upon
emotional education. From this can grow a real discipline, discovered
through experience, rather than a false – and indeed evil – discipline,
imposed by authority, aimed at conformity, based in repression and
punishment, and destructive of responsibility. Like Etzioni, Macmurray believed that 'the foundations of [the] development of disciplined
community can only be laid properly in early life'[104] – but he did not
mean quite the same thing.

CONCLUSION

In different ways, all three writers discussed in this chapter are
addressing similar problems. All agree that social cohesion depends
upon moral integration of some kind, and that this is not independent
of social structure; they see economic interdependence, especially that
of the market, as an insufficient basis for social solidarity, and itself
dependent on prior moral claims. All three see the self as fundamentally socially embedded, and are concerned with the relationships
between freedom or autonomy and community, arguing that these are
not in opposition to each other. All see community as embodying
rights, responsibilities and trust – and all, including Macmurray, see
actual communities as supporting solidarity through informal sanctions. All see community as governed by different rules from economic
life – although Etzioni barely discusses economic relations, and Gray
and Macmurray differ fundamentally in their evaluation of capitalism,
and their understanding of the proper relationship between communal
and economic life. The articulation of these themes differs enormously, and raises a question about the relationship between moral
integration and MUD.

As argued in Chapter 1, just as RED, SID and MUD rely on integration through work, they all assume an element of moral integration

as well. What distinguishes MUD is that it defines the boundary between included and excluded in terms of moral deficiency, and thus implies the imposition of moral order on the excluded. Communitarianism claims to seek a consensual moral order, but tends to rely on formal or informal imposition when the consensus fails or the conditions for it are absent. The parallels with MUD are thus both partial and covert. Etzioni is the most conservative and the closest to MUD; Gray remains liberal in his continued endorsement of the market which community must moderate, oscillating between MUD and SID; while Macmurray's emphasis on personal freedom is grounded in a commitment to material equality which is now deeply unfashionable, and is much closer to RED. All see economic life as embedded in communal morality, while simultaneously being separate and different from it. This uneasy relationship between economy and community runs also through the rhetoric and policies of New Labour, where it is played out in profound contradictions.

6 New Labour, New Discourse

THE BLAIR REVOLUTION AND THE THIRD WAY

The new discourse consolidated in 1995 and 1996 drew on the rhetoric of both stakeholding and communitarianism. It defined the politics of New Labour as a third way between the New Right and the 'old left' or 'old Labour', committed to economic efficiency and social justice. The new Clause IV, ratified at a special conference in April 1995 after intense conflict in the Party, removed the phrase 'common ownership of the means of production, distribution and exchange'. It encapsulated a different set of political priorities, and a different underpinning model of society, cast in a different language. Gone were questions of equity of distribution; of political, social and economic emancipation; a higher standard of social and economic life; and improvement in conditions of work. Gone too was the primary commitment to work with the trade union movement. In their place were some of the phrases which echoed like mantras through the 1997 election campaign: 'the many not the few'; 'the rights we enjoy reflect the duties that we owe'; and the words enterprise, partnership, opportunity, community, security, and trust. (See Appendix).

The third way is variously described as left of centre, the centre-left, the radical centre, or simply the centre. *New Labour, New Britain*, the draft manifesto, said 'New Labour is neither Old Left nor New Right, for neither remotely corresponds to the nature of the challenges facing us. Instead we offer a new way ahead, that leads from the centre, but is profoundly radical in the changes it promises'. In the pre-election period, this positioning was crucial. Differentiation from the New Right established Labour as an alternative to the Thatcher-Major regimes, while retaining Labour's traditional voters. Differentiation from the old left announced that Labour had changed, appealing to new constituencies of support. But the new discourse misrepresents both New Right and old left. Like John Gray, New Labour identifies the New Right with neo-liberalism, and ignores the social authoritarianism which imbued the synthesis of the free market and the strong state. By presenting the New Right as solely oriented to the market, and referring frequently to Thatcher's claim that 'there is no such thing as society', New Labour could be presented as left of centre simply by arguing that markets alone produce socially damaging results which are simultaneously inequitable and inefficient.

Recognizing that markets are necessarily embedded in social structures does distinguish New Labour from extreme neo-liberalism. But the New Right naturalization of 'markets' is replaced by appeals to the inevitability of 'globalization'. The participation of national governments and international institutions in the active construction of a global market, for example through the Multilateral Agreement on Investment (MAI), is ignored.[1] The global economy is repeatedly invoked as an external factor which limits the possibility of government intervention in general and its responsibility for economic insecurity in particular. It is also deployed to support the argument that we are one nation with one interest in successful competition. New Labour embraces the market: it will 'accept and welcome the new global economy' while rejecting 'market infallibility'.[2] Its distinctive message is that 'it does not seek to limit markets', but 'recognises that they need to operate within a fair framework of rules'. At the national level, it 'expands' the ideal of social co-operation 'into a more dynamic view of the need for a strong society and an active community' – a 'new tough, concept of community, where rights and responsibilities go hand in hand'.[3] The embedded market and the strong society of New Labour replace the free market and the strong state of Thatcherism.

'Newness' marks off the Blairite project from old Labour. 'New' and 'modern' are good, 'old' is bad. Britain is to be a 'young country' oriented to 'renewal' and to 'the future not the past'. New Labour is modern, fair and strong. Old Labour is decried as the party of 'tax and spend', New Labour celebrated as the party of 'save and invest', echoing the Borrie contrast between 'levellers' and 'investors'. The old left is portrayed as comprehensively hostile to markets, over-keen on public ownership, statist, centralizing, corporatist and wedded to the power of trade unions. The third way ostensibly lies 'between state control of industry and laissez faire',[4] but everything to the left of New Labour is compressed into the terms old left and old Labour, from Marxists to Croslandite social democrats like Roy Hattersley, previously seen as on the right of the Party. The left-hand boundary of the arena within which New Labour is 'central' is thus placed in this Croslandite position. An extreme version of this strategy contrasts 'ethical socialism' with a travesty of Marxism, and implicates old Labour in the latter:

While never being Marxist, old Labour was influenced by Marxist thought. This quasi-scientific view of the world rests on economic determinism and class analysis, propounded by those who claim to speak for 'the working class'. Always out of kilter with the real world, this socialism of state control of industry offers nothing to an understanding of how the modern market economy can be helped to prosper. Its blind belief in the state is unable to recognise that the public sector too can become prey to vested interests and require reform. Its narrow view of class offers no insights into today's pluralist society in which wrongs of race and gender matter just as much as those caused by social background.[5]

Blair himself referred to the 'struggle to return the Labour Party to [its] guiding values' and to 'strip away from it outdated ideology and the quasi-Marxist doctrines . . . of state control' in favour of the market. 'The abandonment of old-style collectivism puts the dividing lines with the new right in a different place. My criticism of them is nothing to do with living in a market economy'.[6] New Labour 'stands firmly in the social-democratic tradition – but with a new hard edge to its economic thinking'.[7]

Barratt Brown and Coates have criticized New Labour's – and particularly Mandelson and Liddle's – misrepresentation of history, concerned especially at their attempts to delegitimize the links between the Party and the trade union movement.[8] These distortions are not accidental. They work to eradicate the image of the Labour Party as the party of the organized working class, by rejecting a class analysis of society altogether in favour of a pluralist model. Divisions of ethnicity and gender are invoked, as above, as alternatives to class, not as intertwined with it. While Labour has historically been committed to a mixed economy, part publicly owned and part private, it has, of course, always been based on the assumption of conflicting class interests as a structural feature of capitalism. This is not an exclusively Marxist position; previous Labour governments, and many pre-Thatcherite Conservative ones, have seen the role of the state as one of managing these conflicts, rather than either abolishing or denying them. But a central element in third way politics is the denial of structural conflicts of interests. Blair insisted in his 1996 Conference speech: 'Forget the past. No more bosses versus workers. You are on the same side. The same team. Britain united'. Even the need for 'hard choices' invoked the following year referred to priorities, not conflicting interests. In this consensual world, where economic efficiency and social justice go hand in hand, conflict is the outcome of outdated adversarial attitudes, not structural relations, and can be resolved by people being 'fair', 'sensible' and 'responsible' – terms which are also used to support the claim that New Labour is not ideological, but pragmatic. Efficiency, accountability, opportunity and fairness replace the neo-liberal legitimizing principles of efficiency, accountability and freedom.[9]

STAKEHOLDING: A STRATEGIC RETREAT

Mandelson and Liddle define New Labour in terms of five insights, three of which position it as a third way. The two substantive points are that in 1990s Britain people experience high levels of insecurity as a result of global change; and that Britain's decline calls for investment, partnership and education to stimulate economic efficiency, together with political reform. These issues echo the concerns of the stake-holding debate, and refer back explicitly to Hutton's analysis. When Blair took up stakeholding in January 1996, he consulted Hutton before writing the speech in which he said:

> We need to build a relationship of trust not just within a firm but within society. By trust, I mean the recognition of a mutual purpose for which we work together and in which we all benefit. It is a Stakeholder Economy in which opportunity is available to all, advancement is through merit and from which no group or class is set apart or excluded. This is the economic justification for social cohesion, for a fair and strong society.[10]

He argued that a stakeholder economy meant tackling unemployment and establishing a stakeholder welfare system. However, since 'we cannot by legislation guarantee that a company will behave in a way conducive to trust and long term commitment', where business is concerned the challenge is to 'shift the emphasis in corporate ethos... towards a vision of the company as a community or partner-ship in which each employee has a stake, and where a company's responsibilities are more clearly delineated'. Despite the focus on ethos rather than legislation, Blair had at least mentioned the respons-ibilities of companies. Three weeks later, he developed the idea of a stakeholder society as the context of the stakeholder economy. Here, Blair argued that 'the most meaningful stake anyone can have in society is the ability to earn a living and support a family'. But stakeholding is as much about the obligation to work as the right to a stake in society: 'the purpose is ... to ensure that the country works for the good of everybody, and everybody works for the good of the country'. While 'we accept our duty as a society to give each person a stake in its future', 'in return each person accepts the responsibility to respond, to work to improve themselves'.[11]

Although the language of stakeholding spread in popularity and became commonplace in Labour documents and speeches, it lacked any real substance. The draft manifesto equated the 'vision of a stake-holder Britain' with 'economic opportunities for all', and extolled the virtues of partnership between companies and their employees: 'The best companies recognise their employees as partners in the enterprise.... Many unions are enthusiastically embracing the new notion of social partnership, replacing conflict'. The 'new Labour approach' is 'based on partnership, on stakeholding, not an old-fash-ioned war between bosses and workers'. In setting out to create a 'genuine one nation, stakeholder society', we should 'aim to give everyone a stake in our society, a chance in life'.

Blair stopped talking about a stakeholding economy long before the election, although stakeholding rhetoric continued to be deployed in some quarters. Wright's *Why Vote Labour?* argued the superiority of Labour's 'stakeholding approach' not only over the 'inertia-as-ideology' approach of the Conservatives, but over the more long-standing 'negative "two sides of industry approach"' which has been 'allowed ... to dog our industrial relations'. Wright cited Charles Handy's view that 'Companies are communities of people united by common aspirations rather than bundles of assets owned by share-holders', and suggested that 'stakeholding offers the basis for a new kind of partnership in business', involving 'an acceptance of a mu-tuality of obligations'. Conflict is unnecessary: 'commitment to long-term stakeholding makes more commercial sense'. Indeed, 'one of the biggest prizes the election can deliver' is 'the prospect ... of a con-structive partnership between all the stakeholders in the British economy directed towards agreed goals'.[12]

However, stakeholding could be criticized as corporatism, as implying too close a relationship with trade unions. David Willetts, having attacked Hutton on these and other grounds, accused Labour of a neo-corporatist agenda.[13] In *Why Vote Conservative?* he argued that a key choice in the election was between 'a free-market economy and ... a stakeholder economy with "social cohesion" delivered by more regulations and taxation'. He claimed that Labour's stakeholding language expressed 'hostility to the modern enterprise economy', involving legislation for stakeholder representation on company boards; and that 'Labour and the TUC have made it clear that what they mean by stakeholder talk is old-fashioned, organized trade unions'.[14]

Alistair Darling's contribution to *Stakeholder Capitalism* illustrates the attempt to defend stakeholding from such attacks by evacuating it of all meaning.[15] He argued that stakeholding is a general philosophical concept which, contrary to the feelings of insecurity deriving from globalization, 'describes how...we are rooted in society' and 'aims to show how individuals working together can affect the forces that shape society'.[16] It is explicitly not about interventionism, corporatism, or legislative change, but about changing the way in which people think: 'It does not rely on new rules or regulations or new acts of Parliament', but is 'about creating a change of culture in the country'.[17] To build the stakeholder economy means to 'foster the kind of environment in which businesses and companies are likely to prosper'.[18] This may involve increasing participation in the workplace in the interests of 'proper motivation', 'improved performance', and 'partnership' which is 'a far more productive and profitable relationship than adversarial workplace relations'.[19] Darling distinguished between primary stakeholders, who have a real interest in the company – investors, managers and employees; secondary stakeholders, who have an indirect interest – suppliers and customers; and others, such as citizens in the local area, who are not stakeholders at all. In the broader sense, however, everyone should have a stake in the future, a stake in their government, a stake in the country, and a stake in the economy. But in Darling's framework, to be a stakeholder does not entail any particular rights: to have a stake in the economy and in the nation's prosperity simply means to have a job.

The final manifesto – besides removing the residual references to democratic socialism, and replacing them with New Labour – dropped most of the references to stakeholding. It retained only the vaguest formulation of 'having a stake in' society: Blair wanted 'a Britain which we all feel a part of, in whose future we all have a stake'. And it repeated his earlier construction of the idea of stakeholding as a responsibility rather than a right: 'Our longterm objective is high and stable levels of employment. This is the true meaning of the stakeholder economy – where everyone has a stake in society and owes responsibility to it'. Stakeholding survived mainly in plans for 'stakeholder pensions' (Chapter 7).

FROM INSECURITY TO EMPLOYABILITY

Hutton's attention to rising insecurity, even among those who were in employment and in some cases reasonably well paid, found a wide audience. The popularity of *The State We're In* was attributable in part to its articulation and reflection of this experience. Late 1996 saw an intense media debate about the reality or otherwise of employment insecurity. Tory ministers argued that average job tenure had decreased only slightly over the previous decade, and that opinion pollsters were 'registering an exaggerated "state of mind" on the part of many workers about the risks of losing their jobs'.[20] More detailed analysis by the Employment Policy Institute (EPI) showed that job insecurity was increasing for men, and for workers under 25 and over 50 years of age. Paul Gregg and Jonathan Wadsworth argued that job tenure is an inadequate measure of objective insecurity, which depends also on protection against dismissal and the financial costs of job loss.[21] Compared with the 1970s, spells of unemployment had lengthened, and the value of out of work benefits decreased relative to average wages. The drop in wages even for those finding new employment had also increased. Others argued that the insecurity traditionally experienced by many manual workers had simply spread into the middle class, creating an anxiety which was not so much job insecurity as standard of living insecurity.

Labour was not slow to capitalize on public disquiet, and insecurity became a central theme in Party rhetoric. Blair said 'Job insecurity ... stalks the land'; and 'security is life's most precious commodity', yet in Britain 'a few at the top are secure and well-off; but there is an insecure majority'.[22] Meacher insisted that job insecurity was 'the central fact of the British economy'.[23] What might be done about it was more problematic. Some parts of the Party clung to a stakeholding agenda in which employers would moderate their hire and fire practices. Agreements between United Distillers and the GMB, and between Blue Circle and the GMB and TGWU were cited as exemplary. Blue Circle's 124 distribution drivers and 2000 process workers and other staff were to have a guarantee of 'job security' – that is, no compulsory redundancies for five years – in return for pay restraint and increased productivity. Allan Black of the GMB was quoted as saying that 'the pressure from our members is on job se-curity, not pay. This reflects a change of emphasis over the past few years'.[24] He also noted the merits of such deals for employers seeking to secure their staff in times of skill shortages. The agreement, however, was of more direct financial benefit to the company, with Blue Circle conceding that the deal with the drivers alone would save £1.2 million a year. The contribution to job security was more rhetorical than real. The protection from redundancy was effectively a temporary five-year contract, giving only limited security, and it seemed that it was not legally binding. Moreover, it is improbable that employers would enter into such deals where there was a strong likelihood of compulsory redundancies to begin with. Blue Circle had shed 20 per cent of its workforce in the recession, and was operating on very lean staffing levels in an industry with a high labour turnover (of 20 per cent a year), while voluntary redundancy and early retirement remained as ways of shedding labour. And rather than workers being 'given' job security in return for flexibility, increased productivity and pay restraint, such agreements can be read as enforcing changes in conditions and effective pay cuts, under threat of job losses. The Blue Circle agreement with the drivers involved a 3 per cent rise in the first year, and a pay freeze in the second, against a background of rising inflation. The attention given to the very real problem of job insecurity may thus have helped employers to impose changes in pay and conditions which were deleterious to workers without altering the overall levels of insecure employment in the labour market. As in the 1980s, the threat of unemployment was used to drive down pay and conditions, but under the guise of partnership.

Peter Hain, one of Labour's shadow employment team, said that in government, 'Labour will encourage such agreements because we want businesses to think long-term and focus upon jobs, skills, and flexibility as the best passport for Britain's economic success'. And 'since job insecurity is the curse of the British labour market, from the highest manager to the lowest cleaner, what we need to do to get a long-term perspective is to encourage these social partnership deals'.[25] Hain denied that a corporatist pay restraint policy was being surreptitiously introduced. But he also argued that 'Labour's stakeholding agenda' requires a 'change in the national psyche'. This means 'giving a priority to jobs over high pay increases...the focus should be upon job security, skills, flexibility and work reorganisation'. Hain described the three-year deal between the GMB and United Distillers, which was being extended for a fourth year, as having 'matched job security with a commitment to flexibility and retraining, pegging pay increases just above inflation'. Moreover, 'the priority given to jobs has released a basis for partnership and trust to enable the company to strive for world-class status'.[26] This argument would have been a little more convincing if there had been any evidence that United Distillers or Blue Circle intended to impose the same pay restraint upon their chief executives and shareholders, and restrict price rises to those other 'stakeholders', their customers! In February 1997, Hain announced that the Labour Party would propose job security in return for flexibility in public sector employment. But the overwhelming emphasis in policy documents and speeches was on supply-side measures of skills and training, not on a 'stakeholding' agenda.

Although job insecurity was the spectre haunting the land, it was chiefly presented by Labour as an inevitable consequence of the global economy. New Labour would not or could not reduce objective insecurity, so the focus switched to reducing its consequences. 'People feel and are less economically secure' as a result of globalization, but 'jobs for life are a thing of the past'.[27] Blunkett argued that 'part-time and flexible working arrangements will increase', and that 'people will change jobs more often and will need to be equipped to cope with the insecurity this brings'. This did not mean greater social provision for those who become unemployed, despite the EPI's observation that the sense of insecurity was exacerbated by the increased financial consequences of job loss, as welfare benefits had been progressively reduced. Labour blamed the problems of unemployment and low pay on the poor skills of the potential workforce. Employment security was redescribed in terms of the capacity to find new employment, rather than the security of individual jobs: people would 'gain security through moving from one job to another with ease'.[28] The focus was thus shifted to the 'employability' of individuals: 'employability is not only a question of people keeping the job they have now and developing within it. It is about people being able constantly to update their skills so that they can find a better job or a different one if they need to'.[29] At the launch of *Promoting Prosperity* Blair insisted that 'our aim is not...to regulate for job security, but to make people more employable in the labour market, thus enhancing their skills, talents and mobility', and the business manifesto repeated that 'real job security...will come about only through...enhancing people's employability'.[30]

Insecurity had ceased to be presented as a structural feature of the economy and the labour market. Rather, job security had become something individuals achieve. They 'build up their own skills and plan their future and so improve their ability to earn and achieve job security'.[31] It follows that insecurity is a question of individual deficiency – the absence of appropriate skills, and thus lack of 'employability'. The language of opportunity is used to construct employability as an individual responsibility. 'Lifelong learning' is the answer. People must 'update their own potential as the world changes around them'.[32] 'Individual learning accounts', with small government contributions for the unemployed, and possible employer contributions or tax relief for those in work, will 'enable individuals to invest in training'.[33] Making people pay to improve their own skills is presented as empowerment. It will 'give the individual the opportunity to take more control of his or her destiny';[34] we must 'broaden the opportunities for individuals to take responsibility for their own development'.[35] Improved education and training are no longer the basis of secure employment, but 'improved access to learning *opportunities* leads to improved job *prospects* and security'.[36] Placing the onus on individuals is justified because 'the more you learn, the more you earn'.[37] Those without work have the duty not only to seek it, but to make themselves fit for it: 'The young unemployed have a responsibility to seek work, accept reasonable opportunities and upgrade their skills. In return for the new opportunities which we will offer they in turn have an obligation to avail themselves of one of the options and make their best efforts to develop their own skills and training'.[38] Security has been discursively constructed as something individuals achieve through employability, and employability as an individual obligation. What is described as 'a lifetime entitlement to learning'[39] is effectively a lifetime obligation to acquire and maintain marketable skills. And lifelong learning starts early, with 'family learning – from the day a child is born – as the centrepiece of education policy'. Blunkett said 'We would...like to see health visitors broadening their role, equipping parents to support the educational development of their child from day one, and making appropriate learning materials available in the immediate post-natal period'.[40] The project of employability begins at the cradle, if it has not yet been extended to the grave.

COMMUNITY

'Security' also acts as a shifter between discourses about economy and community: much of Labour's discussion of both security and community concerns the problem of crime and its prevention. Labour policy statements, speeches and interviews are saturated with a communitarian rhetoric about obligations and responsibilities which owes more to Etzioni and Gray than it does to Macmurray. Blunkett argues, like Etzioni, that stable and secure communities rest on shared basic values. Mandelson and Liddle assert that 'New Labour's distinctive emphasis is on its concept of community', a 'robust and powerful idea ... at the heart of the stakeholder economy', a 'tough and active concept of community', based on rights and responsibilities.[41] 'Rebuilding a sense of mutual responsibility as individuals, as families and within the local community is right at the heart of Labour's project to build a stakeholder society'.[42] The concept of community is used to identify 'New Labour's enemies', in terms reminiscent of Keith Joseph's infamous remarks about the idle, the feckless and the failures. For Mandelson, the enemies are 'the vested interests who want decisions taken to benefit them, not the community as a whole'; they are also those 'who ignore the feelings of the community', together with 'the inefficient who let the community down and impede its success' and 'the irresponsible who fall down on their obligations to their families and therefore their community'.[43]

Successful communities are, as for Etzioni and Gray, founded on successful families 'where partners show long-term commitment to each other, children learn discipline and mutual respect, and family members help each other to cope with their personal crises and achieve their individual potential'.[44] 'Strong families build the social cohesion of our nation and its communities'.[45] Families are primarily institutions of social control and social welfare. They are 'where the difference between right and wrong is learned, and where a sense of mutual obligation is founded and practised'.[46] 'It is largely from family discipline that social discipline and a sense of responsibility is learned'; and 'if we do not learn and then teach the value of what is right and what is wrong, then the result is simply moral chaos which engulfs us all'.[47] In the manifesto, this became 'Families are the core of our society. They should teach right from wrong. They should be the first defence against anti-social behaviour. The breakdown of family life damages the fabric of our society'.

The fear of moral chaos means that the emphasis is on responsibilities, not rights. Thus Jack Straw claimed that to prevent crime, it is necessary to 'change the moral climate in which people live and behave. People have come to grab rights without recognising you can only exercise rights if you first accept responsibility'.[48] It is difficult for New Labour, however, simply to drop the aura of reciprocity which is embodied in the dyad 'rights and responsibilities'. Rather, the concept of opportunity is deployed instead. Blair's claim that 'a society geared to opportunity is one then able to demand responsibility' had transmuted into the slogan 'opportunity plus responsibility equals community'.[49]

A series of policy and consultation documents, mainly by Jack Straw, elaborated recurrent themes. Danger arises when 'communities fracture and whole areas tip into decline'; 'the breakdown in law and order is intimately bound up with the break-up of strong and cohesive local communities'.[50] Blair repeatedly used the slogan 'tough on crime, tough on the causes of crime' – although the election pledge mug, the best-selling item at the 1997 Party Conference, simply said 'tough on crime'. (Cabinet members did not appear to realize that delegates regarded it as an ironic totem.) Poverty, deprivation and unemployment had all been acknowledged as part of the causes of crime. *Tackling Youth Crime: Reforming Youth Justice* declared: 'We will also be tougher on the causes of crime by tackling the problems of unemployment and poverty, conditions in which crime breeds'. The welfare to work policy was promoted as an anti-crime policy: 'the best way of cutting crime is to give people jobs'.[51] But in so far as the problem of crime was laid at the door of fractured communities, and the strength of communities attributed to the strength of families, crime was blamed on poor parenting. 'The public believes that more responsible parenting is the top priority for improving community safety.'[52]

Mandelson and Liddle had argued that 'parents should...be called to account for their children's unacceptable behaviour, with the possibility of fines, and requirements to attend parenting classes'.[53] In November 1996, the discussion document *Parenting* argued 'that a decent society, based on cohesive communities, demands wider public discussion about parenting' and that 'good parenting is an investment for the future which society cannot afford to neglect'. It claimed that newspapers and magazines were silent about parenting and children – suggesting profound ignorance of the content of many women's magazines. Its main concern was with the contribution of poor parenting to crime: 'parental supervision is one of the most important factors in determining juvenile delinquency'. Reducing crime means 'tackling the issue of parental responsibility and helping people to exercise it' and 'a more rigorous approach to the enforcement of parental responsibility'. A future Labour government would support 'lone parents in carrying out their responsibilities'. They should be given more support 'in the interests of the children', rather than scapegoated. For while lone-parent families are 'not necessarily less caring', nor are they 'criminogenic', they are nevertheless listed with children in need, children in care, and children with attention deficit disorders as 'parenting danger zones'.

Part of the problem of poor parenting is 'our low level of investment as a society in parenting skills'. Besides raising public awareness of the importance of parenting, parenting education programmes are proposed. While some might take place in schools, or in extreme cases through the NHS, the document proposes expanded reliance on voluntary sector programmes, and 'the development of good quality self-help programmes that can be purchased by parents'. Ultimately, 'parental responsibility orders' might be necessary which would require parents 'to attend counselling and guidance sessions', in cases where 'it is clear that parental attitudes and behaviour are a key factor in a child's offending'.

In these discussions, 'the community' appears in different guises. It is the locality in which crime occurs, and that which has broken down, allowing the rise of crime. Crime threatens the community, which is potential victim – and thus also potential recipient of restitution: reparation orders would 'require...specific reparation either to the individual victim...or to the community'.[54] The community is a potential judge, as well as the instrument of social control: 'local councils working with the police and the local community can use by-laws to enforce child protection curfews' where their behaviour is 'a cause of concern in the local community';[55] and 'our aim is to encourage local communities to develop coherent strategies for dealing with all forms of neighbourhood disorder from noise nuisance to serious violent harassment'.[56] Mandelson and Liddle were more specific about the community agencies involved: 'The police, schools and local-authority services must work more closely together to crack down on vandalism and other antisocial behaviour. It is excessive tolerance of this low-level subcriminal behaviour by unruly young people which...provides the breeding-ground for more serious crime'.[57] This is the thinking behind 'zero tolerance', which appears in the manifesto, running together 'anti-social behaviour and crime' and 'crime and disorder'. It is not a new elision. In 1995, Straw wrote in *A Quiet Life* that 'serious anti-social behaviour by neighbours is perhaps the best example of chronic crime'. The different guises of community are blended in the idea of community safety – which always means safety from crime and disorder, and not safety from traffic, air pollution, poisonous food, contaminated water supplies, collapsing sewers or exposure to radiation leaks from nuclear installations. In *Safer communities, safer Britain,*[58] the safety of individuals in the community, the safety of the community itself, and safety ensured by the community are interwoven. *A Quiet Life* proposed 'Community safety orders' to 'restrain anti-social behaviour', using exclusion from particular areas, or curfews, as a form of discipline. Many of these ideas resurfaced in the 1997 Crime and Disorder Bill.

Communities do not only figure as places of danger or instruments of social control. They are also the arena of political inclusion. Labour's emphasis on devolution of power – not only to Wales and Scotland, but also to English regions, and to local government, is justified in terms of reducing centralization, and making government more responsive. One premise is that accountability and responsiveness are most easily achieved at local level, although the emphasis on local government can also be read as an attempt to disperse responsibility and thus deflect blame from the centre. Certainly the various additional requirements which may be laid on local authorities – for example in relation to homelessness, policing and education – will cost money. If this comes from increased council taxes, rather than from income tax through central funding, local authorities rather than central government will take the rap. The second premise is that locality, like ethnicity and gender, but not class, is central to identity: 'most people have a sense of place, of local loyalty, of commitment to the other people who live in their area'. This commitment is also the basis of 'active citizenship', which Blunkett argued would be crucial in regenerating our communities. Fortunately, 'local communities and individuals want to play their part in the process of renewing our country'.[59] Communities are also the space for – and dependent on and generated by – unpaid work, or volunteering.

The third way depends heavily on what is sometimes called the third sector. At its widest, this covers 'all those organisations which are neither purely commercial nor part of government'.[60] Besides families, schools and churches, this broad definition incorporates universities, sports clubs and trade unions within the 'voluntary sector', as well as co-operatives, charities and voluntary organizations. Even more narrowly understood as charities, social service, self-help and advocacy groups, the range and diversity of voluntary organizations is huge. The practical importance of many voluntary organizations lies in the unpaid work they co-ordinate and the social needs they may meet and represent. In his speech to the 1997 TUC Congress, Blair talked of maintaining 'high levels of social inclusion based on values of community and social justice, but where the role of government is not necessarily to provide all social provision but to organise and regulate it most efficiently and fairly'. The importance of voluntary organizations to New Labour's ideology also lies in the importance of 'volunteering' to the generation of 'community'. Alun Michael stressed the 'importance of the voluntary sector to civic society and to healthy communities',[61] while the manifesto insisted that 'an independent and creative voluntary sector, committed to voluntary activity as an expression of citizenship, is central to our vision of a stakeholder society'.

The trouble with active citizenship is that volunteering begins to appear not all that voluntary. 'Volunteering is a key element in active citizenship'. Citizenship itself is a matter of responsibilities – or 'contribution' – rather than rights: 'It is part of renewing a sense of citizenship to ensure that people feel that there is a role for them and that they can make a worthwhile contribution'. The statement that 'the essence of a volunteer is that s/he chooses to help the community in a way acceptable to her/him' muddies the question of whether the choice is over helping at all, or simply the form of help. Ostensibly, the concern is for the benefits to individuals: 'it is the capacity for personal development that makes the voluntary sector central to creating a decent community'.[62] But those who do not choose to help are by implication lesser citizens, as well as less 'developed' as individuals. The suggestion that 'many people do not volunteer simply because they have not been asked to do so' leads on to suggestions that individuals may be persuaded more assiduously to 'volunteer':

> Voluntary action should be given a higher priority within the school curriculum and those reaching retirement should be made aware of the opportunities available locally. Employers also have a role to play in encouraging employees to play an active part in local voluntary activities – recognising that it is to the benefit of the community and the company. The company's employees are, after all, themselves stakeholders in the community.[63]

In these discussions too there is considerable confusion about what 'community' is. The term sometimes refers to communities of interests – the business community or ethnic minority communities. It appears, as we have seen, in a variety of roles in relation to crime. It refers to local communities, either as neighbourhoods or the rather wider constituency for local government. It may refer to that complex of institutions, part of neither market nor state, sometimes called civil society. It may have a wider reference – including local government, perhaps better understood as the local state; or including market institutions – to the point where it is hard to see what is excluded. The intrinsic problems with the term 'community' are compounded by its use as a substitute for, rather than alternative to, 'society' in the insistence on a third way between left and right. Thus before his election to the leadership, Blair said :

> I think it is time we abandoned the notion of leaving everything to some nebulous concept of society or focusing entirely on individual responsibility. We should replace these ideas instead with a concept of shared responsibility in which we act as a country to create communities in which individuals are given opportunities but accept their obligations, where they are given rights but have responsibilities, and where we understand that...the well developed individual, capable of playing a strong and vibrant part in society, is likely to arise best from a strong and vibrant community.[64]

Shortly before the ratification of the new Clause IV, he counterposed the acquisitive anti-social individualism of Thatcherism to the 'confusion of early left thinking' between a strong society, a strong state and collectivist institutions. Community bridges this gap:

> People don't want an overbearing state. But they do not want to live in a social vacuum either. It is in the search for this different reconstructed, relationship between individual and society that ideas about 'community' are to be found. 'Community' implies a recognition of inter-dependence but not overweening government power. It accepts that we are better equipped to meet the forces of change and insecurity through working together.[65]

Socialism itself was reduced to the banal claim in the new Clause IV that 'by the strength of our common endeavour, we achieve more than we achieve alone', or 'a creed that tries to help the many and not just the few', or 'the recognition that individuals prosper best when they recognise their obligations and responsibilities to each other'.[66] The rhetoric of the third way thus transforms democratic socialism into a synthesis of stakeholding and communitarianism. But it is a synthesis in which individual responsibility is to be enforced as obligation through the twin pressures of the global economy and the community as policeman.

7 From Equality to Inclusion

How does New Labour's development of the third way bear on their treatment of inclusion? Is social inclusion, as distinct from political inclusiveness, connected to broad, social democratic definitions of citizenship and thus to civil, political and social equality, or is it more narrowly construed in terms of waged work? To what extent does it reflect the moral inclusion which Room sees as contained in continental versions of social exclusion, and which is present both in discourses about the underclass and in the communitariansim of Etzioni and Gray?[1] Political inclusiveness has a high profile, connected to the consensual assumptions of Labour's third way. While this commitment is consistent with RED, the flight from equality means that discussions of social exclusion omit or actively debar redistribution towards the poor. Like stakeholders, and consistent with SID, Labour understands social inclusion primarily in terms of participation in paid work. This is most obviously the case in the New Deal or welfare to work policies – although the justifications for benefit cuts in conjunction with these policies have overtones of MUD. The Social Exclusion Unit (SEU) combines a broader conception of social exclusion with an emphasis on questions of social order, and is strongly imbued with MUD. Both the New Deal and the SEU emphasize opportunity and employability. As employability is represented as something individuals must actively achieve, it is transformed into an individual obligation. Inclusion becomes a duty rather than a right, and something which requires active performance.

THE FLIGHT FROM RED

The 1997 election was fought on the basis of commitments not to raise standard or top rates of income tax for the whole of the parliamentary term, and to stick to Conservative spending plans for the first two years of office. These policies, imposed by Blair and announced by Brown early in 1997, were seen at the time as a defensive strategy to prevent a repetition of 1992, when Labour lost the election at least in part because of Tory scare stories about the tax rises implied by their expenditure commitments. The subsequent landslide victory could be seen either as a vindication of promised fiscal restraint, or as evidence

128

that the self-imposed straitjacket was entirely unnecessary. Some argued throughout that the parallel with 1992 was false. The opinion polls had been solidly in Labour's favour for over four years, even if the extent to which the Conservatives remained mired in sleaze throughout the election campaign could not have been predicted. But even opponents of the self-imposed constraints interpreted them as an electoral strategy, rather than an essential part of an overall programme. Yet the development of New Labour rhetoric and the policy changes which were effected between 1992 and 1997 constitute a continuation of the flight from redistribution and equality towards a mixture of market-oriented and socially authoritarian policies.

In contrast with 1997, the 1992 manifesto had proposed the introduction of a new top rate of income tax of 50 per cent, together with the abolition of the ceiling on National Insurance contributions, and adjustments to personal allowances which would exempt 740 000 people from paying tax. It also promised to increase Child Benefit for all children, with the full value going to every family (implying that the increase would not be taxed or deducted from income support payments); to replace the Social Fund; to restore benefit rights to 16 and 17 year-olds; and to increase pensions. These commitments were notably absent from the 1997 manifesto. Labour was hardly recognizable as the party which five years before had insisted that 'the most effective way to reduce poverty quickly is to increase child benefit and pensions and take low-paid people out of taxation'.

Blair's stated priorities were 'education, education and education'. He offered less funding and more policing – or standards, not structures. The promise of training and support for teachers in 1992 was accompanied in 1997 by the promise of new and speedier procedures to sack them. The home-school contracts in 1992 were to tell parents what the school undertook to deliver as much as to set out what might be expected of parents; by 1997 the balance had shifted to 'a culture of responsibility for learning within the family', with homework targets. The 1992 commitments to the abolition of selection at 11 and the return of opted-out schools to local authority control were both dropped. The 1997 manifesto promised that the system of funding would not 'discriminate unfairly' between schools – without comment on what level of discrimination might be fair. In May 1992, additional investment was promised; by 1997, the commitment was simply a reversal of the trend of cutting expenditure, with increases dependent upon 'savings' from the social security budget, although both manifestos promised to reduce class sizes.

In 1992 there had been no suggestion that free university education – from which virtually all members of the Government had benefited – might be under threat. The 1997 manifesto pre-empted the Dearing report on the future of higher education by insisting that expansion and improvement could not be financed out of general taxation, and that maintenance costs should be entirely met by loans repaid on an income-contingent basis, but 'with fairness ensured'. When Dearing was published, Labour ignored its strictures about increasing participation rates among poorer families, and within hours announced policies requiring students to repay not only maintenance costs but a substantial proportion of their tuition fees. There was little sustained opposition to these proposals at the 1997 Party Conference, even when it became clear that the intention was not to use the fee income to restore university funding, but at least in part to cross-subsidize the further education sector. The justification was that higher education led to higher earnings, and those who benefited should pay – directly, rather than simply through taxation; Tessa Blackstone described the plans as progressive, even socialist. Education was treated as a commodity which individuals possess and profit from; the collective, social good of an educated citizenry did not figure.

If the costs of higher education were transferred from the state to the individual, the costs of training were similarly shifted – this time from the corporate sector. The 'Learn as You Earn' policy was in place in 1992 – to be financed by a compulsory training levy on employers. By 1997, two metamorphoses had taken place, again redefining education as a marketable commodity and an individual good, and altering the basis of funding. The new system entailed Individual Learning Accounts, largely financed by individuals, although kick-started by small government grants in some cases. Whereas the training levy would have required all but small firms to contribute, by 1997, in the new spirit of partnership, employers were simply encouraged to make voluntary contributions. This was consistent with Labour's generally reduced willingness to assert the rights and interests of workers over those of employers. By 1997 Labour had retained the formal commitment to insisting on union recognition where a majority of the workforce wanted it (leading to a series of bizarre fudges about the definition of the 'relevant' workforce to be balloted). Otherwise, Tory legislation was to stay in place. Even the commitment to giving all employees protection against unfair dismissal from day one was dropped in June 1996 with the publication of *Building Prosperity: Flexibility, Efficiency and Fairness at Work*.

Labour's changing policy on pensions illustrates the shift from social to individual provision, and from RED to SID. In 1975, increases in the basic state pension were linked to increases in average earnings or prices, whichever was higher. In 1980, the Tories abolished the earnings link. By 1996, the consequent reduction in the value of the pension meant that a single person received £61.15 rather than £80.25, a couple £97.75 rather than £128.65. The pension for a single person had fallen from 20 per cent of average male earnings to 14 per cent, and was predicted to drop to 9 per cent by 2020. In 1992, Labour's commitment to redistribution was such that the manifesto pledged immediate increases of £5 (or £8 for a couple), with restoration of the earnings link. Earnings-related pensions payable under SERPS would be tied to the best 20 years' earnings. In the summer of 1996, the commitment to restoring the earnings link was dropped, together with all mention of immediate pension increases. It was said that increasing basic pensions – and restoring benefits under SERPS which had also been cut by the Tories – was too expensive; and that since the basic pension went to those with private or occupational pensions who were deemed not to need it, it was not a cost-effective way of preventing poverty among the retired population. Instead Labour proposed the introduction of 'stakeholder pensions' – individual top-up pension accounts for those with modest earnings, which differed from existing private pensions in that they would be run by non-profit making bodies such as trade unions, or employer/employee partnerships, and thus be more cost-effective than the private market.

But Labour's plans for stakeholder pensions, like SERPS and all occupational and private schemes, would link income in retirement to earnings when in work. Even the basic pension is dependent on National Insurance contributions paid during a working life or credited during periods of registered unemployment, throwing those with incomplete records on to means-tested benefits. But at least for those who qualify, the basic pension is egalitarian. Other pension schemes reproduce in retirement the inequalities of working lives – inequalities between paid and unpaid workers, between high and low earners, and between women and men. The term 'stakeholder' here is a piece of individualizing rhetoric, changing pension provision from a collective insurance against risk to an individual one. When Brown argued that inequalities at work were the root of all other inequalities, he did not point out that this is a consequence of policy decisions. Although Labour did suggest that the state might credit the accounts of carers to produce a citizen's pension, the clear thrust of the policy was to reinforce the link with lifetime earnings. Such plans also had no bearing on the needs of existing pensioners. But Harman used the poverty of some pensioners as an argument against a general uprating. The 700 000 pensioners not currently receiving the income support to which they were entitled should be 'targeted'; but those who did draw income support would lose it if the basic pension were raised, and would not benefit.

Labour's apostasy provoked a pamphlet by Barbara Castle and Peter Townsend insisting that since National Insurance contributions are earnings-related, there is no reason why benefits should not be.[2] They also argued that the administrative costs of universal benefit schemes are much lower than those of means-tested schemes like income support, and the administrative costs of state pensions far lower than occupational, private, or the putative stakeholder schemes. In the only serious policy debate at the 1996 Conference, Castle argued passionately and cogently for the restoration of the earnings link and of SERPS and extracted from Harman the promise that a pensions review would be set up immediately. The feeling of Conference was clearly with Castle rather than with Harman. The issue went to a card vote, and much back-room arm-twisting was needed to avoid a defeat for the leadership. Six months later, the 1997 manifesto contained only the commitment to uprate pensions 'at least' in line with prices, to 'examine means of delivering more automatic help to the poorest pensioners' – and to set up a review. Although Castle addressed the 1997 Conference on the same issue, the hall was half empty, and the resolution on restoring the earnings link remitted for government consideration rather than put to a vote. Well before the outcome of the pensions review in early 1998, the direction of Labour's pensions policy clearly led away from equality and collective provision, towards individual provision, individual risk, and inequality.

In November 1997, Brown's preliminary budget statement announced supplementary payments of £20 to all pensioner households, and £50 to pensioners receiving income support, to assist with winter fuel bills. Some commentators argued this indicated Brown was more egalitarian than Blair, that he would spend money when resources allowed and that his reluctance to do so stemmed from prudence – although others, including Hutton, claimed that public finances were better than had been projected, and Brown had much more scope to spend. The suggestion that Red Gordon was held in check by Iron Brown glossed over the evidence that he had changed his name to Sid, and was wholly complicit in the flight from equality, pushing through

benefit cuts for lone parents and their children, and threatening benefit cuts for disabled people. These cuts and their legitimation involved
redrawing the line between deserving and undeserving poor in terms
of working age. Harman argued repeatedly that the best form of welfare for people of working age is work: 'we want to make the mainstream economy – with its opportunities and risks – the main path out
of exclusion for all people of working age'.[3]

HATTERSLEY'S LAST STAND

Before the end of Labour's first hundred days in office, an argument
broke out about how far, and in what sense, Labour remained committed to equality. The catalyst was an article by Roy Hattersley.[4]
Although Blair occasionally acknowledged that the modernization of
the party was started not by him, nor even by John Smith, but by Neil
Kinnock in 1983, Hattersley's role as Kinnock's deputy was rarely
mentioned. Still less visible was the fact that the Kinnock/Hattersley
'dream ticket' was one in which the left-wing Kinnock was com-
plemented by the more right-wing Hattersley. Hattersley cast the old
dividing line in the Labour Party as 'between advocates of extended
public ownership and proponents of greater equality', an antithesis
which is as much an ideological construction as New Labour's division
between themselves and the old Labour camp of which Hattersley is
part. It is also one which implies that the commitment to common
ownership – in whatever form – represented opposition to egalitarianism, rather than being seen as a route to it. Hattersley's objection to
changing Clause IV was not to shedding the old, but to the substance
of the new: 'Most egalitarians support the view that change was
important. We hoped that a commitment to create an equal society
would replace the promise of wholesale nationalisation'. That Hattersley should in 1997 become the standard-bearer of the left in British
politics thus has a certain irony – while underlining the effectiveness
with which Thatcherism, aided by 'centre-left' ideologues like John
Gray, succeeded in establishing new boundaries of political debate. As
Ian Aitken put it 'Hattersley was an unapologetic rightwinger...and
has only become a dangerous lefty because the party, not him, has
changed'.[5]

Hattersley took Gray to task for his argument in *After Social Democracy* that 'The pursuit of greater equality...through redistributive
tax and welfare policy, the promotion of full employment through

economic growth, a cradle to grave welfare state ... and the support for and co-operation with a strong Labour movement as the principal protectors of workers' interests' are all outdated notions. He was less concerned, however, by Gray's belief that 'the use of tax and welfare systems for egalitarian redistribution is now precluded by voter resistance and the global mobility of capital' than by Blunkett's argument that 'the truth is that any government entering the 21st century cannot hope to create a more equal or egalitarian society simply by taking from one set of people and redistributing it to others, as envisaged when the rich were very rich and the poor made up the rest'. Hattersley argued for both the necessity and the possibility of redistribution: tackling poverty through tackling unemployment took too long for those who could work, and was irrelevant to the needs of those who could not. Egalitarians no longer had an obligation of loyalty to the Party and its policies, since its 'ideological apostasy' involved abandoning both socialism and equality:

> In truth, it is hard to describe New Labour as a democratic socialist party, and much to his credit, Tony Blair has always been frank about his wish to create what he calls the radical centre ground of politics. That creates problems for us for whom equality is an article of faith. We should rejoice at the victory of May 1. The Blair government is not only incomparably better than its predecessor. In many ways it is admirable in its own right. But it is not a force for a more equal society.

'Blair' replied in the *Sun*: 'People like them [Hattersley and Benn] were in charge of the party for almost 20 years while we were losing general elections'.[6] Aitken contrasted this 'sneeringly offensive response' with Brown's more courteous response in the *Guardian*.[7] But Brown's response was, in fact, rather less courteous than it appeared, for he had not written a reply to Hattersley's argument, but recycled an edited version of his Anthony Crosland Memorial Lecture given the previous February, adding the usual puff about the policies being put in place by the new Government.

While Brown accepted Crosland's designation of equality as the fundamental principle distinguishing Labour from the Conservatives, he reconstructed its meaning in 'the context of the 1990s' as equality of opportunity rather than equality of outcome – just as Mandelson and Liddle had contrasted the left's desire for 'equality of outcome' with New Labour's goal of 'equal opportunity for all'.[8] In terms essentially similar to those of New Right apologists throughout the 1980s, Brown argued that 'equality of outcome ... is neither desirable nor feasible'. It requires excessive state intervention to enforce uniformity: 'predetermined results imposed, as they would have to be, by a central authority and decided irrespective of work, effort or contribution to the community, is not a socialist dream but other people's nightmare of socialism. It denies humanity rather than liberates it.'

Contrasting 1956 and 1997, Brown argued, like Gray, that globalization means national governments have less economic power, and must therefore focus on supply-side measures to enhance competitiveness, rather than on demand management. Full employment can no longer be assumed; nor can jobs for life. The new 'information economy' relies less on physical capital: 'the truly indispensable ... capital is intellectual and human capital'. From these premises, it follows that since 'skills ... are the assets that matter', today it is 'unemployment and the absence of skills that is the biggest source of poverty'. In these new circumstances, while 'our commitment to equality is as strong as ever', its implications are different. Starting from 'a fundamental belief in the equal worth of every human being', Brown deduced that 'all deserve to be given an equal chance in life to fulfil the potential with which they are born' – no more or less logical a deduction than that all are entitled to an equal share of the social product. But equal life chances demand equality of opportunity: 'employment opportunity for all because work is central ... to individual fulfilment'; lifelong educational opportunity; and 'genuine access to culture' together with 'a redistribution of power that offers people real control over the decisions that affect their lives'. Even this last point, which broadened the concept of equal opportunities beyond the labour market, was used to hammer home the message of a decrease in collective provision: 'the issue for socialists is not so much about what the state can do for you, but about what the state can enable you to do for yourself'.

Hattersley responded sharply that the equation of equality and uniformity is absurd: 'true diversity is only possible in a society which avoids great discrepancies in wealth and income. No-one who lives on social security at its present levels can afford to be different'.[9] But the central question at issue in the Hattersley/Brown exchange was not whether equality of opportunity was a good thing, but whether it was attainable with current levels of inequality and poverty. Hattersley argued that greater equality, and thus redistribution, was necessary to increase opportunities for the poorest. Blunkett, in contrast, had argued that poverty was not a bar to educational achievement and thus future success: 'Poverty cannot be an excuse for failure. It is poverty of aspiration and not poverty of income which prevents a child from taking full advantage of their talent'[10] – a position Hattersley consistently disputed. Brown's response deployed the false antithesis. A new welfare state should concentrate on employment and educational opportunity, on the causes of poverty, *rather than* on the alleviation of poverty through benefits. 'I know that the answer is not a few pounds on benefit, but the chance for real work' – a formulation which in the *Guardian* became 'they do not want a few pounds on benefit'. Confusing necessary and sufficient conditions, he used the fact that 'increased spending does *not necessarily* increase social justice' to imply that it was not even necessary. The emphasis was firmly upon inclusion through labour market attachment: 'Egalitarians must start from the premise that no-one in our society...should be excluded from the opportunity to work'.

Brown reiterated Labour's intention to 're-establish the work ethic at the centre of our welfare system', and to 'reform...the benefit system to make work pay'. His emphasis on the centrality of work is one indicator of the transition from RED to SID. The increasing use of the terms justice and fairness rather than equality – evading the question of what is just or fair and who decides – intensifies this shift. Fairness, like equality of opportunity, is as much a procedural as a distributional concept. Thus fairness and equality of opportunity can both be used to justify inequalities of outcome on the basis of 'hard work'; the rich are entitled to more because they have earned it. Overtly, Brown criticized inequality: 'Inequalities can only be justified if they are in the interests of the least fortunate', and 'unjustifiable inequalities' must be tackled. He supported a 'guaranteed minimum' including 'a minimum wage, a tax and benefit system that helps people into work', and the somewhat vague 'best possible level of health and social services for all and the assurance of dignity and security for those who are retired or unable to work through infirmity'. But he also endorsed inequality, while appealing to the populist criterion of public resentment: 'What people resent about Britain today is not that some people who have worked hard have done well'.

Labour's rejection of redistribution from rich to poor is not, however, a rejection of redistribution in itself. Rather, it is a legitimation of the major redistribution from poor to rich which marked the 1979–97 Conservative regime – and a relegitimation of wealth and inequality themselves. Whereas for egalitarians, 'fairness' implies fewer rich as well as fewer poor, Blair is happy to see more millionaires in Britain 'so long as they are benefiting the community at large'.[11] Within weeks, millionaire MP Geoffrey Robinson, the Paymaster General, was in the public eye for alleged tax avoidance through the use of offshore trusts. Mandelson and Liddle had argued that 'belief in the dynamic market economy involves recognition that substantial personal incentives and rewards are necessary to encourage risk-taking and entrepreneurialism'; unearned income was equally legitimate, since 'profits are accepted as the motor of private enterprise'.[12] Given the incomes of some of Labour's political advisers, this is just as well. Sir Peter Davis, Chief Executive of the Prudential since 1995, reportedly 'earns' £621 000 a year; he was brought in to head the welfare to work task force. But risk at 'the Pru' falls most heavily on its customers, not on its senior management: the company was one of the worst offenders in the mis-selling of private pensions from 1986. In 1997, firms were repeatedly criticized by Treasury minister Helen Liddell for taking too little action too slowly to compensate their victims. The Securities and Investments Board said the Prudential had 'failed to exercise the requisite due skill, care and diligence in its conduct of the pensions review'.[13] Martin Taylor, Chief Executive of Barclays Bank (and a member of the advisory council of Demos), was co-opted to head a task force on the tax and benefits system; at Barclays, risk was arguably greater for the thousands of staff who had been thrown out of work.

Even great inherited wealth received implicit sanction. Blair's Prime Ministerial role might explain his considerable involvement in the funeral arrangements for Princess Diana, and his participation in the ceremony. It subsequently emerged that Blair and Diana had agreed she should be given a semi-official ambassadorial role: political inclusion extended to the aristocracy if not quite to the monarchy itself. New Labour shows no inclination to challenge the entrenched wealth and privilege that the Spencer family, as well as the Windsors, represents. The funeral appeared to endorse the consensual, one-nation message of New Labour, exploited in Blair's phrase 'the people's princess'. But among Diana's symbolic functions was an endorsement of material inequality. Representation of her eating disorders, her unhappy marriage, her love for her sons all had the subtext money does not buy happiness and that wealth is unimportant. Her supposed capacity to make human contact with all across boundaries of class and culture – whether real or not – signalled not their eradication, but their removal from recognition, their irrelevance. Her 'talent for including the excluded'[14] included them as objects of charity. The increasing focus on charity, both in the persona of Princess Diana, and in the

Lottery, which Labour refers to as the people's Lottery, has two effects. It underpins the reconstruction of categories of deserving and undeserving causes and persons on entirely populist criteria, and it shifts the balance away from collective provision of welfare rights and public services towards voluntary and charitable activity, eroding the citizenship of recipients. Charity also endorses the wealth and power of those for whom charitable donation may be seen as a form of entirely voluntary taxation – which in the United States has led to the very rich to seek social approbation through competitive giving. Diana's charitable 'work' endorsed and depended on her aristocratic position as a member of a rich and powerful class.

SID'S NEW DEAL

Having abandoned redistribution as a means of tackling poverty, Labour produced two sets of policies for addressing social exclusion. The first, the New Deal or welfare to work, was laid out before the election and launched with the July 1997 budget, financed by the long-promised windfall tax on the excess profits of the privatized utilities. The second, the formation of the Social Exclusion Unit, was announced by Mandelson in August and launched in December 1997. Welfare to work was primarily driven by the desire to reduce Treasury spending on social security, and the Social Exclusion Unit by questions of social order, but the justifications of both combine elements of SID and MUD.

Brown's emphasis on inclusion through work reflected the general shift in Labour's rhetoric. It did not in itself represent a break from traditional Labour priorities, but there was a change from emphasizing the need for full employment as part of an assault on unemployment and poverty to emphasizing employment – and increasingly 'employment opportunity' – as the only route out of poverty. This sidelined the question of the support available to different groups of the unemployed and 'economically inactive', redefined the groups legitimately exempted from participation in paid work, and, notwithstanding the commitment to some level of minimum wage at least for those over the age of 26, largely ignored the question of in-work poverty. Brown might be committed to 'a national crusade against unemployment and poverty' but this meant 'action against unemployment as action against inequality and poverty'.[15] Blair talked not about the poor, but about a new workless class which must be 'brought back into society and into useful work'.[16] For some, the emphasis on employment went beyond its provision of an income. Brown insisted that 'The core value is work...work and employment will be our first priority', and 'work offers self-esteem and inclusion', while Straw insisted that 'work is a precondition in our society to self-esteem and self-worth'.[17] Inclusion through paid work rests on the work itself, not simply the pay, just as it does for exponents of stakeholding.

In its pre-election version, the welfare to work strategy was aimed at three groups: young unemployed people aged between 18 and 24 years, the long-term unemployed, and lone parents. Young people unemployed for six months or more would have four options. Those without basic educational qualifications might, with the approval of the Employment Service, keep their benefit for a minimum of six months to study full-time on an approved education or training course. The second option, intended to form 40 per cent of the placements, was subsidized employment with a private sector employer. Employers recruiting someone who had been unemployed for over six months would receive a £60-per-week rebate for six months, conditional upon the provision of approved training for one day a week. Where such work was unavailable, young people would have the option of working in the voluntary sector or in the new Environmental Task Force for 'benefit plus'. It was emphasized that there would be no fifth option of a life on benefit. Subsequently, an additional option of assisted self-employment was added. A 'Gateway' was announced, consisting of up to four months of intensive counselling and/or training before entry into the main part of the scheme.

Job subsidies of £75 per week were also on offer for those over the age of 25, who had been unemployed for over two years. For this older group there was no 'guarantee' of a job offer; in 1992, the manifesto had promised the choice of work experience or training for all those out of work for more than six months. Because of the imbalance in registered unemployment, both groups – the young unemployed and the long-term unemployed – were disproportionately male. In March 1997, Labour estimated that the target group of 250 000 young unemployed was about three quarters men and one quarter women. However, attention was also drawn to the problem of workless households where both members of couples were unemployed, but only one (usually male) claiming and therefore registered. They proposed that both members of unemployed couples should have access to advice on job search and training.

The third group targeted under the New Deal was lone parents, principally women, with school-aged children. Proposals for moving them into paid work were set out in a document by Harman in October 1996, and flagged by Blair in speeches in Amsterdam in January 1997, and in Southwark in June. Lone parents whose youngest child was in the second term of full-time school (which, with the promised changes to nursery education, meant those aged four) would be approached by the DSS and Employment Service and offered a careers interview to discuss job opportunities, training and child care with a personal adviser. A national child-care strategy would be funded with the proceeds of the National Lottery. Child-care facilities had long been an issue for women, especially given their scarcity in Britain compared with most of Europe. The 1992 manifesto had promised out-of-school and holiday activities for older children as well as nursery care for three and four year olds. The 1997 manifesto promised publicly-funded nursery places for all four year olds, with provision for three year olds to be implemented through targets for local education authorities together with private and voluntary agencies. 'Early excellence centres', incorporating nursery education, child care, training and information services into local health centres were also proposed. The national child-care strategy turned out to mean initially a network of homework and after-school clubs to be partly staffed by volunteer workers and young people themselves mobilized through the New Deal.

The New Deal for lone parents was welcomed by the National Council for One-Parent Families although Gingerbread, another lone-parent pressure group, was more cautious. Many lone parents with school-aged children would like paid employment if good jobs at reasonable rates of pay within practicable travelling distance and affordable child care were available, although in many areas such jobs were simply not available. Even where employment was a possibility, the transition would not be from welfare to work, but from welfare to work plus welfare, with inadequate incomes supplemented by in-work benefits such as Family Credit. The implementation of a minimum wage was presented by Brown as an integral part of the welfare to work strategy. Despite low pay, and an increase in women's total workload, labour market attachment could be argued to be in women's best interests, since future earnings are adversely affected by spells of absence from the labour market – and lifetime earnings increasingly have an impact upon pension entitlement, and thus on the probability of poverty in later life. The policy was, however, clearly cost-driven. It was accompanied by a commitment to increase the numbers of fathers paying maintenance, reducing the costs to the state and increasing the financial incentives for lone mothers to seek employment. In the months before the election, Harman had issued a flurry of press releases repeating the consequences for public expenditure: 'The cost of keeping a single parent on benefit is greater than for any other group. On average it costs £155 a week, or £8000 a year to keep a single mother with two children on benefit. When lost taxes are taken into account, the [Conservative] Government's failure to get lone mothers off benefit and into work costs £10000 a year for every lone parent trapped on benefit'.

Reservations about the New Deal for those under the age of 25 concerned the quality of placements potentially available, and the potentially coercive nature of the scheme. The pre-election version of welfare to work effectively had a gendered approach to compulsion. Coercion in the form of benefit sanctions was central to the New Deal for the young unemployed; the existing rules of the Jobseeker's Allowance implied a 40 per cent benefit reduction for failing to actively seek work, translating into sanctions for non-participation in the New Deal. The programme for lone parents – who might be in the same age group – was consistently presented as optional. In January 1997, Blair insisted that the proposals were 'not about compelling [lone parents] to work or interfering with their arrangements for their children', but about increasing choice. In February, Brown said that single parents would not be compelled to work. Lone parents were portrayed as victims of a benefit system which traps them in dependency, and as needing employment to escape poverty, but also to achieve independence and self-esteem. Above all, the policy was presented as an opportunity for women, 90 per cent of whom, it was claimed, wanted to work. The principally male targets of the other parts of the New Deal, potential agents of social disruption, needed to be forced into work by withdrawal of benefits.

After the election, compulsion tightened. Young people could be sanctioned by total benefit withdrawal for refusing placements under the New Deal. At the same time, there were a series of disputes over potential exemptions from or regional variations in the minimum wage, as well as continued uncertainty about its level. In 1992, the manifesto commitment was that a minimum wage would be introduced at half, and progressively increased to two thirds, of average male earnings. The 1997 manifesto made no commitment about the level of the minimum wage, but proposed a Low Pay Commission to set the level after extensive consultation with industry to ensure that it would not damage competitiveness or employment levels. By the autumn, well before the Low Pay Commission had reported, those under the age of 26 seemed likely to be exempt.

The enabling character of the programme for lone parents as 'empowerment not punishment' was stressed again by Blair in June, and by Alan Howarth in July. But the election manifesto did not rule out compulsion:

> Today the main connection between unemployed lone parents and the state is their benefits. Most lone parents want to work, but are given no help to find it. New Labour has a positive policy. Once the youngest child is in the second term of full-time school, lone parents will be offered advice by a proactive Employment Service to develop a package of job search, training and after-school care to help them off benefit.

Before the election, Richard Layard, appointed in June as an adviser to the welfare to work programme, had suggested that the programme should be made compulsory:

> When children are young, it is reasonable that mothers should have a choice about whether to seek work. But there is a real question of whether, in today's world, mothers of older children who ask for Income Support should not be expected to look for work... This issue arises both for lone mothers and for wives of unemployed men.[18]

Frank Field, given responsibility for overseeing Labour's overall reform of welfare provision, had argued both before and after the election that lone mothers of school-aged children should be required to seek work as a condition of receiving benefit. Formal compulsion was not introduced; but benefit cuts announced in the last Conservative budget were pushed through. The extension of the welfare to work programme to disabled people was announced at the 1997 Party Conference, again presented as a long-needed opportunity. By December, they too were threatened with cuts to Industrial Injuries Benefit, Incapacity Benefit and the Disabled Living Allowance. Blair, like Brown, insisted that the welfare state would be reconstructed on the basis of the work ethic.

PENALIZING LONE PARENTS

The benefit cuts announced in November 1996 and vociferously opposed by Labour at the time affected all new claims by lone parents.

Abolition of lone-parent premiums for Child Benefit, income support and housing benefit would result in reductions of up to £11 per week. The reduction of Child Benefit meant lone parents in employment would lose £5.65. For several months, Labour MPs argued for reversal of these changes. An amendment by the Liberal Democrat Steve Webb proposed restoration of the lone-parent addition to Child Benefit, culminating in the first rebellion against the Government. In the vote on 10 December 1997, the amendment was defeated by 457 to 107, with the Labour Government which implemented the cuts passing through the division lobby with the Conservatives who had proposed them. Forty-seven Labour members voted with the Liberal Democrats against the Government, including Malcolm Chisholm and Gordon Prentice who resigned their Government posts, and Alice Mahon who was sacked. A further thirteen Labour MPs present in the House abstained, while others were strategically absent. Far more had expressed disquiet, signing a private letter to Blair asking for a change in policy. Opinion polls suggested that the cuts were opposed by three quarters of the population.

The debate took place against a background of repeated assertions that the costs of the welfare state were escalating out of control, with benefits described as the costs of failure. Bill Cash suggested that lone parents were being sacrificed to Treasury needs to meet the Maastricht criteria for monetary union. The arguments illustrate the uneasy mixture of SID and MUD in Labour's rhetorical armoury. The famous incoherence of Harman's attempt to justify the cuts in an interview with John Humphreys on the *Today* programme on the morning of the debate resulted in part from her oscillation between these discourses, but also from her reluctance to publicly appeal to MUD. The arguments mounted by the rebels show the continuing strength of RED within the Parliamentary Labour Party, including the specific linking of social exclusion to poverty, as well as themselves drawing on SID. The repeated appeal to the manifesto commitment to stick to Tory spending plans, which as Ken Livingstone put it, sounded increasingly like a 'used-car salesman drawing attention to the small print', cast this commitment itself in a different light. Rather than a constraint, it was a necessary excuse which looked suspiciously like a calculated element in Government strategy.

Harman's promotion of the New Deal for lone parents had always rested on the claim that 90 per cent of lone parents wanted to work, and that they would be on average £50 per week better off than on benefits. Both claims were tendentious: the first rested on research more accurately cited in the Borrie report as showing that most would like to work at some time in the future;[19] the second was based on the incomes of a small and unrepresentative sample of employed lone mothers, taking no account of in-work costs. Her defence in this debate rested on reiteration of the opportunities offered to lone parents by the New Deal. Work for lone parents would increase self-esteem and independence, and tackle the causes of poverty, not just the symptom. Patricia Hewitt argued that 'changes in the benefit system alone would not make opportunities possible', while Lorna Fitzsimons said that 'although £5 on benefit will buy things, in the long term it will not alleviate the poverty trap'. In the Alice in Wonderland world of New Labour, lone-parent families would be released from this trap by a drop in income: Fitzsimons said 'this is a short-term measure that will reap long-term gain by creating a modern economy and liberating from poverty all the children and single parents whom I represent'.

Harman's reply in the debate slid inexorably into MUD. The claim that work is about more than money meant not just self-esteem, but independence – and, crucially, as a role model for the young, teaching them that 'work is better than benefit dependency'. Lone mothers themselves were invoked as saying 'we want to work – we do not want to be dependent on benefit because we want to set an example to our children'. She added that 'the public clearly want an active approach to welfare so that everyone works for his or her living if that is possible'. She repeatedly refused to rule out compulsion. Her reply that 'there is no intention that the New Deal should drive lone parents with young children out to work' could be interpreted as foreboding coercion of those whose children were not so young. The extension of the opportunities of the New Deal to those with pre-school children might then seem like the thin end of a worrying wedge – especially given Clive Soley's reference to those who did not wish to work in the early years of their children's lives as a 'difficult group'.

The objections levelled from within the logic of the welfare to work strategy itself concerned the disincentive effects of the benefit cuts. Those currently receiving means-tested benefits in many cases claimed the lone-parent premium to Income Support, not to Child Benefit, and would lose this if they moved into work. They would be ill-advised to take seasonal or insecure work, as they risked returning as 'new claimants' to a lower rate of benefit. Both Alice Mahon and Audrey Wise, the principal Labour speakers against the Government, expressed support for providing opportunities for education, work and child care through the New Deal, but not as an alternative to decent levels of benefit. Their central argument was that reducing the benefits of the poorest families was morally unacceptable. Wise argued that inclusion would imply raising the incomes of the poor to increase equality of opportunity, suggesting that 'if we want social inclusion …we should make it possible for children to do what my grand-children can do: go swimming, watch football and have piano lessons', and detailing the substantial costs of these activities.

UNPAID WORK

Critics of benefit cuts for lone parents also raised the question of unpaid work. The very phrase welfare to work when applied to lone parents carries the message that parenting is not work. While demonstrators outside parliament chanted 'every mother is a working mother', Webb argued that 'all lone parents are working lone parents, but only some of them get paid for it'. The issue of child care was central to the New Deal for lone parents. Harman argued that the higher costs incurred by lone-parent families were chiefly child-care costs, and that the loss of benefit would be compensated for by the direct provision of child-care services. Wise questioned 'why child care is work when it is done by a stranger but not when it is done by the child's mother or father'. Mahon stressed the contradiction between the acknowledged importance of parenting and pressurizing lone parents into paid work.

It cannot be argued that Labour ignores unpaid work, which is both recognized and to some extent recognized as gendered. The national child-care strategy, however inadequate, demonstrates this. In addition, policy documents acknowledge the unpaid work of personal caring and other forms of voluntary action which sustain social life in 'communities'. They anticipate an increase rather than a drop in informal caring, and recognize the added burden that has been created by community care. They also acknowledge that support services are inadequate, leaving carers feeling isolated and restricted (although this is not described in terms of social exclusion). But there is a profound contradiction between treating paid work as the defining factor in social inclusion, and recognizing the value of unpaid work. How can Labour's claims to recognize the value of unpaid work be reconciled with their insistence on inclusion through paid work?

Firstly, inclusion may be effected by proxy. While lone parents are deemed to need paid work for social inclusion, self esteem and independence, full-time parenting remains an option for those not in receipt of income support, including for those with working partners but eligible for family credit. In such cases, social exclusion is not deemed to result from absence from the labour market. If social inclusion is effected through work, this makes little sense. However, Labour's concern is not with individual inclusion, but with those *households* where no-one of working age is in work. Whereas dependence on the state is a moral hazard, personal economic dependency apparently is not – although for women who are only a divorce or separation away from lone-parent status and poverty, it may be a practical hazard. Paid work is, it seems, only necessary for social inclusion for those who would otherwise become a charge on the state.

Secondly, the recognition of unpaid work is itself ambiguous. The activity of parenting is recognized as socially necessary. There is pressure for greater parental involvement in children's education, as well as repeated reference to the importance of parenting in preventing crime. But parenting is not referred to as work; it is referred to as a 'responsibility', while the associated domestic labour of shopping, washing, ironing, cleaning and cooking is ignored. Thus affordable child care 'can help men and women lead more balanced, fulfilling lives by enabling women to return to work and let both parents share more equally the responsibilities of caring for children'.[20] More often, it is women who are expected to juggle the conflicting demands of paid and unpaid work: Brown argued that the welfare state must become more responsive to women's needs, 'allowing them to combine family responsibilities with employment'.[21] The costs to women of juggling in this way do surface occasionally: 'working mothers with young children...were exhausted at the end of the day and felt they were spending too little time with their children'.[22] But Blair's lack of grasp of what mothers do was reflected in his suggestion that maternity leave is an opportunity for women to improve their marketable skills: 'The mother on maternity leave' might learn 'a new skill or language to equip her for her return to work'.[23] Paradoxically, Brown's acclaimed recognition in his first budget speech that child care was an economic issue was not a recognition that it was work, but rather the reverse. Child-care provision was necessary to draw women into economic activity, that is, into the labour market – precisely because their unpaid work did not itself constitute an economic contribution. In terms of Glucksmann's model of the total social organization of labour, non-market activities are looked at from a perspective which privileges paid work, so that although unpaid work is visible, it is not consistently interpreted as work, or valorized as economic activity. Thirdly, the capacity of unpaid work to generate social inclusion depends in part on where it takes place. Unpaid work for family members within the private sphere can only generate proxy inclusion, whereas voluntary work or 'active citizenship' – which at least crosses the boundary between public and private – is seen as socially inclusive. It is a way of including the retired population, through unpaid work in schools or as surrogate grandparents, and a secondary route to inclusion for those for whom paid work is not available. People must not, therefore, be excluded from the opportunity to volunteer. Barriers to volunteering include poverty and the rules of the benefit system, so that 'idleness is... fostered by the operation of the welfare state'.[24] In the context of active citizenship, lack of child care is argued to be as 'relevant to volunteering as it is to work'.[25] Volunteering is a route to self-worth, especially for 'unemployed people and those on long-term benefits'.[26] It also enhances employability: 'it makes people more employable, cultivating their skills, their capacity to work with others and to solve problems'.[27] This establishes a hierarchy of forms of work: the unpaid activity or 'responsibility' of parenting, the unpaid activity of volunteering, and paid work, with only the last constituting real work and delivering real social inclusion.

THE SOCIAL EXCLUSION UNIT

Social inclusion was explicitly brought to the centre of Government policy in December 1997 with the creation of a new unit dedicated to tackling social exclusion. This commitment was, said Blair, 'in many ways the defining difference between ourselves and the previous government'. The Social Exclusion Unit was, like welfare to work, presented as a flagship policy. It was set up for two years in the first instance, although the task of overcoming exclusion was predicted to take ten years, or two full parliamentary terms. It was part of the Economic and Domestic Affairs Secretariat in the Cabinet Office, reporting to the Prime Minister and working with the No. 10 Policy Unit. Besides twelve full- and part-time co-opted members incorporating representatives from the police, business, the voluntary sector and the civil service, a network of ministers from relevant departments was identified to both guide and present the unit's work. They included Hilary Armstrong (Environment), Keith Bradley

(Social Security), Stephen Byers (Education and Employment), Tessa Jowell (Health), Peter Mandelson (Cabinet Office), Alun Michael (Home Office), Geoffrey Robinson (Treasury) and Barbara Roche (Trade and Industry).

In the remit of the Unit, social exclusion was defined as 'a shorthand label for what can happen when individuals or areas suffer from a combination of linked problems such as unemployment, poor skills, low incomes, poor housing, high crime environments, bad health and family breakdown'. The Unit's purpose was to break the vicious circle of interaction between these problems by 'improving understanding of the key characteristics of social exclusion, and the impact on it of Government policies'; and 'promoting solutions, encouraging co-operation, disseminating best practice and, where necessary, making recommendations for changes in policies, machinery or delivery mechanisms'. The emphasis was on co-ordinating policy across Government departments, and exploring with local authority and voluntary agencies integrated approaches to overcoming social exclusion – joined-up policies for joined-up problems.

The programme for the first six months was clearly specified. The first priorities were the reduction of truancy and school exclusions, together with better provision for those necessarily excluded from school; the reduction of rough sleeping 'to as near zero as possible'; and 'developing integrated and sustainable approaches to the problems of the worst housing estates, including crime, drugs, unemployment, community breakdown, bad schools'. Potential areas for late 1998 included 'preventive interventions with children and young people'; looking at aspects of exclusion disproportionately affecting ethnic minority groups; 'options for improving access to services, public and private, for low income areas or individuals'; and 'ways to encourage individual and business involvement in tackling social exclusion'. The Unit had no spending budget. Its purpose was to direct existing funding more effectively, by making recommendations which would feed into Departmental spending reviews. It was also expected to develop key indicators of social exclusion, to be used in evaluating Government policy.

A definition of social exclusion similar to that of the Social Exclusion Unit was given by Harriet Harman in November 1997 at the new Centre for the Analysis of Social Exclusion (CASE) at the London School of Economics (a research centre funded by the Economic and Social Research Council with no formal connection with the Social Exclusion Unit): 'what we mean by "social exclusion" is complex. We mean adults deprived of work, and children deprived of a decent education. We mean families deprived of the material goods that many of us take for granted. We mean whole communities deprived of proper access to transport, to healthcare and to financial services'. The problem, she argued, was multi-dimensional and dynamic, 'about exclusion from the opportunities provided by education, by work, and by participation in the wider society'. In the initial announcement about the Unit in his Fabian Society lecture the previous August, Mandelson had offered a similarly broad view of exclusion. It was, he said, 'about more than poverty and unemployment', and 'about being cut off from what the rest of us regard as normal life'. The excluded were 'the growing number of our fellow citizens who lack the means, material and otherwise, to participate in economic, social, cultural and political life in Britain today'.

But despite a broad definition which looked superficially compatible with RED, it was clear from the outset that the SEU's brief was located in SID and MUD. Mandelson described its purpose as 'to seek lasting solutions to the problems of those without hope and a stake in society', and to spend less money alleviating the effects of social exclusion by preventing it from happening. As so often, the statement that exclusion was about 'more than' poverty became the justification for not addressing poverty directly. Mandelson attacked Hattersley's attempts to reinstate the cause of distributive equality, claiming that Labour's policies would deliver greater equality, of a superior kind: 'one of the fruits of our success will be that Britain has become a more equal society' and 'we will have achieved that result by many different routes, *not just* the redistribution of cash from rich to poor which others artificially choose as their own limited definition of egalitarianism'. Harman similarly argued that 'if social exclusion is about much more than just poverty, then tackling it has to go far beyond changes to the rate of benefit'. In the week of the Labour Party Conference, fifty-four professors of social policy and sociology, led by Ruth Lister and Robert Moore, wrote to the *Financial Times,* drawing attention to the false dichotomy between welfare to work and improving living standards for the poorest, and arguing that the Government was trying 'to tackle social exclusion with one hand tied behind its back'.

Mandelson described the excluded as those 'at best on the edge of the labour force': five million families with no-one in work, single parents, the homeless, children not attending school, and '3 million people living in the worst... housing estates experiencing multiple deprivation, rising poverty, unemployment, educational failure and crime'. The emphasis was on those groups who were identified as potential workers, or as a moral danger. Those in poverty but neither perceived as workers nor a threat to social order took second place. Although for groups such as poor pensioners and the chronically sick and disabled 'the message of opportunity must seem hollow', Mandelson argued that 'we must concentrate effort on helping individuals who can escape their situation to do so'. The top priorities were moving people from welfare to work, and addressing low educational standards and expectations – already promoted as priority areas for the new Government. Although these were only the first steps in tackling multiple deprivation, the comprehensive policies promised for the future covered public health, education, housing, the youth justice system, and new jobs; they notably did not include redistribution through the tax and benefit systems.

When the Social Exclusion Unit was launched in December – two days before the debate on lone parents' benefits – Blair declared its priority to be dealing with the 'thousands of truant children hanging around on street corners'.[28] Truancy and school exclusion bridge SID and MUD, the agendas of employability and crime prevention:

> I've asked the unit to make truancy and school exclusions a top priority because we know that the prospects for kids who miss school are so dismal. It's bad enough if kids are missing out on the education they'll need to get a job and make a life. What's worse is that, for many, being out of school is the beginning of a slippery slope to crime, drugs and exploitation by others. They pay a high price. But in the long run we all end up paying for it as well.[29]

The unit's first practical target was therefore to set up homework clubs, to which parents might be 'strongly advised' to send their children – although children who truant from school may of course be reluctant to attend the clubs as well.

The discourse surrounding the Social Exclusion Unit showed an alarming tendency to slip from SID to MUD. The plans for the Unit were intimately linked to the New Deal, and there was a strong emphasis on the transition from welfare to work. A Downing Street source interviewed about the Unit suggested that the problem of unemployment was attributable less to lack of jobs than to the absence of child care and transport – and to the fact that the excluded were not psychologically equipped for work. 'The culture on workless estates has to be changed by...visits to lone parents and even door-to-door knocking to encourage people to come on training courses'. Cultural change would be backed up by coercion. It was suggested that Benefits Agency staff should 'be able to offer unemployed drug addicts a training programme and jobs placement in three months, and in the meantime dock benefit if they do not attend a rehabilitation programme'.[30]

For Harman, at the launch of CASE, the emphasis was firmly on work as the route to inclusion:

> Work is central to the Government's attack on social exclusion. Work is the only route to sustained financial independence. But it is also much more. Work is not just about earning a living. It is a way of life...[W]ork is an important element of the human condition. We hear a lot about the non-wage *costs* of work. But very little about the non-wage *motivation* for work. Work helps fulfil our aspirations – it is the key to independence, self-respect and opportunities for advancement....Work brings a sense of order that is missing from the lives of many unemployed young men. Work provides access to social networks. And work is not just important while we are working. It is through work that we support ourselves in retirement.

The many factors contributing to exclusion did not, in Harman's list, include low income, but 'low educational achievement, truancy, drug abuse, worklessness, poor health and poor housing'. And as the argument shifted to the consequences for the included, so MUD dominated over SID: 'we all suffer...the fall-out of low educational achievement, truancy, school exclusion, drug abuse, juvenile crime'. Her characterization of the excluded echoed this moral agenda:

> They and their families are trapped in dependency. They inhabit a parallel world where: income is derived from benefits, not work; where school is an option not the key to opportunity; and where the dominant influence on young people is the culture of the street, not the values that bind families and communities together. There are some estates in my constituency where: the common currency is the giro; where the black economy involves much more than moonlighting – it involves the twilight world of drugs; and where relentless anti-social behaviour grinds people down, particularly the old who live in constant fear. These are whole communities which are completely disconnected from the world of work.

The slipperiness of New Labour's thinking about social exclusion is illustrated by Mandelson:

Many of those who are socially excluded are experiencing multiple deprivation and there is no one simple quick fix. Obviously their outstanding need is for a job, but many of them are so distanced from the labour market that they have very many bridges to cross just to bring them back into any sort of mainstream living. If you have someone who is experiencing family breakdown or has a criminal record and is involved in drugs or is on the verge of homelessness then they are not going to last very long in employment or on a work-experience scheme.[31]

The first sentence is a straightforward acknowledgement, entirely compatible with RED, that poverty is multi-dimensional. It then leaps to the assumption that employment is the answer, which may often be true, but in some cases may be quite inappropriate. Distance from the labour market is linked to distance from mainstream living; we are now apparently in SID. But the statement that 'they have very many bridges to cross' implies a measure of unemployability – then elaborated in terms of family breakdown, crime, drug use and homelessness, as if these were characteristics peculiar to the poor. The last sentence has shifted decisively into the moral discourse of the underclass. It ignores the facts that many people in employment use illegal recreational drugs. Having a criminal record makes it more difficult to find employment, but does not necessarily have any direct bearing on the capacity or motivation to work, while homelessness is a practical problem, not a moral failing. There was a particular irony in the suggestion that family breakdown means people will not 'last long in employment', as this statement was made within days of the public announcement of the ending of the Foreign Secretary Robin Cook's own marriage, with no suggestion that he had suddenly become unemployable.

THE DEMOS FACTOR

The key influence behind the Social Exclusion Unit was Geoff Mulgan, Director of Demos and part-time adviser to the No. 10 Policy Unit. Not surprisingly, Demos took up the issue of exclusion. Perri 6 described social exclusion in broad terms as referring to 'the ways in which significant minorities are excluded from participating in the mainstream life of society: from jobs, education, homes, leisure, civic organisations and even voting, and on how this disconnection tends to coincide with vulnerability to poverty, crime and family breakdown'.[32] The framework is not RED. 'There is no case for increases in the generosity [sic] of income support for able-bodied unemployed people of working age.' There may be a case for modest increase in state support for retired or 'very severely disabled' people – but not to the extent that this would diminish the incentive for others to take out second pensions. There is a strong element of SID: the concern is explicitly to get more people 'into the labour market, as the principal strategy for getting out of social exclusion'. Cultural factors are central. While Perri 6 argues that this is not blaming poverty on the culture of the poor, since the cultural problems are a consequence rather than a cause of poverty, he nevertheless draws heavily on MUD in endorsing the 'powerful tools of regulation and incentive' in changing cultures: 'The proper role of time-limited benefits and tight conditions of active job search and duties to accept certain kinds of offers is cultural, rather than part of controlling public spending, and ministers and officials should take every opportunity to make this clear'.[33] The Demos approach also differs from RED in being unconcerned with equality. Kruger argues that 'social exclusion can be defined as exclusion from access to the ladders of social improvement, being cut off from the paths of upward mobility', while Perri 6 defined social exclusion as 'loss of access to ... life chances'.[34]

Mulgan himself is an exponent of the third way, beyond what he describes as the two exhausted political projects of social democracy and Thatcherism. He describes social democracy as 'a combination of faith in government, moderately egalitarian welfare and the mixed economy'; its failure was succeeded by Thatcherism, 'a bold project of national renewal which tackled head on many deep structural problems, but then ran out of steam'.[35] He insists on employability as the basis of security, arguing that private investment in education should become the norm rather than the exception. He does concede that employability is worthless unless jobs are created, but his is no Keynesian prescription for demand management: 'the old Keynesian way to tackle unemployment was to dig holes, the modern way is to fill brains and release potential'. He suggests those old Thatcherite remedies, entrepreneurial activity and self-employment: 'those out of work should ... be trained more effectively to create jobs for themselves'.[36] A change in the role of trade unions is implied; they should be more committed to 'helping people become employable, rather than protecting them in existing jobs'.[37] For Mulgan, politics is at least in part about 'attempting ... to mobilise changes in public behaviour such as harder work, better parenting or greater willingness to obey laws'.[38]

Mulgan characterizes capitalism as a system of exchange 'born out of an ethos of work and sacrifice'.[39] Participation in exchange defines inclusion: 'exchange ... is the main means of inclusion: without being able to sell your labour, and without the cash that comes from successful exchange of labour, you are effectively excluded from participation in most forms of communal life'.[40] Exclusion is not, for Mulgan simply or primarily a matter of the resources which paid work provides: the work itself, as for Hutton, is essential to both self-esteem and identity. Work is 'the prime source of status'; 'the worst thing that can happen is to fall out of work, and lose your employability, your skills, your personal qualities, as well as friends and contacts'.[41] The importance of work does not depend on it being decently paid: 'we need deliberately to cultivate useful work, albeit often on low wages, from short periods of work experience for 14 year olds to two-day weeks for 70 year olds, as the key to self-esteem, employability and social cohesion'.[42] And 'whereas earlier generations without jobs might have thought of themselves as unlucky, today those without jobs are likely to think of themselves as literally valueless'.[43] This, for Mulgan, explains the long working hours of those with jobs: 'For those who have it, work defines their identity, and motivates them to devote ever longer hours to it. For those without a job, its absence cuts them off from the normal life of friends and neighbourhoods, citizenship and sociability'.[44] This, together with the contradictory concern that the work ethic is weakening, is why there must be 'appropriate sticks and carrots for getting someone who has been unemployed for several years back into work'.[45]

But Mulgan's view of inclusion also reflects Murray's concern about the moral consequences of welfare benefits, although he rejects the word underclass. 'If governments spend vast sums of money on welfare, they have to be concerned if the dependency thus created undermines the character of the recipient' and 'when welfare systems become more generous they tend to promote the very behaviour they are designed to alleviate'.[46] More specifically, 'If welfare is given to people more generously where there is no father, then women respond to the incentives by being more likely to choose to bring children up on their own'; while it is right to provide support for parents it is 'wrong to make it too easy for them to dump their children onto the responsibility of the state'.[47] Those in receipt of benefits are described not only in terms of dependency, but parasitism, especially 'the form of parasitism in which people take advantage of the community to do the work needed to pass on their own genes'. Mulgan is not referring to assisted conception, but mothers and fathers who must be prevented 'from taking advantage of the state to pay for their children's upbringing'.[48]

Like Murray, Mulgan does not see all of the poor as a problem. Many of those in Hutton's lowest 30 per cent drift in and out of poverty and/or unemployment and thus are not 'really' excluded. Mulgan is concerned principally with those whose exclusion is semi-permanent, which he estimates at 8 to 10 per cent of the population: those 'who leave school with no qualifications after a school life of inattention, truancy and disruption; who live in the areas where nearly 50 per cent of all crimes are committed; who provide most of the single-parent families, the drug addicts – the chronic losers'.[49] Even the public sanctification of the Princess of Wales does not dent the routine condemnation of lone parenthood. Mulgan's concern with the evils of dependency, however, stretches beyond the conventional target groups of those who rely on means-tested benefits. He deplores a widespread modern mentality of 'disobedient dependence', giving as an example 'the grumbling assembly-line workers who would never dream of setting up in business on their own'.[50] And he intimates that reliance on the state pension and the NHS are less obviously legitimate than social democrats suppose. He implies that more generous benefits even for those not expected to work are socially damaging and should not be encouraged: 'If states choose to fund the old, then, not suprisingly, the extended family weakens'.[51] And he describes as 'parasites' those people 'who abuse their own health when health care is socialised, safe in the knowledge that others will pick up the bill'[52] – a charge which could to some degree be levelled at large sections of the population, and which is reminiscent of Edwina Currie's criticisms of the lifestyles of the poor.[53]

Mulgan's views would be less disturbing if they were less typical of New Labour's uneasy oscillation between social exclusion as worklessness and as moral hazard. Although Mulgan avoids the term underclass, Blair uses it repeatedly. His portrayal of the underclass simultaneously contains a description of multiple deprivation and of moral failure: 'often their life is marked by unemployment, poor education, crime, drug abuse and family instability'. Young men and young women pose different problems. 'For a generation of young men, little has come to replace the third of all manufacturing jobs that have been lost. For part of a generation of young women early pregnancies and the absence of a reliable father almost guarantee a life of poverty'.[54] Unemployment, poverty and deprivation are routinely juxtaposed to drug abuse and criminality; 'family instability' is a recurrent theme; and welfare dependency a moral problem, in an economy 'built on benefits, crime, petty thieving and drugs'.[55] The underclass is morally distinct. They are, says Blair, 'living in a culture that is becoming more and more alienated'.[56] They are 'without any sense of shared purpose' with the rest of society, whereas 'to be a citizen of Britain is . . . to share its aspirations, to be part of the British family'.[57] America offers the warning of what will happen if this goes on. There, 'millions have simply dropped out of society, forming alternative systems of living and language . . . that is the threat if we do not stop the break-up of our society'.[58]

OPPORTUNITY KNOCKS

The combination of SID and MUD gives rise to a highly specific understanding of inclusion as an active obligation, in which opportunity is the crucial term. Blair argued: 'For the new Millennium we need a war on exclusion and a determination to extend opportunity to all.'[59] Harman spoke of 'promoting employability, adaptability and inclusion', together with 'a fair distribution of economic opportunity'.[60] Just as security is reduced to employability, the question of inclusion through work is ultimately addressed through the provision not of jobs, but of employment opportunities. Thus Brown declared:

> So we must create a country where there are new opportunities for everyone – millions of points of opportunity. Opportunities for work and the qualifications for work. Opportunities to start businesses. Opportunities to become self-employed. And I make no apologies for saying government has a responsibility in creating this new ladder of opportunity – a new ladder of opportunity from the school to the workplace. That will allow the many, by their own efforts, to benefit from the opportunities once open only to a few.[61]

Social inclusion now has nothing to do with distributional equality, but means lifting the poor over the boundary of a minimum standard – or to be more accurate, inducing those who are sufficiently sound in wind and limb to jump over it – while leaving untouched the overall pattern of inequality, especially the rich. Just as the Commission on Social Justice argued for the redistribution of opportunities rather than of income, Mandelson's concern was with those 'dropping off the end of the ladder of opportunity' – not with the length of the ladder or the distance between the rungs.[62]

Moreover, inclusion is an active process, not a status; and agency – and hence resposibility – lies with the individual. The combination of employability and opportunity renders inclusion something which individuals achieve and perform through the exploitation of opportunity. If opportunity plus responsibility equals community, New Labour's implicit message is that opportunity plus employability equals inclusion. Both in the labour market and as active citizens in the community, people are called upon to perform their inclusion. They are morally obliged to do so: 'Everybody has a duty to take part in society'.[63] This performative inclusion, which Raymond Plant[64] has described as supply-side citizenship, is enforced through the carrots of SID and the sticks of MUD – the pecuniary and non-pecuniary benefits of paid work and the direct compulsion of benefit withdrawals and reductions. In the process, the total work load of women is increased, as they are expected to perform both paid and unpaid work.

But there is also indirect pressure exerted through the twin processes of condemning 'dependency' and increasing the extent to which social identities are discursively constructed primarily on the basis of participation in paid work. SID hinges on the argument that self-esteem and identity are predicated on paid employment. The repetition of these claims is part of a discursive construction of the self in which the claims themselves become true. If there is a contradiction between pressing people into paid work while worrying about the quality of parenting, this attempt at social control through the very nature of the self produces a deeper contradiction between SID and MUD. The film *The Full Monty* illustrates the importance of work (and certain kinds of work), and the consequences of worklessness, for male identity. Bea Campbell's discussion of social exclusion and masculinity in *Goliath* suggests that the problems of social disorder are both real and gendered: it is not just that 'the poor' suffer most, but that poor women have to resist the aggressive colonization of space by poor men.[65] Her central point is that this behaviour is *not*, as MUD would imply, a pathological form of masculinity produced by unemployment and poverty. Rather, unemployment *reveals* the way in which masculinity is constructed across society, a model of masculinity into which low-skilled young men are only too well socialized, but for whom it frequently finds anti-social expression. The experience of men illustrates the consequences of constructing self-esteem and social status as attaching almost exclusively to participation in paid work – and graded according to pay levels – in a society which then denies that participation. Paid work is important to the identity of women, but not yet so for all women in the same way or to the same extent as for men, precisely because of their involvement in unpaid work. A more rational response might be to argue for strategies to *detach* self-esteem from paid work as Gray (Chapter 5) suggests – to make men more like women, rather than making women more like men.

The repetition of arguments about the importance of work to independence, self-respect, and identity is an active project, not a description of a naturally occurring event – just as the manipulation of benefit levels and eligibility criteria constructs the objective conditions within which people make their personal histories. Performative inclusion involves the attempted coercive and discursive creation of the self as first and foremost a worker. People – or perhaps just embodied worker-selves – are then invited to perform their social inclusion, in paid work if they can get it, but if not in various forms of voluntary activity where they can carry out necessary labour without payment. Social inclusion cannot be performed within the family, so unpaid work in the private sphere does not count. But other forms of unpaid work in 'the community' may be a stage for inclusion. Where paid work is unavailable, voluntary work is a second choice: those citizens who have no professional opportunities to perform their inclusion are redirected to the theatres of community, to practice active citizenship.

8 Delivering Social Inclusion

How far will Labour succeed in delivering social inclusion? Blair would prefer this question deferred for ten years, but at least a provisional assessment will be needed before the election in 2001 or 2002. As the policies are put in place, it is possible to ask what kind of inclusion Labour seeks to deliver, what the criteria of success would be, and how likely it is that the policies will achieve this. None of the discourses has a well-developed set of indicators of social exclusion, partly because the centrality of the term in British politics is so new – and partly because to clarify the definition would undermine the very flexibility of the concept which makes it politically useful. Because the meaning and imputed causes of exclusion differ in RED, SID and MUD, so too will some of the indicators of success in producing greater inclusion. The prospects for inclusion depend on which discourse you are situated in. Both provisional and later assessments can be made in Labour's own terms, and against other understandings of social exclusion and other criteria. Success in combating exclusion will be as contested as the concept itself. The most obvious critical yardsticks are those implied by RED, and the main part of this chapter considers the prospects for welfare to work and the Social Exclusion Unit from the different standpoints of RED, SID and MUD. Questions are also raised about the nature of the 'social' in social inclusion, and about unpaid work, transport, participation in common institutions and political inclusion – and the contradictions and tensions between aspects of inclusion.

WELFARE TO WORK: THE VIEW FROM SID

There are aspects of both welfare to work and the remit of the Social Exclusion Unit which are consistent with RED, SID and MUD. The welfare to work programme has widespread support. For RED, involuntary unemployment is one important cause of poverty; for SID, work in itself delivers inclusion; for MUD, work is a moral necessity to counter dependence. In the broadest sense, all would interpret the programme as successful if it: reduces the number of people dependent on benefit; moves the people concerned into socially useful paid employment which delivers self-esteem, social relationships and a reasonable standard of living; provides high quality, affordable care for their children; reduces poverty; reduces social security spending, thus releasing more money to be spent on health and education; and does so without coercion. Pigs might fly. The difference between the discourses lies in the priority given to these various aims.

From the perspective of SID, the most important indicators of success would be a rise in labour force participation rates, especially for the target groups of young people, lone parents and people with disabilities; and a drop in the number of workless households among those of working age. Falling registered unemployment is not an adequate measure of the success of the New Deal, since it excludes those forced off the register and a range of people deemed economically inactive. In 1997, the unemployment figures fell sharply, and there were no longer 250 000 young people eligible for the New Deal, but roughly half that number. This was partly due to the effect on the count of the Jobseeker's Allowance, but also to a real drop in youth unemployment. A rise in unemployment was forecast for 1998 as the New Deal came into effect. The test of rising participation rates avoids the measurement problems associated with unemployment, but it is complicated by how far any change can be attributed to the welfare to work programme itself. Evaluating changes against a background of changing economic conditions is not so easy.

There is a further complication to relying on unemployment rates as an indicator of exclusion. Unemployment rates are higher in France and Germany, and Labour, like the Conservatives, attributes Britain's lower recorded unemployment – and that in the USA – to the greater flexibility of the economy. But the USA has a much higher proportion of its male population in prison. If incarceration rates and unemployment rates are taken together, the difference between Europe and the United States lies principally in the proportion of young (predominantly black) men in jail.[1] While levels of imprisonment in Britain are not comparable with those in the US, they are high by European Standards. This has implications for benefit budgets. The proportion of GDP spent on social security in the UK, as in the USA, is relatively low compared to France and Germany, but the costs of social security payments for the unemployed must be balanced against the greater costs of incarceration. While unemployment is the key form of social exclusion for SID, the greater social exclusion of imprisonment is neglected.

Rising participation rates are more important to SID than the numbers passing through the programmes who find some form of work. Before the pilot schemes for lone parents and their evaluation were completed, Harman vaunted their success in terms of the percentage of participants moving into employment. These early figures were disputed because they related to those taking up the offer of an interview, not those approached or eligible. It was also suggested that these were the very women who would have taken employment without help. Some of those moving into work under the New Deal would do so anyway. Simply looking at outcomes for participants in welfare to work ignores two further problems: substitution and churning. Participants may be given a competitive advantage, so that they get jobs at the expense of others in the labour market, for example privileging the young unemployed at the expense of older workers. This substitution effect is a particular problem with subsidised employment. As Hutton said, the programmes may also result in only temporary and short-term work placements, and a churning in and out of employment. Increased labour force participation rates indicate the success of the programmes over and above substitution, churning, or existing levels of movement into work.

The likely success of welfare to work in SID's terms is – and will remain – disputable. Its supply-side assumptions may undermine it. There is no consensus about how far unemployment is a problem of employability, and how far it is caused by a lack of demand for labour. Although the lead indicator for SID is labour market attachment, and this has priority over the quality and pay of jobs, SID differs from MUD on the issue of compulsion. The emphasis on the positive utility of work means compulsion should not be necessary; the emphasis on work as a route to self-esteem makes compulsion, especially in the shape of thinly-disguised workfare schemes, counter-productive. It is therefore important whether the New Deal results in people moving into real jobs, rather than being forced into make-work schemes for benefit, or even 'benefit plus'. The quality of the scheme, and therefore of the work, is not irrelevant.

Without investment to provide real jobs, improved training and skills may simply equip individuals for a competitive struggle for employment in which some must lose. The initial response of the private sector to pleas to provide opportunities for young people under the New Deal was disappointing, even with the subsidies offered. This is partly because employers do not want unwilling conscripts as workers, but it does not bode well for the expansion of jobs when the subsidies run out. One suggestion has been that local authorities might compensate for this shortfall. In a roundabout way, the local state would thus become the employer of last resort, in a return to limited Keynesian demand management – a solution compatible with SID, but one which will cost money. But SID emphasizes carrots, not sticks. Within SID, the prime concern is not saving money: increased expenditure on in-work benefits, on child care, on training, and even on job creation might be wholly legitimate in promoting inclusion through work.

WELFARE TO WORK: THE VIEW FROM MUD

From within MUD, the central criterion of success is the reduction in the numbers of people of working age wholly dependent on benefit. A drop in the number of workless households is important. Since the central element in MUD is the moral necessity of work, neither the level of pay nor the quality of the work is important. Coercion is legitimate – even justified as tough love. MUD may appear to be directed primarily at reducing public spending, but the discourse and the policies are ambiguous in this respect. Labour's welfare to work policies as originally floated in the Borrie report owed much to the Australian Working Nation programme,[2] and especially to the JET (Jobs, Education, Training) scheme for lone mothers. Both the rhetoric, in the use of the term welfare and the phrase New Deal, and the substantive policies, moved closer to an American model. In office, Labour showed increasing interest in Wisconsin Works or W–2, and in September 1997 Jean Rogers, the W–2 administrator, attended the post-election conference at the London School of Economics on 'How Labour can Deliver'. Experience in both Australia and Wisconsin showed that the provision of child care to enable lone parents to work is expensive. This is so even before posing serious questions about the quality of child care, whether parents or children suffer as a result, or the pay and conditions of the carers.

MUD has other features. Work is also a prophylactic against crime. For the young unemployed, it is a means of social discipline – or, as Labour put it, 'our policy against crime is jobs'. It is important both for workers and for their children, who need to be set an example, and to learn the work ethic – not at their parent's knee, but through separation from it. Those same children, especially in lone-parent families, are seen as in need of parental supervision to curb their criminal tendencies. This points either to an irresolvable contradiction between welfare to work and the agenda of social order – or to Murray's agenda, of attempting to make lone parenthood as difficult as possible to enforce moral conformity. Success, for MUD, would mean not just a decrease in benefit dependency, but a decrease in crime and in lone parenthood, all perceived as indissolubly linked.

WELFARE TO WORK: THE VIEW FROM RED

For RED, the most pressing question is the effect on the lives of the excluded. The central indicator of success or failure in tackling social exclusion is the prevalence of poverty, and whether there is both absolute and relative improvement in the living standards of the poor. The availability of information to monitor these changes was undermined by changes to the statistical base during the Thatcher years; restoration and improvement is needed.[3] The question will not just be whether more people are in paid work, but whether those in and out of employment, above and below working age, are better or worse off.

The reduction of involuntary unemployment is one element in this. As for SID, the emphasis is on the benefits of paid work, financial and otherwise. The quality of work matters. Coercion is generally rejected because benefit penalties may be unjustly applied, and themselves cause greater poverty and exclusion – as well as potentially undermining the New Deal by turning it effectively into a workfare programme. Compulsion is viewed as unnecessary in almost all cases if there is reasonable, reasonably paid work available, and pointless or worse if there is not. RED, like SID, sees exclusion from paid work as a form of and a factor in social exclusion. But increased rates of labour market participation will be an indicator of success only if they result in a reduction in poverty. The level of the minimum wage is crucial to RED. And whatever the success of welfare to work, it will not improve the situation of those who remain dependent on benefits or state pensions. Moreover, because RED recognizes parenting as unpaid work, lone parents dependent on benefit are not viewed as not working. The implication is an increase in benefits to relieve poverty, rather than an across the board cut or the introduction of coercion into the New Deal to force them into paid employment. For RED, welfare to work can be at best a partial solution to the problem of social exclusion.

DELIVERING SOCIAL INCLUSION: THE SOCIAL EXCLUSION UNIT

One of the first tasks set for the Unit in its first six months was the development of indicators of exclusion. In one sense, this will make assessment of the success of the Unit in the Government's own terms relatively straightforward. But as in the case of welfare to work, different indicators will be preferred or prioritized from the standpoint of the different discourses. Perri 6, writing for Demos, says social exclusion 'can best be measured by looking at how many people are cut off from work, learning and other forms of social participation' – the priorities of SID – and goes on to suggest as indicators measures of both the causal processes and the condition of social exclusion. The former include 'mobility, promotion and redundancy, social stratification and limited social mobility, educational failure or family breakdown'; the latter 'worklessness and unemployment, homelessness, lack of membership of voluntary organisations, denial of services, isolation or lack of effective social contacts, lack of a car or a telephone'.[4] It is notable that poverty does not appear as an indicator of either the cause or condition of exclusion.

For RED, income data is a proxy indicator, though not a measure, of the wider multi-faceted process of exclusion. Although poverty is a prime cause of social exclusion, the two are not synonymous. Improving the material living standards of the poor is a necessary but insufficient condition for combating exclusion. The Social Exclusion Unit also sees exclusion as a complex and multi-dimensional problem. Its concern with multiple deprivation, homelessness, joblessness, and the concentration of these in areas which also suffer from high levels of crime is not immediately different from RED, and the pursuit of a co-ordinated approach to these is wholly consistent with it. To some extent, the indicators will overlap. But whether the perceived causes and thus proposed solutions coincide is another matter. In MUD, if exclusion is the result of poverty, poverty itself is largely attributed to a failure of employability – which, given the responsibility of individuals for their own employability, is in large part a moral problem. If MUD says 'the poor are different from us', RED says 'yes; they have less money'. The obvious difference is that RED implies improved levels of benefits, while MUD does not. Government policy rules out additional expenditure in this form, so that for RED, as Lister said, the Social Exclusion Unit tackles exclusion with one hand tied behind its back.

In some instances, the relationship between the two approaches is as straightforward as Lister suggests. For example, the Unit is concerned about the exclusion of sectors of society from financial services. Residents in some areas may be unable to open bank accounts, obtain credit cards, or obtain credit because of their postcode. Poorer people pay more for credit – especially from loan sharks. Competitive strategies in the privatized utilities discriminate against poorer customers. Potential future work for the Unit includes looking at 'options for improving access to services, public and private, for low income individuals or areas'. These issues may be addressed through pressure on utilities and financial institutions to alter their practice, and through encouraging credit unions – non profit-making self-help groups which foster saving and provide small loans. There is nothing here that would conflict with a RED agenda; Child Poverty Action Group has long documented the fact that the poor pay more for most goods and services. There is, simply, a gap: one aspect of financial exclusion is that the poor have less money, and inadequate income is an important factor in debt.

In other respects, the RED approach and that of the Social Exclusion Unit differ rather more. The range of goals may largely coincide, but the priority given to them is different; and since the perceived causes of exclusion are different, so too are the means of reaching those goals. If RED emphasizes social and economic inclusion, and understands poverty in material and structural terms, MUD emphasizes moral inclusion, and understands poverty as primarily cultural in origin. Explanations of poverty as a cultural problem lead all too easily into policies to control the poor. The more the thinking behind the Unit is consistent with MUD, the more the policies for achieving inclusion are likely to be ambiguous from the standpoint of RED.

The most obvious example of this is the focus on social order. In terms of its initial priorities, the reduction in crime and disorder particularly on the targeted estates would be a key indicator of the Social Exclusion Unit's success – although the measurement of crime is fraught with difficulty, and the measurement of disorder even more so. When Jack Straw was asked by Jonathan Dimbleby on 28 September 1997 what changes would take place during Labour's first term of office, he replied that communities would be safer – but that the Government also aimed to change the norms and values of a generation, and to establish that parenting is not a purely private matter in which next door neighbours have no say. Some of the policies for delivering these outcomes rely not only on repression, but forms of repression which are themselves directly exclusionary – an increased use of exclusion orders against individuals, curfews which exclude young people from public spaces, and eviction orders. As the Social Exclusion Unit started work, it was reported that there were 'nearly 10 000 people ... on the council's exclusions list for anti-social behaviour' in Manchester alone.[5] A general increase in the use of eviction orders is anticipated. It may even be necessary – but it is important to recognize that the inclusion of some is predicated on the further exclusion of others. If the control of crime and disorder leads to more prison sentences, this too represents an increase in social exclusion. The 1997 Crime and Disorder Bill makes provision for 'anti-social behaviour orders' which may be sought by local councils or by the police for any person aged ten or over who has acted 'in a manner that caused or was likely to cause harassment, alarm or distress to two or more persons not of the same household as himself'. The orders may contain those prohibitions 'necessary for protecting persons in the local government area from further anti-social acts by the defendant'. Breaches of the order carry penalties of up to five years imprisonment. The problem lies in the catch-all formula, which does not rest on any specific offence being committed – and does not even require that alarm and distress be reasonable responses to the behaviour in question.

The early priority given to tackling truancy is again ambiguous. Although the remit of the Social Exclusion Unit referred also to exclusions from school, it was truancy which Blair stressed at the Unit's launch. In a police report to the Unit, children aged between 10 and 16 were said to be responsible for 40 per cent of all street robberies, 33 per cent of car thefts and 30 per cent of house break-ins in London, mostly during school hours. The link between truancy and crime seemed clear – although it does not follow that most children illicitly absent from school or even most persistent truants are engaged in crime, or that they should be publicly regarded as actual or potential offenders. Other research presented to the Unit referred to the low educational achievement of young offenders, and suggested that persistent truanting was the result of poor educational attainment (mainly by boys) rather than its primary cause. Again, an improvement in educational achievement, a reduction in persistent truanting, and a reduction in crime would all be regarded as good outcomes by RED, SID and MUD. But the connections posited between them, and the policies for addressing them differ. The link long made by RED between unemployment and crime, a social and structural problem, becomes in MUD a link between unemployability and crime, a problem of individual behaviour. In MUD, 'tough on crime, tough on the causes of crime' points to truancy and poor parental supervision as the 'causes'; in RED, the emphasis is on poverty and its role in educational underachievement. The danger is not just that one hand is tied behind the Unit's back, but that repression will substitute for inclusion. The attraction for MUD of focusing on truancy is that parental responsibility can be invoked as a solution. The Crime and Disorder Bill, consistent with pre-election policy, provides for the use of parenting orders. These would apply to the parents of convicted young offenders, and to the parents of children or young people subject to child safety orders, anti-social behaviour orders, or who do not regularly attend school. They may require parents to attend weekly counselling sessions for up to three months, and to comply with other specified requirements for up to a year. Jack Straw elaborated likely requirements as being home at specified times to supervise their child and accompanying that child to school. Breaches of the order will be punishable by a substantial fine. It is not clear whether the orders will be made against the parents severally or jointly, and who will be liable for the fine, especially where parents are not married and are thus not legally liable for each other's debts. The potential conflict between meeting the requirements of a parenting order and earning a living is implicit in the suggestion that the stipulations should 'as far as practicable' not interfere with times when the parent normally works. Where truanting is the problem, the children who cause most concern are those of secondary school age – the age group where there is growing pressure within New Labour that lone parents should be compelled to seek paid employment.

A suggestion that the Foyer movement be extended to single mothers is also ambiguous. Pioneered in France and developed in Britain since 1992, Foyers provide hostel accommodation for homeless young people, with help and advice to enable them to move into more permanent accommodation and training or work. They are entirely voluntary, although residents are required to keep house rules. Their encouragement by the Social Exclusion Unit would be appropriate from RED, SID and MUD – in RED's case, especially if supported by additional funds, and a benefit system which facilitated a move on from Foyer life. But the suggestion that 'young mothers would be encouraged to move into...hostels with their babies, and would get advice on training, access to creches and support workers, including health care visitors to monitor their children' does not seem quite in the Foyer spirit.[6] There may be some young women for whom such facilities would be welcome and wholly appropriate, offering practical and social support not available elsewhere; some units already exist. As a policy for inclusion, it is double edged. Encouraging young single mothers into institutions – having reduced the benefits available to them – marks them out as a group, and is potentially exclusionary. And it rests on a presumption of moral exclusion. MUD sees single parenthood as a form of delinquency, and as a 'parenting danger zone' in need of early intervention. The provision of suitable services, including housing, in a non-institutional manner is not only more expensive, but offers less possibility of social control.

'SOCIAL' INCLUSION

The wide brief of the Social Exclusion Unit makes its success more difficult to define than that of the welfare to work scheme. More, the potential breadth of the idea of social exclusion itself means that a very wide range of policies may bear on the delivery of inclusion. In RED, the question of social participation, not just participation in work, is central. Exclusion is exclusion from participation – in economic, political, social or cultural systems.

However the understanding of the 'social' in social inclusion is under-developed. Demos addresses this in terms of networks and social capital. Social capital refers to 'the quality of contacts people have and networks they plug into, and the norms of trust, reciprocity and goodwill, sense of shared life across the classes, and capacities to organise that these ties afford'; or more simply to 'those relationships which provide people with a sense of trust and community'.[7] The potential fruitfulness of this is undermined by the treatment of social networks as means to ends – either of work or of social control. Thus for individuals, network poverty means lack of access to the kinds of contacts helpful in finding employment.[8] For society, networks are important because 'an organized citizenry can alleviate many social problems and ease the implementation of various kinds of public policy, for instance by using neighbourhood watch groups to minimise crime. As a result, nations as a whole lose a resource when the ties between individuals erode'.[9]

Discussions of social exclusion in contemporary political discourses do not collapse the social into the economic, although economic inclusion is paramount. There is recurrent reference in stakeholding and communitarian literature to the importance of intermediate institutions and to civil society – those places where people live their lives beyond the workplace. But there is a disturbing tendency for civil society and the community to be reduced to an arena of unpaid work, a means of mopping up problems created by the market or a mediator of social discipline. Social inclusion, social networks, and sociability as ends in themselves scarcely figure: the meaning of the social needs clarification and elaboration.

The presumption shared by RED, SID and MUD is that inclusion in paid work leads to greater social inclusion – in the case of RED, provided that it also reduces poverty. There is little attention paid to the ways in which paid work may impede inclusion. Although Hutton indirectly acknowledges this where people work very long hours, and the problem of 'juggling' is a constant issue in relation to women's employment, the downside of paid work is not thought of in terms of social exclusion. Yet not being able to collect young children from school affects participation in the social networks that develop around the school and in the neighbourhood as well as the relationship between parent and child. Paid work leaves less time for many other activities. The same may be true of unpaid work.

UNPAID WORK

The contradiction between welfare to work and parenting in Labour's policies can hardly be overstressed. It arises from thinking about parenting as a responsibility, rather than something which involves work which is currently unpaid. The unpaid work of parenting includes domestic labour as well as direct engagement with the child – engagement which takes place through daily practicalities and which can also be describe as emotional labour. Even if welfare to work for lone parents is a success, and they move voluntarily into employment, their children are adequately cared for, and they are materially better off, there is a hidden cost. It is a cost to women of a major increase in their total workload, not a cost to society of inadequate parenting. Looking at social production from the point of view of the total social organization of labour and acknowledging the prevalence of unpaid work calls into question how we understand the meaning of work itself and the justice of using the wage relation as a means of distributing the social product, as well as the reliance on paid work as a mechanism of social inclusion. Solutions to this are not obvious, and are limited by the structural dominance of the market.

One approach is to bring as much unpaid work as is possible into the market sector. This is the direction in which current policies point. However, even if all adults of working age are expected to be in paid work, and all children in collective day care, a great deal of unpaid work remains to be done – and is done chiefly by women. Its implication is an increase in women's overall workload.

A second approach would be to reward unpaid work directly, in proportion to its value. This, on the ONS figures, would imply a huge shift of resources from the market to the non-market sector. One common objection is the difficulty of evaluating how well unpaid work is carried out. While one can imagine that attempting to do this might be an attractive idea to Jack Straw, it is not necessary; most jobs in the market sector are not rewarded on the basis of performance related pay. A more intractable difficulty is the danger of ghettoizing women in domestic labour, the criticism levelled at the Wages for Housework Campaign in the 1970s. And a principled objection might be that distribution in relation to unpaid work, like distribution through the wage relation, rests on a redefinition of what constitutes a social contribution, not on a shift to distribution on the basis of need; it is in this sense less radical and less egalitarian that RED. It would also meet the same limits as RED. The redistribution of resources from market to non-market sector would, as Townsend said of radical redistribution through the benefits system, run up against the limits of what is possible in a system which depends fundamentally on distribution through the wage relation.

A third possibility would be a major redistribution of both paid and unpaid work. This would mean breaking down the gender inequalities in both forms of work. It would also require limitations on paid working time more draconian than anything likely to be contemplated by the European Union, but affording an acceptable standard of living on the basis of much shorter hours. Movements in this direction are possible, and favoured by the French. But significant changes which do not increase poverty and inequality would be possible only on the basis of a large reduction in wage differentials, and limited by the requirements of a capitalist economy.

GETTING THERE

Participation in social life, whether that be paid work, voluntary work, family life, or the ragbag category leisure, depends on being able to get to the sites of these activities. It requires mobility; it requires transport. The promised development of an integrated transport system is fundamental to the development of social inclusion. This is an issue for SID as well as RED, for transport problems affect employment prospects. For RED, it is a wider question: the social life of those without cars can be very limited. This is particularly true in rural areas, where in many cases public transport is almost or wholly non-existent. Such a system needs to be affordable – although affordability depends on income, so increasing the incomes of the poorest might be a useful contributory factor. It also needs to be accessible to disabled people, whose social exclusion is caused not only by lack of money, but by lack of transport and the general inaccessibility of public spaces. The response of the green pressure group SERA's response to the transport White Paper argues that an inclusive transport system would mean 'a rail system that is adequately staffed, affordable and fully accessible to all disabled people' and that 'all buses running on the streets of Britain are fully accessible to all the nation's citizens'.[10]

The promotion of an integrated transport system has a number of motivations. Reducing traffic congestion is partly about managing capitalism more efficiently; traffic jams cost firms money. It is partly environmentally driven, both in terms of the global need to reduce greenhouse emissions, and the local need to reduce asthma-inducing air pollution. Reducing car use, once a fringe concern, is now Government policy and has wide support. But this is not a straightforward matter. First, the projected need for new homes is likely to be met by increased building in rural areas. Many people want to move out of cities. The land available for building in cities is limited – although it could be substantially increased by reducing the amount of land used for parking. Some brownfield sites are heavily polluted, and decontamination makes them more expensive to develop than greenfield sites. Increased rural development means more car use, not less. Secondly, the exhortation to individuals to use their cars less must not be a way of subordinating their needs to industry's preference for a clear run. Switching freight to rail is part of the plan, and success in this is essential to an inclusive system. This is particularly important because most of the discussions of reduced car use focus on switching short journeys to walking or cycling, on the supposition that these are most amenable to modal change. But many short journeys are made to ferry children around or carry shopping. SERA concedes that 'the car can bring people into the mainstream of life who might otherwise feel excluded', notes its importance to 'mothers who have a thousand and one things to do with...children', and says that the challenge is to make sure the right sort of journeys are made by car, 'for they add to, and don't detract from, social inclusion'.[11] This implicitly recognizes the third potential bar to and negative effect of changing public behaviour. Walking to and from a school a mile away with young children involves four miles and the best part of two hours a day. If the distances are greater, so is the time involved; if the children are at different schools, the logistics may be impossible – and certainly impossible to combine with getting to work. Many mothers already juggle with these difficulties. Reducing car use may mean an increase in women's unpaid work.

COMMON INSTITUTIONS

Hutton's focus on the rich as well as the poor suggests that inclusion requires that people use the same services and institutions. Transport is one example. Others are health and education, where Hutton's concern was with the divide between public and private provision. There is a body of opinion that the combination of medical advances leading to new treatments, an ageing population and rising demands make some form of rationing in the National Health Service inevitable. Without greatly increased funding, the likely outcome of this is an increase in private health provision among those who can afford it. In both health and education there is talk of 'partnership' – the NHS buying treatments in private hospitals, private schools opening up their sports facilities to state school pupils. This will not address the fundamental inequality of provision. Short of making private health and education illegal, the only ways of radically reducing the possibility of a large and influential minority deserting collective provision are to provide public services which match those privately available, or to radically reduce the inequalities which make this desertion possible. The first route is enormously expensive, and New Labour has no intention of promoting inclusion by the second means.

In both school and university sectors of education, newly divisive policies are being pursued. The introduction of fees and the abolition of maintenance grants for higher education is likely to narrow rather than broaden access. The education action zones promised in the Education Bill in late 1997 pose a different kind of problem. The purpose of the zones, described by Government officials as 'the centrepiece of our modernisation agenda' is to improve educational standards in the designated areas. Their connection to addressing social exclusion is clear. But schools in these zones will be able to employ 'innovative methods'; they will be not be bound by the requirements of the national curriculum, but be allowed to concentrate on core skills. They will also be exempt from national agreements on teachers' pay and conditions, and be able to extend their working week, extending the school day and opening schools at weekends (compare Etzioni, Chapter 5). Management of the zones will be put out to tender, and while most are expected to be run by 'partnerships' of local authorities, community groups and businesses, zones may be imposed against local authority wishes and may be run solely by private businesses. This potentially places large parts of the education system in private hands, where the curriculum can be increasingly bent to the needs of industry rather than the wider needs of pupils. It also removes democratic accountability, and further undermines the role of local education authorities and local government – continuing, rather than reversing the trends of the last twenty years. The question of democratic accountability raises the issue of political inclusion.

POLITICAL INCLUSION

One important wider aspect of inclusion is the question of political inclusion or inclusiveness. This addresses the structures and processes of political decision making, how these are conducted, and who is involved in them; social inclusion and exclusion more often refer to the experiences of citizens whose participation in normal social life, however this is understood, is facilitated or prevented. Social and political inclusion are doubly connected: political inclusiveness may be expected to deliver greater social inclusion; and among the aspects of social life in which participation is sought is the political process itself. From the perspective of RED, political inclusion is an aspect of social inclusion.

In one sense, the whole agenda of political reform, including policies for Scottish, Welsh and regional devolution could be presented as an attempt to bring government closer to the people. Whether they could or will deliver greater political inclusion is a large and important question, beyond the scope of this book. Inclusion would mean greater participation in processes broadly defined as political – and with the outcome of giving people greater real power over decisions affecting their lives. The reconstruction of local government would be an important part of this. Some of the problems about the idea and reality of political inclusion can be illustrated by looking at the early stages of the Blair Government itself.

On election, Blair promised to govern inclusively. Most of Labour's references in the pre-election and immediate post-election period were to political inclusiveness; they were about consultation and 'dialogue', about political rather than social or economic inclusion, about process rather than outcome. Government should be democratic, open, accountable and responsive and should eschew sectarian exclusion, hierarchical exclusivity and adversarial style. Wider consultation and public involvement, as well as the devolution of decisions according to the principle of subsidiarity, should supplement elections. Such processes might include community forums, citizens' juries, public hearings, as well as referendums. The inclusion of those groups in society hitherto excluded from or under-represented in the political process should be increased in both formal and informal processes. The most frequently stated concern was the under-representation of women; less frequent, but regular, mention was also made of ethnic minorities and disabled people. The inclusive society would be one where everyone – or every significant group – has a voice, and where these voices are heard either through representation on the basis of identity – women speak for women, black people for black people – or indirectly through advocacy groups or voluntary associations. Inclusive government was signalled by the presence of women MPs and ministers, as well as those disabled, openly lesbian or gay, or from ethnic minorities.

Some of the problems deriving from constructing identities rather than collectivities as the proper basis of representation can be seen by looking at Labour's best case, women – which also illustrates that political inclusion may be necessary, but it is scarcely sufficient. There were more women elected to the 1997 Parliament, and more women in Blair's first Government, than ever before in Britain. This resulted from a policy of having all women short-lists for a proportion of parliamentary candidates – a policy dropped after it was challenged as illegal by two male party members. It may thus prove to be a fragile achievement. Blair's honouring of the long-standing promise of a Minister for Women with cabinet status did not inspire confidence. The job was given to Harriet Harman as an afterthought, in addition to the potentially conflicting brief of Secretary of State for Social Security. Then, in an attempt to patch up the damage, Joan Ruddock was asked to take on ministerial responsibility at a more junior level.

However, by this time, all the salaried ministerial positions had been distributed (including Mandelson's post of Minister without Portfolio) – so she acquired the work, the status, but not the pay. A Women's Unit was set up, part of its brief being to assess the impact on women of all policy proposals. It was given no spending budget, and some argued that to be effective, it would need to be based in the Treasury, with gender impact statements central to Treasury policy. Fears were expressed that the inclusion of women in the Blair Government meant a feminization of politics rather than an advance for feminism and the interests of women. Skjeie argues from the Norwegian experience that the political inclusion of women does not necessarily transform substantive outcomes.[12] Increased representation does give a higher profile to some issues – notably, and importantly, child care – but responses to these issues are routinely subordinated to conventional party political agendas. This is exactly what happened in the dispute over benefit cuts for lone parents – a dispute which also illustrated how the inclusion of women meant not only their co-option to, but their active role in legitimizing, policies damaging to women's interests.

Processes of informal inclusion and consultation are at least as significant as formal presence. Blair greatly increased the number of political advisers at Downing Street, many recruited from think-tanks like the IPPR and Demos; these advisers were unelected, unaccountable and overwhelmingly male. Appointments to the large number of task forces and review bodies set up after the election continued the co-option of unelected individuals to the policy-making process, particularly those from the business sector or 'community'. Political inclusion crossed party boundaries. David Mellor, a Conservative minister forced to resign after a sexual scandal, was asked to chair the Football Task Force. Alan Howarth, who defected to Labour from the Tories in 1996, was rewarded with a ministerial post at the Department for Education and Employment. Pre-election collaboration with the Liberal Democrats over plans for constitutional reform continued after the election with a cross-party Cabinet Committee – although in the week of the 1997 Liberal Democrat Conference, both Peter Mandelson and Alistair Darling warned that if the Liberal Democrats wanted co-operation between the parties to continue, they should stop criticizing the Government's economic policies.

Daniel argues that outside groups did gain greater access to ministers and civil servants – consistent with the new Clause IV commitment to working with voluntary organizations, consumer groups and other representative bodies.[13] However, she said, this inclusion was 'not about participatory democracy so much as about participation in the delivery of policy', and that 'those who confuse the two things are in for a disappointment'. Nowhere was this more apposite than in relation to the trade unions, who were repeatedly warned to expect no special treatment – 'fairness not favours'. Unions constituted a sectional interest, while the business community, apparently, was not. They were not altogether excluded from participation in the task forces, but their representation was meagre. Trade union representatives were invited to Downing Street in the late summer of 1997 to discuss the manifesto commitment to union recognition, but not involved in wider policy questions. Blair spoke at the 1997 TUC Congress, which met under the slogan 'Partners for Progress', and made it clear that any political inclusion of the unions was conditional upon their conforming to the new 'responsible' unionism epitomized by John Monks, which would not challenge either the policies of government or the consensual image of the new Britain it sought to promote. Blair said he would 'watch very carefully to see how the culture of modern trade unionism' developed. He told the unions that there were more important battles than those over 'labour law', and that they should be concentrating on issues of skills, training, welfare to work, pensions and the reform of the National Health Service. He ordered them to modernize: 'Modernise your political structures as we have done in the Labour Party. Influence with this government and with me is not determined by anything other than the persuasiveness of your arguments. The old ways – resolutionitis, the committee rooms, the fixing, the small groups trying to run the show have no future. New trade unionism – that is your aim. Partners for Progress. That is your slogan'. But there was no doubt who was the senior, and who the junior, partner. Appropriate behaviour for trade unions was to be defined by Blairite fiat, not by trade unionists themselves, and their inclusion dependent upon this effective co-option. And it is notable that the constituencies of legitimate identity eligible for inclusion did not include class: for this would be to import 'old' categories of conflict into the new era of partnership.

The central question is who, and whose interests, are represented at any level of government – and whose interests prevail. The general problem about the contemporary emphasis on dialogue and on 'having a voice', which in political and social theory is based on the ideas of Jurgen Habermas, is that it gives too little recognition to the structures of power within which that discussion takes place. Emergent decisions take on the appearance of consensus, and political inclusion risks becoming political co-option. Moreover because there are presumed to be only differences of opinion, not conflicts of interest, dissenting voices outside the consensus are marginalized as trouble makers. Genuine political inclusiveness may be necessary to overcoming social exclusion, though it is certainly not sufficient. Rhetoric about inclusiveness, and even actual inclusion, in the processes of policy formation must be distinguished from the outcomes of these policies.

The dirigiste management of Blair's Government is easily understandable as repressing conflicts which might otherwise divide the Party within and beyond Parliament. What is less immediately obvious is that the underpinning model of society on which the third way is based is one in which conflicts of interest are suppressed. It is this which leads to the instability of the third way and its tendency to fall into authoritarianism. This model, with its consequences and limits, is the subject of the final chapter.

9 The New Durkheimian Hegemony

Social exclusion is a powerful concept, not because of its analytical clarity which is conspicuously lacking, but because of its flexibility. At an individual level, it mobilizes personal fears of being excluded or left out, which reach back into childhood as well as having immediate reference. At a political level, it has a broad appeal, both to those who value increased participation and those who seek greater social control. Crucially, social exclusion facilitates a shift between the different discourses in which it is embedded, so that the contested meaning of social exclusion now lies at the heart of political debate. The boundaries of this debate are set both by the real configuration of political forces and by the language in which it takes place. That language reflects and reproduces underlying ideas about what society is and how it works. The character of the new political discourse very clearly reflects the language of Durkheim, with its appeal to social integration, solidarity and social cohesion. What is less immediately obvious is that the model of social process embedded in contemporary political thought is also fundamentally Durkheimian; in a deep, as well as a superficial way, we live in a new Durkheimian hegemony. This is true of all three discourses of exclusion, despite their profound differences. They correspond to different possible (and occasionally impossible) interpretations of Durkheim's sociology. The limits of political debate, and the possible manoeuvre between discourses of social exclusion, are set by the fact that we are all Durkheimians now.

The central themes in Durkheim's work are social order, social cohesion and solidarity – and particularly how these may be effected in advanced industrial societies. *The Division of Labour in Society* argues that small-scale undifferentiated societies are held together by mechanical solidarity, in which there is a shared body of beliefs and sentiments called the *conscience collective*; social cohesion depends upon similarity.[1] As the division of labour develops, society becomes more complex, and so too do the ties that bind. Organic solidarity replaces mechanical solidarity. Advanced societies are held together by the functional interdependence of their members. *The Division of Labour in Society* sees the integration and cohesion of advanced societies as brought about through interdependence in the sphere of social production. Occupational specialization limits the scope of shared beliefs and sentiments as mechanical solidarity recedes. This does not mean the disappearance of the *conscience collective*, rather a change in its character; the shared elements become increasingly abstract and the concrete, substantive beliefs more differentiated and specific to particular social and occupational groups. That abstract element includes a commitment to individualism, in the sense of respect for the rights of individual persons rather than self-interest. Organic solidarity rests on difference, both in terms of functional interdependence and in the development of moral individualism. Social integration rests on a combination of integration through work and moral integration.

The mixture of SID and MUD which permeates current political thinking reflects this same combination, though in different proportions. Stakeholding, communitarianism and New Labour are all centrally concerned with how social cohesion may be maintained, under perceived conditions of disintegration. They draw, in different ways and to differing extents, on integration through work and interdependence, and through moral solidarity. Communitarianism focuses on the issue of moral order, and Etzioni makes direct reference to Durkheim. In one sense, Etzioni can be understood as a right-wing reading of Durkheim, emphasizing the dependence of social order on moral consensus. His struggle to establish that there is no contradiction between this and individual liberty recalls Durkheim's argument that industrial societies both produce and depend on moral individualism, as well as on a transformed *conscience collective*. Etzioni contrasts the 'thin' social order sought by liberal individualists with the 'thick' social order pursued by communitarians which 'contains a set of shared values, to which individuals are taught that they are obligated', whereas Durkheim suggested that modernity necessarily involves a movement, if not from a thick to a thin consensus, at least from a concrete to an abstract one. Here Gray reflects Durkheim more precisely when he insists that 'we cannot recapture a 'thick' common culture', but must cultivate 'a thinner...common culture of common understandings of fairness and tolerance', and rejects Etzioni's position as delusive.[2] Elsewhere, Etzioni himself distinguishes his own position from that of more conservative communitarians in terms of pursuing a smaller, consensual core rather than an extensive monolithic set of values.

Willie Watts Miller develops the implications of the increasing abstraction of the *conscience collective* for a global ethic, in which specific and different national ideals all involve 'a recognizable regard for everyone as a person, in a society of persons, as a core value and belief'.[3] Similar ideas recur in contemporary discourse. Compare, for example, George Soros's description of the cohesive role of commitment to the open society on a global scale:

> There has to be a common interest to hold a community together, but the open society is not a community in the traditional sense of the word. It is an abstract idea, a universal concept. Admittedly there is such a thing as a global community; there are common interests on a global level... But these interests are relatively weak in comparison with special interests.... Moreover, the open society as a universal concept transcends all boundaries. Societies derive their cohesion from shared values. These values are rooted in culture, religion, history and tradition. When a society does not have boundaries, where are the shared values to be found? I believe there is only one possible source: the concept of the open society itself.[4]

The moral element in organic solidarity includes a complex body of assumptions about obligations and justice in which contractual and exchange relationships are embedded, so that 'everything in the contract is not contractual'.[5] The embeddedness of markets is a central plank in the arguments of stakeholders including Hutton, as well as Gray: markets alone cannot produce a cohesive society, but require social and moral frameworks, both to operate at all, and to mute their potentially disruptive effects. The parallels go beyond the assertion of embeddedness. The pursuit of a third way, integration through work, work as the basis of identity, and the treatment of social conflict as pathological rather than endemic, are shared themes, as is the neglect of unpaid work. Durkheim and Hutton also both mount passionate but ultimately equivocal critiques of inequality.[6]

Durkheim was trying to negotiate a route between free market capitalism and state socialism, both deemed unacceptable. Adamantly opposed to Spencer's view that social cohesion could arise from the pursuit of self-interest, he was trying to avoid the Scylla and Charybdis of a 'conflict of unfettered egoisms, and 'despotic socialism'.[7] This was, in a sense, a third way – which rejected the alternatives as being based in forms of utilitarian economism, and as neglecting the necessary moral dimension in social life. Durkheim stressed the importance of intermediate groups between the individual and the state, bastions against the excesses of the market and the potential excesses of a hypertrophied state. He was not concerned to limit the range of activities of the state, which necessarily become more extensive as the division of labour and the complexity of society develop. The state has a key role in articulating the moral content of the *conscience collective*, establishing the conditions for individualism, and sustaining a 'sentiment of common solidarity'.[8] It is also properly involved in the regulation of economic activity. For Durkheim, democratic government depends on the degree of communication between state and society, which is facilitated by the increasing reach of the state into society. Intermediate associations are crucial to this communication, and play a dual role. They 'are essential if the state is not to oppress the individual: they are also necessary if the state is to be sufficiently free of the individual... They liberate the two conflicting forces, whilst linking them at the same time'.[9]

Durkheim both predicted and prescribed the development of these intermediate groups in the form of 'corporations' or 'occupational groups'. The integration of individuals into the whole, both institutionally and morally, would take place primarily through their occupational roles. The functions of occupational groups might, as Sorel suggests for syndicates,[10] extend beyond the workplace to the provision of welfare and leisure services. They were in some sense 'the heir of the family', since 'man passes a notable part of his existence far from all domestic influence'.[11] The 'sphere of influence of a corporation is... more restricted' than that of the family. But 'we must not lose sight of the increasingly important position the occupation takes in life as work becomes more specialized, for the field of each individual activity tends steadily to become delimited by the functions with which the individual is particularly charged'.[12] Durkheim even suggested that political constituencies should be based upon occupational rather than geographical groups, since individual attachment and identification lies increasingly with these: 'the professional association is the true electoral unit... because the links attaching us to one another derive from our calling rather than from any regional bonds of loyalty'.[13] Despite this, Durkheim did not overplay the positive aspects of work, saying 'let us not forget... that work is still for most men a punishment and a scourge'.[14] While commitment to individualism and thus the importance of individual identity arise from the increasingly abstract nature of the *conscience collective*, specific individual identities are largely constituted by occupational roles and the network of roles in society. Individual identity as well as individual integration into society is primarily constituted through work.

Contemporary writers also emphasize the importance of intermediate institutions, not just between individual and state, but in civil society between the family and the state. Like Durkheim, they insist that markets exist only in societies, and that their operations depend upon social relations and moral assumptions beyond the market. Some favour regulation of the market, and are reluctant to leave corporate governance to the vicissitudes of business ethics. Where Hutton refers to the gap between the rhetoric about high ethical standards in British business and the grubby reality, Durkheim suggested the importance of developing business ethics, and the inadequacy of relying on these alone:

> Indeed, in the economic order, occupational ethics exist only in the most rudimentary state. There is a professional ethic of the lawyer and the judge, the soldier and the priest, etc. But if one attempted to fix in a little more precise language the current ideas on what ought to be the relations of employer and employee, of worker and manager, of tradesmen in competition, to themselves or the public, what indecisive formulas would be obtained! Some generalizations, without point, about the faithfulness and devotion workers of all sorts owe to those who employ them, about the moderation with which employers must use their economic advantages, a certain reprobation of all competition openly dishonest, for all untempered exploitation of the consumer; that is about all the moral conscience of these trades contains. Moreover, most of these precepts are devoid of all juridical character, they are sanctioned only by opinion, not by law; and it is well known how indulgent opinion is concerning the manner in which these vague obligations are fulfilled.[15]

Pahl drew attention to the unpopularity during the Thatcher years of intermediate institutions, notably trade unions, local government and even the Church of England, arguing that the 'capacity of occupational associations to generate social cohesion is at best partial and at worst seen to be dangerous'.[16] But this was before stakeholding was on the political agenda. There has been little or no reversal in the suspicion of trade unions as solidaristic entities – but the stakeholding company takes their place. The most important intermediate institution in stakeholding and in SID is the firm itself, and it is through the attachments of the workplace that identity and social integration are effected. As we have seen, unpaid work is neglected.

For Durkheim too, work meant paid work in the public sphere, and the workers integrated by the division of labour are primarily men. As

Jennifer Lehmann points out, Durkheim saw women's labour as biological, not social, and his concern was with social labour, men's work, not with labour in society.[17] He was not addressing the total social organization of labour. If work is a vehicle of integration and identity only in relation to the public sphere, where does this leave women? Durkheim argued – as did Charlotte Perkins Gilman, writing almost at the same time – that the division of labour itself has been partly responsible for the evolution of physical and psychological differences between the sexes. Unlike Gilman he did not develop this into a critique of the sexual division of labour.[18] This is, argues Watts Miller, because Durkheim's insistence on the importance of real attachments rather than abstract contractual relationships led him to place a high value on the family as a locus of such particular attachments. Lehmann suggests, however, that 'conjugal solidarity' complements the organic solidarity in the public sphere, both being based on difference. Durkheim forsaw a great difficulty: 'the equality of the two sexes cannot increase unless woman becomes more involved in public life; but then how will the family have to be transformed? Profound changes will be necessary, which we perhaps cannot avoid, but must anticipate'. Durkheim was alarmed at the prospect of 'the weakening of the organic unity of the family and marriage' which are likely to come about if the roles of men and women become more similar.[19] The continued importance of the family in effecting the integration of individuals, and especially men, into society is made plain in *Suicide*.[20] Durkheim's typology of suicidogenic factors rests on the two dimensions of moral regulation and social integration. Suicide rates rise under conditions of anomie, where moral regulation is too weak, and under conditions of egoism, where individuals are insufficiently attached to the collective life of society.

The most fundamental parallel between Durkheim and 'centre-left' writers, especially Hutton, lies in the treatment of the evident problems of the capitalist societies around them as pathological. Durkheim's model of organic solidarity suggested a degree of integration and cohesion, both institutionally and morally, which manifestly did not exist. He could hardly fail to recognize that the real world was more unjust and exploitative than a model of organic solidarity suggests it should be, and riven by class conflict: 'there are two main classes of society, linked by all sorts of intermediate classes: the one which in order to live has to make its services acceptable to the other at whatever the cost; the other class which can do without these services, because it can call upon certain resources'.[21] But he regarded these deep divisions as abnormal and potentially avoidable. At the end of *The Division of Labour*, Durkheim discussed 'abnormal forms', including the anomic division of labour, where there is too little regulation; the forced division of labour, where there are the wrong rules rather than simply too few; and a failure of co-ordination which leads to insufficient economic activity. Visible conflicts resulted from the incomplete transition to the proper form of organic society. Hutton's general argument similarly rests on the pathological character of British capitalism, more benign versions being identifiable elsewhere as well as conceivable as a practical possibility.

The idea of 'abnormal forms' for Durkheim and the peculiar perversities of 'gentlemanly capitalism' for Hutton form a bridge between what is and what should be – the goal being an efficient and socially cohesive capitalism. In both cases there is a gap between diagnosis and prescription – but in Durkheim's case the prescription is arguably more radical than the diagnosis, whereas in Hutton's case the reverse is true. The contrast lies in their treatments of conflict and of equality. Durkheim's diagnosis was that conflicts of interest are not structurally necessary. This, together with his emphasis on moral order and his endorsing of extensive state intervention, meant that he was read by a generation of undergraduates – including Hutton – as profoundly conservative. But Durkheim's prescribed cure for the pathology of current conditions, and the instigation of a 'normal' state of affairs, required not only regulation of economic activity by the state: it involved a potentially radical claim for equality.

Durkheim argued that inequality – except in so far as it is an expression of natural inequality – compromises organic solidarity. He suggested that inherited wealth introduces a differential power and thus an inherent injustice into contractual relationships. He did not attack the institution of property itself, arguing that to limit rights of disposal – as in inheritance – is 'in no way an attack on the individual concept of property'.[22] The problem is not inequality itself, but the fact that it impedes equality of opportunity – and indeed it was only the latter which concerned Durkheim: 'as the progress of the division of labor implies ... an ever growing inequality', therefore 'the equality which public conscience affirms can only be ... equality in the external conditions of conflict'. There is a gap between the model of a consensual, regulated, organic society and the existence of a structural conflict of interest between classes which Durkheim recognized as an empirical reality. Recognition of this conflict pushed Durkheim to the questions of inequality and property; the supposition of its transcendence invokes a moral consensus supported by the state in which inequalities resulting from individual capacities to succeed in the market are accepted and endorsed. But hereditary wealth undermines equality of opportunity, which is necessary so that individuals occupy 'the place in the social framework which is compatible with their faculties'; substantive inequalities may interfere with this process.[23]

Hutton, more clearly than Durkheim, sees capitalism as intrinsically throwing up conflicts and inequities. Recalling the criticisms of Durkheim by his generation of students, Hutton said 'he didn't understand class, he didn't understand conflict, he didn't understand property'; and went on to suggest that the success of *The State We're In* was that it was 'Durkheimian and One Nation in tone whilst...recognising the fundamental challenge that class and power...bear to that'. But Hutton's pragmatic commitment to a possible political project, and his belief in the positive merits of capitalism, again lead him to a limited challenge. The stakeholding agenda does call into question the rights attaching to property, especially in the call for a legal framework acknowledging the interests of stakeholders other than shareholders. The wish to limit property rights or reconstruct them in the interests of social equity and cohesion, while not fundamentally challenging the institution of property itself, is a notable point of correspondence with Durkheim. More often, moral responsibility in the exercise of those rights is called for. But on the issue of equality, Hutton, while trenchantly critical of the effects of inequality, is more muted in his prescription: he merely proposes an increase in inheritance tax.

It is the very reliance on the necessity of moral integration which drives Hutton to this position. The rich are to be persuaded to inclusion rather than exclusivity by appeal to values. In this respect, Hutton, Kay, Etzioni and Gray – in tune with most contemporary political discourse – understand morality in a more colloquial sense than did Durkheim. As the European White Papers appealed to solidarity as an attitude (and potentially resultant practice), so they largely understand morality as a set of beliefs, precepts and behaviours we may individually and collectively choose to adopt and foster. Where Durkheim differs is in understanding the nature of the moral order to be predicated on the structure of that society. The move from mechanical to organic solidarity is not voluntaristic, but brought about by structural changes. Solidarity is an emergent property of the structure of society; it might be a moral fact, but it is not brought about by moral exhortation. Thus Durkheim said, 'to will a morality other than that implied by the nature of society is to deny the latter'.[24] Appeals to moral integration do not in themselves represent a slide into MUD. As argued above (Chapter 1), RED, SID and MUD all appeal to moral precepts, just as they all see work as a factor in social integration. What distinguishes MUD is its view of the poor as morally deficient, whereas Hutton is more concerned with the moral deficiencies of the rich. The problem with Durkheim's own argument, though, is that just as he represses the structural conflict of interest within society, so he simultaneously suppresses the question of whose interests are served by the morality that is implied by the nature of the society, and thus the problem of its imposition.

There are, of course, different possible readings of Durkheim.[25] Lockwood has contrasted Durkheimian and Marxist treatments of conflict and order.[26] Mike Gane and Jennifer Lehmann have assessed Durkheim's scattered writing on women.[27] Willie Watts Miller has explored Durkheim's arguments and their implications in terms of morality, identity and the self in ways which go beyond the issues dealt with here.[28] The sketch of Durkheim's position presented here is just that, showing the broad parallels with contemporary debates. While an essentially Durkheimian model can be slanted in different directions, and thus be visible in positions as different as Hutton's and Etzioni's, there are limits to this flexibility. And in Durkheim himself, as well as in what might be called neo-Durkheimian political economy, there is a central failure to resolve the problem of conflicting interests in society.

This has implications for the fate of New Labour's third way, and both discursively and materially for the future of social exclusion. Durkheim had an intellectual problem because the reality of class conflict kept forcing itself upon his consciousness, to be kept in check by the idea of abnormal forms. In contemporary politics, the concept of social exclusion itself is part of the discursive construction of social conflicts as pathological. But discursive containment may not hold, and the denial of fundamental conflicts of interest renders the third way unstable. This denial is present even in the post-election formulation, in which New Labour's insistence that all former dilemmas were in fact win-win situations gave way to warnings of hard choices. For these hard choices mean spending priorities within (chosen) budget constraints, not between groups whose interests are structurally opposed. It is a politics which barely accepts that there may be conflicts of opinion, let alone deep-seated conflicts of interest. As real conflicts force their way into visibility, the third way must resolve either leftwards, to the limiting position of social democracy, where equal opportunities are recognized to rest on a degree of substantive equality – or rightwards, replacing the Thatcherite symbiosis between free market and strong state with the soft synthesis of a market embedded in a consensus supported by the community as moral policeman. These polar positions correspond to the boundaries set on political debate by New Labour and especially by John Gray. If social exclusion acts as a shifter between discourses, it does so within these boundaries, with RED and MUD representing the possible limits. Movement in either direction is possible: if New Labour has so far been shifting to the right at every point of conflict, Hutton has been moving to the left, towards a stronger position on equality and redistribution, opening up an increasing gap between them. Labour's future trajectory through, and deployment of, the discourses of exclusion will determine what kind of inclusion they may ultimately deliver.

BEYOND INCLUSION

Egalitarians should not give up constructive engagement in the debate over what constitutes inclusion, how it may be measured and how it may be fostered. Although some versions of inclusion require only minimal access to 'opportunities', others imply equality of opportunity. The question then becomes, as Hattersley insists, the degree of substantive equality on which equality of opportunity (or 'fairness') depends. Inclusion can be used to advance the cause of equality. But there are definite, if not definable, limits to this. For those who believe, like Hutton, that more equality is a necessary though insufficient condition for an inclusive society, the question is how much more? The claim is prevented from becoming radically egalitarian by market constraints, just as there are market constraints on the valorization of unpaid work. To challenge the limits placed by the market on inclusion and equality is, ultimately, to challenge the legitimacy of the market itself. My point is not, like Gray's, that globalization makes social democracy a defunct project, but that the inclusion potentially offered by social democracy is limited by the nature of capitalism and the nature of social democracy themselves.

Thus beyond the question of who is included and on what terms lies the question of what they are included in. The term social exclusion presumes that inclusion is beneficial, but it is salutary to remember that even if the unemployed, women, ethnic minorities and disabled people achieve equal opportunities in the labour market, this will still mean participation in a capitalist economy driven by profit, based upon exploitation and fundamentally divided by class. Capitalism is not, as Mulgan suggests, a system based on an ethos of sacrifice, but a system based on production for profit. It needs expansion of its markets in order to survive. Its need for growth is incompatible with the finite resources of the planet.

Capitalism also, as Durkheim observed but had difficulty theorizing, embodies profound conflicts of interest. The contemporary political discourses within which social inclusion is deployed are primarily based on Durkheimian and third way models which repress conflict. The dichotomous model of social exclusion and integration or inclusion itself contributes to this repression. Much of what Westergaard said about the term 'underclass' can also be said of the concept of social exclusion.[29] It distracts attention from the essentially class-divided character of society, and allows a view of society as basically benign to co-exist with the visible reality of poverty. It does this by discursively placing the unwanted characteristics outside society. But the real society is not that constituted by the (unequal) 70 per cent, to which the rest are marginal or from which they are excluded; it is made up of the whole 100 per cent, and is a society in which inequality and poverty are endemic. Social exclusion may thus be seen as a conceptual device for bridging the gap between what is empirically observable and what is theoretically claimed about the nature of contemporary society – much like Durkheim's abnormal forms. While we should use the concept of social exclusion to pursue as much equality as is possible, we should remember that the political framework within which it operates is one which itself excludes the possibility of an equal society.

Yet while inclusion, as the obverse of exclusion, is repressive of conflict, it simultaneously, and for the same reason, conjures up a vision of a good society. If this vision is collapsed into the present, as is partly so in Durkheim, it becomes a defence of the status quo. If it is maintained as a utopian other, it invites the possibility of creating a more radical discourse of inclusion. This discourse would explore both the contours of a radically inclusive society and the conditions of our potential inclusion in it. The logic of a more egalitarian radical approach to inclusion leads beyond the metaphor of inclusion and exclusion itself, into that critique of capitalism which the neo-Durkheimian hegemony removes from the political agenda. If we or future generations are to have any hope of living in a society which is built around our needs as persons, and which would make possible the kinds of relationships proposed by Macmurray, the question of alternatives to capitalism must be reopened. It may be countered that capitalism is the only game in town and there is no alternative; but humankind must sometimes set itself questions which it cannot immediately solve.

Appendix
The Changes to Clause IV

THE ORIGINAL CLAUSE IV

National

(1) To organise and maintain in parliament and in the country a political Labour Party.*

(2) To cooperate with the General Council of the Trades Union Congress, or other kindred organisations, in joint political or other action in harmony with the party constitution and standing orders.

(3) To give effect as far as may be practicable to the principles from time to time approved by the party conference.*

(4) To secure for the workers by hand or by brain the full fruits of their industry and the most equitable distribution thereof that may be possible upon the basis of the common ownership of the means of production, distribution, and exchange, and the best obtainable system of popular administration of each industry or service.

(5) Generally to promote the political, social and economic emancipation of the people, and more particularly of those who depend directly upon their own exertions by hand or by brain for the means of life.

Inter-Commonwealth

(6) To cooperate with the labour and socialist organisations in the Commonwealth overseas with a view to promoting the purposes of the party, and to take common action for the promotion of a higher standard of social and economic life for the working population of the respective countries.

International

(7) To cooperate with the labour and socialist organisations in other countries and to support the United Nations Organisation and its various agencies and other international organisations for the promotion of peace, the adjustment and settlement of international disputes by conciliation or judicial arbitration, the establishment and defence of human rights, and the improvement of the social and economic standards and conditions of work of the people of the world.

---

*Retained elsewhere in the constitution

190

THE NEW CLAUSE IV

(1) The Labour Party is a democratic socialist party. It believes that by the strength of our common endeavour, we achieve more than we achieve alone; so as to create for each of us a community in which power, wealth and opportunity are in the hands of the many not the few, where the rights we enjoy reflect the duties that we owe, and where we live together, freely, in a spirit of solidarity, tolerance and respect.

(2) To these ends we work for:

- a dynamic economy, serving the public interest, in which the enterprise of the market and the rigour of competition are joined with the forces of partnership and cooperation to produce the wealth the nation needs and the opportunity for all to work and prosper, with a thriving private sector and high quality public services, where those undertakings essential to the common good are either owned by the public or accountable to them;
- a just society, which judges its strength by the condition of the weak as much as the strong, provides security against fear, and justice at work; which nurtures families, promotes equality of opportunity and delivers people from the tyranny of poverty, prejudice and the abuse of power;
- an open democracy, in which Government is held to account by the people; decisions are taken as far as practicable by the communities they affect; and where fundamental human rights are guaranteed;
- a healthy environment, which we protect, enhance, and hold in trust for future generations.

(3) Labour is committed to the defence and security of the British people, and to co-operating in European institutions, the United Nations, the Commonwealth and other bodies to secure peace, freedom, democracy, economic security and environmental protection for all.

(4) Labour will work in pursuit of these aims with trade unions, cooperative societies and other affiliated organisations, consumer groups and other representative bodies.

(5) On the basis of these principles, Labour seeks the trust of the people to govern.

Notes

NOTES TO INTRODUCTION

1. Andersen, Paul and Mann, Nyta (1997) *Safety First: The Making of New Labour*, London: Granta Books; Davies, A.J. (1996) *To Build a new Jerusalem: The British Labour Party from Kier Hardy to Tony Blair*, London: Abacus; Jones, Tudor (1996) *Remaking the Labour Party: From Gaitskell to Blair*, London: Routledge; Panitch, Leo and Leys, Colin (1997) *The End of Parliamentary Socialism: From New Left to New Labour*, London: Verso; Shaw, Eric (1994) *The Labour Party Since 1979*, London: Routledge.
2. Layard, Richard (1997) *What Labour Can Do*, London: Warner Books.
3. Silver, Hilary (1994) 'Social exclusion and social solidarity: three paradigms' *International Labour Review* Vol. 133, Nos. 5–6, pp. 531–78.

NOTES TO CHAPTER 1

1. Murgatroyd, Linda and Neuburger, Henry (1997) 'A Household Satellite Account for the UK' *Economic Trends* No. 527, October: 63–71; Waring, Marilyn (1988) *If Women Counted*, London: Macmillan.
2. These gender differences are almost certainly understated. The methodology does not allow people to record themselves as doing more than one thing at once. Respondents are expressly instructed that doing housework while caring for children should be recorded as housework *rather than* care of children. If this is extended to activities such as eating and leisure (which are not counted as unpaid work), the child care responsibilities of women will be seriously undercounted, and the differences between men and women reduced.
3. Glucksmann, Miriam (1995) 'Why "Work"? Gender and the "Total Social Organisation of Labour"' *Gender, Work and Organisation* Vol. 2, No. 2, p. 69, 67.
4. Townsend, Peter (1979) *Poverty in the United Kingdom*, Harmondsworth: Penguin p. 32.
5. *Ibid.*, pp. 399, 249.
6. *Ibid.*, p. 564.
7. Duncan, Simon and Edwards, Rosalind (1997) *Single Mothers in an International Context: Mothers or Workers?* London: UCL Press.
8. Townsend's (1979) attitude to unpaid work, and to the position of women more generally, was not wholly consistent. In talking about levels of unemployment, he argued that the numbers would be far higher if the 'under-utilized productive capacity of non-employed women with or without dependants', together with other economically inactive groups were to be included. On the other hand, he was concerned that the shift from manufacturing to service industries would 'create a major new

source of inequality and poverty in society' as older men were displaced from the labour market in favour of women. He predicted that 'a larger number of physically active middle-aged males will be pensioned off to facilitate occupational opportunity for women' p. 682.

9. Townsend, Peter (1997) 'Redistribution: The Strategic Alternative to Privatisation', in Alan Walker and Carol Walker, *Britain Divided: The growth of social exclusion in the 1980s and 1990s*, London: CPAG, p. 269.
10. Walker, Alan and Walker, Carol, (eds) (1997) *Britain Divided: The growth of social exclusion in the 1980s and 1990s*, London: CPAG.
11. *Ibid*: 8.
12. Harker, Lisa (1996) *A Secure Future? Social security and the family in a changing world*, London: CPAG; Harker, Lisa (1997) 'New Paths for Social Security' in Alan Walker and Carol Walker, *Britain Divided: The growth of social exclusion in the 1980s and 1990s*, London: CPAG.
13. Walker, *op cit.*, p. 8.
14. Golding, Peter (1986) *Excluding the Poor*, London: CPAG.
15. Lister, Ruth (1990) *The Exclusive Society: Citizenship and the Poor*, London: CPAG.
16. Goodin, Robert E. (1996) 'Inclusion and Exclusion', *European Journal of Sociology* Vol. 37, No. 2, pp. 343–71.
17. Marshall, T.H. (1950) 'Citizenship and Social Class' in T.H. Marshall and Tom Bottomore, *Citizenship and Social Class*, London: Pluto Press 1992, p. 8.
18. Ibid., p. 44.
19. Pateman, Carole (1988) *The Sexual Contract*, Cambridge: Polity Press; Walby, Sylvia (1994) 'Is Citizenship Gendered?' *Sociology* Vol. 28, No. 2, pp. 379–95.
20. Lister, *op cit.*, p. 68.
21. Hall, Stuart and Jacques, Martin (1983) *The Politics of Thatcherism*, London: Lawrence and Wishart; Levitas, Ruth (1986) (ed.) *The Ideology of the New Right*, Cambridge: Polity; Gamble, Andrew (1988) *The Free Economy and The Strong State*, Basingstoke: Macmillan.
22. *Cole on the Dole*, 19 February 1993.
23. Townsend (1979) *op cit.*, p. 920.
24. Field, Frank (1990) *Losing Out: The Emergence of Britain's Underclass*, Oxford, Basil Blackwell, p. 101.
25. Dahrendorf, Ralf (1987) 'The erosion of citizenship and its consequences for us all' *New Statesman*, 12 June, p. 13.
26. *Ibid*.
27. Field, *op cit.*, pp. 7, 107.
28. *Ibid.*, pp. 155, 107.
29. *Ibid.*, p. 8.
30. Field, Frank (1995) *Making Welfare Work: Reconstructing Welfare for the Millennium*, London: Institute of Community Studies.
31. Murray, Charles (1990) *The Emerging British Underclass*, London: IEA, p. 23.
32. *Ibid.*, pp. 4, 17.
33. *Ibid.*, p. 7.
34. Murray, Charles (1994) *Underclass: The Crisis Deepens*, London: IEA.

35. Bewick, Tom (1997) 'The poverty of US welfare reform: lessons from California', *Working Brief* 87, August/September, pp. 21–7.
36. *Panorama*, 29 September 1997; Rogers, J. Jean (1997) 'Making welfare work', *New Statesman* 29 August, pp. 17–18.
37. Macnicol, John (1987) 'In pursuit of the Underclass', *Journal of Social Policy*, Vol. 16, pp. 293–318; Mann, Kirk (1992) *The Making of an English Underclass*, Milton Keynes: Open University Press; Morris, Lydia (1994) *Dangerous Classes: The Underclass and Social Citizenship*, London: Routledge.
38. *Thinking Aloud*, 12 November 1987, 'Is There a New Underclass in British Society?' Channel 4.
39. Westergaard, John (1992) 'About and Beyond the "Underclass"', *Sociology* Vol. 26, No. 4, pp. 575–87.
40. Oppenheim, Carey (1993) *Poverty: The Facts*, London: CPAG.
41. Dean, Hartley and Taylor-Gooby, Peter (1992) *Dependency Culture: the explosion of a myth*, New York: Harvester-Wheatsheaf.
42. Lister *op cit.*, p. 26.
43. Adonis, Andrew and Pollard, Stephen (1997) *A Class Act: The Myth of Classless Society*, London: Hamish Hamilton, p. 16.
44. *Ibid.*, p. 13.
45. Duffy, K. (1995) *Social Exclusion and Human Dignity in Europe*, Council of Europe.
46. Silver *op cit.*
47. Spicker, Paul (1997) 'Exclusion', *Journal of Common Market Studies* 35(1): 133–143; Evans, Martin, Paugam, Serge and Prelis, Joseph A. (1995) *Chunnel Vision: Poverty, social exclusion and the debate on social welfare in France and Britain*, STICERD working paper WSP/115, London: London School of Economics.
48. Spicker *op cit.*
49. Room, Graham (1995) (ed.) *Beyond the Threshold*, Bristol: Policy Press.
50. Sostris (1997) *Social Strategies in Risk Societies: Social Exclusion in Comparative Perspective*, Sostris Working Paper 1, London: University of East London.
51. EC (1994b) *European Social Policy: a way forward for the Union*, Brussels: European Commission; EC (1994a) *Growth, competitiveness, employment: the challenges and ways forward into the 21st century*, Brussels: European Commission.
52. EC (1994a) *op cit.*, p. 3.
53. EC (1994b) *op cit.*, p. 49.
54. EC (1994a) *op cit.*, pp. 15–16.
55. EC (1994b) *op cit.*, p. 49.
56. *Ibid.*, pp. 35–6, 51–2.
57. EC (1994a) p. 136.
58. EC (1994b) *op cit.*, p. 49; EC (1994a) *op cit.*, p. 134.
59. EC (1994a) *op cit.*, pp. 9,11.
60. *Ibid.*, pp. 148–9.
61. Maier, Friederike (1994) *Equal Opportunities for Women and Men: Wage and Non-wage Labour Costs, Social Security and Public Funds to Combat Unemployment*, Brussels: European Commission; Rees, Teresa (1994)

Equal Opportunities for Women and Men: Equality into Education and Training Policies, Brussels: European Commission.
62. EC (1994a) *op cit.*, pp. 12, 15.
63. *Ibid.*, p. 54.
64. *Ibid.*, pp. 15–16, 139.
65. Ackers, Louise (1998) *Shifting Spaces: Women, Citizenship and migration within the European Union*, Bristol: Policy Press.

NOTES TO CHAPTER 2

1. Thompson and du Gay (1997) 'Future imperfect' *Nexus*, Winter/Spring, pp. 8–9.
2. Twigg, Stephen *Fabian Review* Vol. 109, No. 2, p. 23.
3. Cohen, Nick (1997) 'Totally Wonkers', *Observer*, 9 March, p. 20.
4. *New Statesman* 15 January 1993, p. 5.
5. The membership of the Commission on Social Justice was: Sir Gordon Borrie, QC; Professor A.B. Atkinson, Oxford; Anita Bhalla, Asian Resource Centre, Birmingham; Professor John Gennard, Strathclyde University; The Very Reverend John Gladwin, Provost of Sheffield and Bishop-Elect of Guildford; Christopher Haskins, Chairman, Northern Foods plc; Patricia Hewitt; Dr Penelope Leach, Fellow, British Psychological Society; Professor Ruth Lister, Loughborough University; Professor David Marquand, University of Sheffield; Bert Massie, Director, Royal Association for Disability and Rehabilitation; Emma MacLennan, Vice-Chair, Low Pay Unit; Dr Eithne McLaughlin, Queens University, Belfast; Stephen Webb, Institute for Fiscal Studies; Margaret Wheeler, UNISON; Professor Bernard Williams, Oxford.
6. Beresford, Peter and Turner, Michael (1997) *It's Our Welfare*, Report of the Citizens' Commission on the future of the Welfare State, London: National Institute for Social Work.
7. Commission on Social Justice (CSJ) (1994) *Social Justice: Strategies for Social Renewal*, London: Vintage, p. 96 (emphasis added).
8. Townsend, Peter (1995) 'Persuasion and Conformity: An assessment of the Borrie report on Social Justice', *New Left Review* Vol. 213, pp. 137–50.
9. Milne, Kirsty (1995) 'Welfare Statement', *New Statesman and Society*, 27 January, p. 21.
10. CSJ *op cit.*, p. 95.
11. *Ibid.*
12. Andersen and Mann *op cit.*
13. This was part of the Australian 'Working Nation' initiative, which, like New Labour's New Deal, was introduced by a right-wing Labour administration. See Finn, Dan (1997) *Working Nation: Welfare Reform and the Australian Job Compact for the long term unemployed*, London: Unemployment Unit.
14. Showstack Sassoon, Anne (1996) 'Beyond pessimism of the intellect: Agendas for Social Justice and Change' in Mark Perryman (ed.) *The Blair Agenda*, London: Lawrence and Wishart, p. 159.

15. *CSJ op cit.*, p. 112.
16. *CSJ op cit.*, p. 81.
17. *CSJ op cit.*, p. 103, 111.
18. *CSJ op cit.*, p. 170, 147, 3.
19. *CSJ op cit.*, p. 6, 169, 178.
20. *CSJ op cit.*, p. 166.
21. *CSJ op cit.*, p. 262.
22. *CSJ op cit.*, p. 152.
23. *CSJ op cit.*, p. 104, 151.
24. *CSJ op cit.*, p. 264–5.
25. *CSJ op cit.*, p. 20.
26. *CSJ op cit.*, p. 243.
27. *CSJ op cit.*, pp. 126, 366, 368.
28. *CSJ op cit.*, p. 82.
29. *CSJ op cit.*, p. 187.
30. *CSJ op cit.*, p. 193.
31. *CSJ op cit.*, p. 197.
32. *CSJ op cit.*, p. 189.
33. *CSJ op cit.*, p. 166.
34. *CSJ op cit.*, p. 76.
35. *CSJ op cit.*, p. 18.
36. Milne *op cit.*, p. 21.
37. The members of the Inquiry Group were: Sir Peter Barclay, Trustee of the JRF and former Chairman of the Social Security Advisory Committee; Tessa Baring, Trustee of the Baring Foundation and Chair of Barnados; Michael Bett, Deputy Chairman of British Telecom and Chairman of the Social Security Advisory Committee; Vivienne Coombe, NCH Action for Children; Howard Davies, Director-General of the CBI; Kathleen Kiernan, Senior Research Fellow, Population Studies, LSE; Ruth Lea, Economic Editor, ITN; Pamela Meadows, Director, Policy Studies Institute; John Monks, General Secretary, TUC; Robin Wendt, Chief Executive, Association of County Councils; John Willman, Features Editor, *Financial Times*; Tricia Zipfel, Director, Priority Estates Project. John Hills, LSE, was Secretary to the project.
38. Rowntree (1995) *Joseph Rowntree Foundation Inquiry into Income and Wealth*, 2 vols, York: Joseph Rowntree Foundation, Vol. I, p. 33.
39. *Ibid.*, p. 32.
40. *Ibid.*, p. 38.
41. *Ibid.*, p. 36.
42. *Ibid.*, p. 34.
43. The membership is given in the report as: Lord Dahrendorf, Warden of St. Antony's College, Oxford; Frank Field, Member of Parliament for Birkenhead, Chairman of the House of Commons Social Security Select Committee; Carolyn Hayman, Executive Director, Rutherford Ventures; Ian Hutcheson CBE, Chairman and Chief Executive of Acatos and Hutcheson [who provided the financial support for the Commission]; Will Hutton, Assistant Editor of the Guardian; David Marquand, Professor of Politics, University of Sheffield; Andrew Sentance, Senior Research Fellow, London Business School; Sir Ian Wrigglesworth,

Deputy Chairman John Livingston & Sons Ltd.; Secretary, Dan Trelford. Among those listed as giving advice to the group are Andrew Dilnot from the Institute of Fiscal Studies; Richard Layard (LSE) and John Monks (TUC), both of whom were members of the IPPR Commission on Public Policy and British Business, discussed in Chapter 4; Mark Goyder, similarly acknowledged in the report of that Commission and Howard Davies, who, like Monks, was also part of the Rowntree team. The launch of the Dahrendorf report was sponsored by the Prudential Corporation.

44. Dahrendorf, Ralf *et al.* (1995) *Report on Wealth Creation and Social Cohesion in a Free Society*, London: Commission on Wealth Creation and Social Cohesion, pp. 43, 33.
45. *Ibid.*, pp. 34–5.
46. *Ibid.*, p. 38.
47. *Ibid.*, p. 38.
48. *Ibid.*, p. 15.
49. Dahrendorf, Ralf (1996) 'On the Dahrendorf Report', *Political Quarterly* Vol. 67, No. 3, p. 196.
50. Dahrendorf, Ralf et al., *op cit.*, p. 15.
51. *Ibid.*, p. 103.
52. *Ibid.*, p. 17.
53. *Ibid.*, p. vii.
54. *Ibid.*, p. 26.
55. *Ibid.*, p. 97.
56. *Ibid.*, p. 18.
57. *Ibid.*, p. 26.
58. *Ibid.*, p. 12.
59. *Ibid.*, p. 100.
60. Hewitt, Patricia (1993) *About Time: the revolution in work and family life* London: IPPR/Rivers Oram Press.

NOTES TO CHAPTER 3

1. Willetts, David (1997) *Why Vote Conservative?* Penguin, p. 4.
2. Marquand, David and Seldon, Anthony (1996) *The Ideas that Shaped Post-War Britain*, London: New Statesman/Fontana, p. 3.
3. Hutton, Will (1997a) 'Our Stake in Society', *Observer*, 20 April, p. 29.
4. Hutton, Will (1995a) 'High Risk Strategy', *Guardian*, 30 October, p. 3.
5. Hutton, Will (1997a) 'Our Stake in Society', *Observer*, 20 April, p. 29.
6. Hutton, Will (1997c) *The State to Come*, London: Vintage, p. 4.
7. *Ibid.*, p. 4.
8. *Ibid.*, p. 64.
9. Hutton, *Guardian* 24 April 1995.
10. Hutton, Will (1995b) *The State We're In*, London: Jonathan Cape, p. 114.
11. *Ibid.*, p. 21–2.
12. *Ibid.*, p. 24.
13. Hutton, Will (1996a) *The State We're In*, London: Vintage, p. 169.
14. These figures are as given by Hutton in January 1995.

15. Hutton (1995a) *op cit.*, p. 2.
16. Hutton (1997c) *op cit.*, p33.
17. Hutton, Will (1996b) 'The Stakeholder Society' in Marquand and Seldon *op cit.*, p. 297.
18. Hutton (1995a) *op cit.*, p. 3.
19. Hutton (1995b) *op cit.*, p. 197.
20. Hutton (1995a) *op cit.*, p. 3.
21. Hutton (1995b) *op cit.*, p. 323.
22. Hutton (1996b) *op cit.*, p. 300.
23. Hutton (1996a) *op cit.*, p. xxv.
24. Hutton (1995b) *op cit.*, p. 326.
25. Hutton, *Guardian* 17 January 1996.
26. Hutton, *Guardian* 9 January 1996.
27. Hutton (1997c) *op cit.*, p. 68.
28. *Ibid.*, p. 32.
29. Hutton, *Guardian* 17 January 1996.
30. Hutton and Kay, *Observer* 13 October 1996.
31. Hutton (1995b) *op cit.*, p. 295.
32. Hutton (1996a) *op cit.*, p. 330.
33. Hutton (1997c) *op cit.*, p. 71.
34. *Ibid.*, p. 65.
35. Hutton, *Guardian* 6 March 1996.
36. Hutton (1997c) *op cit.*, p. 81.
37. Hutton (1995b) *op cit.*, p. 296.
38. *Ibid.*, p. 297.
39. GUMG (Glasgow University Media Group) (1976) *Bad News*, London: Routledge and Kegan Paul.
40. Hutton (1997c) *op cit.*, p. 81.
41. Hutton, *Guardian* 17 January 1996.
42. Hutton (1997c) *op cit.*, p. 81.
43. *Ibid.*, p. 81.
44. *Ibid.*
45. Hutton, *Guardian* 17 January 1996.
46. Hutton (1997c) *op cit.*, p. 81.
47. Hutton and Kay, *op cit.*
48. Hutton (1995b) *op cit.*, p. 111.
49. Hutton, *Guardian* 17 January 1996.
50. Hutton (1995b) *op cit.*, p24.
51. Hutton (1995b) *op cit.*, p. 99–100, 111.
52. Hutton and Kay *op cit.*
53. Hutton (1997c) *op cit.*, p. 66–7.
54. *Ibid.*, p. 67.
55. Plant, Raymond (1997a) 'Rights, Obligations and the Reform of the Welfare State', Public Lecture, University of Bristol, 14 May; Moon, J. Donald (1988) 'The Moral Basis of the Democratic Welfare State' in Gutmann (1988) pp. 27–52; Elster, Jon (1988) 'Is There (or Should There Be) a Right to Work?' in Gutmann (1988) pp. 53–78.
56. Hutton (1995a) *op cit.*, p. 3.
57. Hutton (1995b) *op cit.*, p. 231.

58. Hutton, *Guardian* 22 May 1995.
59. Hutton (*Observer*, 2 November 1997).This point appears to be drawn straight from Tony Giddens, whom Hutton admires. Giddens overstates his own case, but at least he does not imply that women are principally affected by the impact of 'reflexive modernity' on personal relationships, nor formulate this in terms of greater 'hard-headedness'. Staying in bad relationships out of economic necessity is at least as hard-headed as leaving them when that necessity is removed.
60. Hutton, *Observer* 2 November 1997.
61. Hutton, (1997b) 'An Overview of Stakeholding' in Kelly *et al.* (1997), p. 8.
62. Hutton, *Guardian* 18 March 1996.
63. Hutton (1997c) *op cit.*, p. 41.
64. Hutton, *Observer* 8 December 1996.
65. Levitas, Ruth (1996a) 'Fiddling while Britain Burns: The 'measurement' of unemployment' in Ruth Levitas and Will Guy (eds) *Interpreting Official Statistics*, London: Routledge, pp. 45–65.
66. Hutton (1995a) *op cit.*, p. 2.
67. Hutton (1997c) *op cit.*, p. 40.
68. Hutton (1995a) *op cit.*, p. 3.
69. Hutton, *Observer* 8 December 1996.
70. Hutton, *Guardian* 27 December 1995.
71. Interview with Will Hutton, July 1997.
72. Freely, Maureen (1997) 'Want to be a stakeholder? Better get a wife', *Guardian*, 23 January, p. 9.
73. Hutton (1997b) *op cit.*, p. 3.
74. Hutton, Will (1996c) 'Left with no illusions', *Prospect*, March, pp. 46–50.
75. Hutton (1997c) *op cit.*, p. 89.
76. *Ibid.*, p. 75–6.
77. *Ibid.*, p. 89.
78. Hutton (1996b) *op cit.*, p. 300.
79. Hutton (1995b) *op cit.*, p. 309.
80. Hutton, *Guardian* 27 March 1995.
81. Hutton (1996a) *op cit.*, p. 341.
82. Hutton (1995b) *op cit.*, p. 310–11.
83. Hutton (1995b) *op cit.*, p. 214.
84. Hutton, *Observer* 20 October 1996.
85. Hutton (1995b) *op cit.*, p. 308.
86. *Ibid.*, p. 311.
87. Hutton, *Guardian* 8 November 1995.
88. Hutton (1997c) *op cit.*, p. 6.
89. *Ibid.*, p. 63.
90. Interview with Will Hutton, July 1997.
91. Perkin, Harold (1996) *The Third Revolution: Professional Elites in the Modern World*, London: Routledge, pp. 174, 168.
92. Hutton (1995b) *op cit.*, p. 323.
93. Plender, John (1997) *A Stake in the Future: The Stakeholding Solution*, London: Nicholas Brealey.
94. The acknowledgements in *The State to Come* suggest that Hutton's connections with the Blairite circle were very strong. They include David

Miliband, Geoff Mulgan, John Gray, and David Marquand as well as Anthony Giddens, Martin Jacques, David Held, Neil Belton, Colin Mayer, David Halpern and Stuart White.

95. Hutton, *Observer* 19 October 1997.

NOTES TO CHAPTER 4

1. *Guardian* 9 December 1996.
2. Willetts (1997) *op cit.*, pp. ,13–14.
3. *Guardian* 16 January 1997.
4. *Newsnight* December 1996.
5. Kelly, Gavin, Kelly, Dominic and Gamble, Andrew, (eds) (1997) *Stakeholder Capitalism*, London: Macmillan, p. 239.
6. *Ibid.*, pp. 255, 248.
7. Lloyd, John (1997b) 'Interview: Clive Hollick', *New Statesman*, 24 January, p. 19.
8. Kay, John (1993) *The Foundations of Corporate Success*, Oxford: Oxford University Press, p. 186.
9. *Ibid.*, p. 50.
10. *Ibid.*, p. 320.
11. *Ibid.*, p. 322.
12. *Ibid.*, p. 326.
13. Kay, John (1996b) *The Business of Economics* Oxford: Oxford University Press.
14. *Ibid.*, pp. 81, 111.
15. *Ibid.*, p. 108.
16. *Ibid.*, p. 112.
17. *Ibid.*, p. 86.
18. *Ibid.*, p. 123.
19. *Ibid.*, p. 131.
20. *Ibid.*, p. 125.
21. *Ibid.*, p. 124.
22. *Ibid.*, p. 131.
23. *Ibid.*, p. 135.
24. *Ibid.*, p. 132.
25. Kay (1996b) *op cit.*; Kay, John (1996a) 'The Good Market', *Prospect*, May: 39–43.
26. Kay (1996b) *op cit.*, p. 139.
27. *Ibid.*, p. 138.
28. *Ibid.*, pp. 140–1.
29. *Ibid.*, p. 143.
30. *Ibid.*, p. 141.
31. *Ibid.*, p. 124.
32. *Ibid.*, p. 146.
33. *Ibid.*, p. 144.
34. Barratt Brown, Michael and Coates, Ken (1996) *The Blair Revelation: Deliverance for Whom?* London: Spokesman.
35. Kay (1996b) *op cit.*, p. 146.

36. *Financial Times* 1 November 1996.
37. Kay (1996) *op cit.*, p. 87.
38. Jones, Nicholas (1997) *Campaign 1997*, London: Indigo.
39. *Financial Times* 22 January 1997.
40. Lloyd (1997b) *op cit.*, p. 19.
41. Commission on Public Policy and British Business (CPPBB) (1997) *Promoting Prosperity: A Business Agenda for Britain*, London: Vintage, p. 29.
42. *Ibid.*, p. 103.
43. *Ibid.*, p. 103.
44. *Ibid.*, p. 104.
45. *Ibid.*, p. 103–4.
46. *Ibid.*, p. 111.
47. Mandelson, Peter and Liddle, Roger (1996) *The Blair Revolution: Can New Labour Deliver?*, London: Faber and Faber, p. 25.
48. CPPBB *op cit.*, p. 49.
49. *Ibid.*, p. 106.
50. *Ibid.*, p. 105.
51. *Ibid.*, p. 105.
52. *Ibid.*, p. 117.
53. *Ibid.*, p. 49.
54. *Ibid.*, p. 112.
55. *Ibid.*, p. 270.
56. *Ibid.*, p. 184.
57. *Ibid.*, pp. 186–7.
58. *Ibid.*, p. 185.
59. *Observer* 16 February 1997.
60. Trades Union Congress (TUC) (1996) *Your Stake at Work: TUC Proposals for a Stakeholding Economy*, London: Trades Union Congress, pp. 5, 15.
61. *Ibid.*, p. 20.
62. *Ibid.*, p. 36.
63. *Ibid.*, p. 7.
64. *Ibid.*, p. 21.
65. *Ibid.*, p. 23.
66. *Guardian* 30 December 1996.
67. Hutton (1996a) *op cit.*, p. 296.
68. Green Party (1993) *Manifesto for a Sustainable Society* London: Green Party, pp. 12–13.
69. *Ibid.*, p. 26.
70. *Ibid.*, p. 7.
71. Hutton (1996a) *op cit.*, pp. xxiii, 342.

NOTES TO CHAPTER 5

1. Tonnies, F. (1963 [1887]) *Community and Society* New York: Harper and Rowe.

2. Mulhall, Stephen and Swift, Adam (1992) *Liberals and Communitarians*, Oxford: Blackwell.
3. Halsey, A.H. and Young, Michael (1995) *Family and Community Socialism*, London: IPPR.
4. Etzioni, Amitai (1995 [1993]) *The Spirit of Community: Rights, Responsibilities and the Communitarian Agenda*, London: Fontana.
5. Etzioni, Amitai (1997 [1996]) *The New Golden Rule: Community and Morality in a Democratic Society*, London: Profile Books.
6. *Ibid.*, p. 7.
7. *Ibid.*, p. 57.
8. Etzioni (1995) *op cit.*, p. ix.
9. Etzioni (1997) *op cit.*, pp. 61, 64.
10. Etzioni (1995) *op cit.*, p. 12.
11. Etzioni (1997) *op cit.*, p. 65.
12. *Ibid.*, pp. 71–3.
13. Etzioni (1995) *op cit.*, pp. 13–4.
14. *Ibid.*, p. 6–7.
15. Etzioni (1997) *op cit.*, p. 167.
16. Etzioni (1995) *op cit.*, p. 91.
17. *Ibid.*, pp. 90, 63, 69.
18. *Ibid.*, p. 85.
19. *Ibid.*, p. 72.
20. Etzioni (1997) *op cit.*, p. 186.
21. *Ibid.*, p. 212.
22. *Ibid.*, p. 187, 172.
23. Etzioni (1995) *op cit.*, p. 25.
24. *Ibid.*, p. 91.
25. Etzioni (1997) *op cit.*, p. 149.
26. Etzioni (1995) *op cit.*, p. 36.
27. *Ibid.*, p. 63.
28. *Ibid.*, p. 61.
29. Etzioni (1997) *op cit.*, p. 146.
30. Etzioni (1995) *op cit.*, p. 15.
31. *Ibid.*, p. 40.
32. Etzioni (1997) *op cit.*, p. 124.
33. Etzioni (1995) *op cit.*, p. 43.
34. *Ibid.*, p. 145, 76.
35. *Ibid.*, p. 130.
36. *Ibid.*, p. 241.
37. *Ibid.*, pp. 251, 252.
38. *Ibid.*, p. 174.
39. Gray, John (1997) *Endgames: Questions in Late Modern Political Thought*, Cambridge: Polity Press, p. 116.
40. Gray, John (1993a) *Beyond the New Right: Markets, government and the common environment*, New York: Routledge, p. 59.
41. Gray, John (1989) *Liberalisms: Essays in Political Philosophy*, London: Routledge; (1993a) *Beyond the New Right: Markets, government and the common environment*, London: Routledge; (1993b) *op cit.*; (1995) *Enlightenment's Wake: Politics and culture at*

the *close of the modern age*, London: Routledge; (1997) *Endgames: Questions in Late Modern Political Thought*, Cambridge: Polity Press.

42. Gray (1995) *op cit.*, p. vii.
43. Gray (1993a) *op cit.*, p. viii.
44. *Ibid.*, p. x.
45. Gray (1995) *op cit.*, pp. 88–9.
46. Gray (1997) *op cit.*, p. 100.
47. Gray (1995) *op cit.*, p. 91.
48. Gray (1997) *op cit.*, p. 18.
49. Gray, John (1992) *The Moral Foundations of Market Institutions*, London: IEA Health and Welfare Unit.
50. Gray (1997) *op cit.*, pp. 19–20.
51. Gray (1993a) *op cit.*, p. 59.
52. Gray (1997) *op cit.*, pp. 16–17.
53. Gray (1993a) *op cit.*
54. Gray (1997) *op cit.*, p. 17.
55. Gray (1993a) *op cit.*, p. 105.
56. *Ibid.*, p. 24.
57. *Ibid.*, pp. 33–4.
58. *Ibid.*, p. 33.
59. *Ibid.*, pp. 33–4, 53.
60. *Ibid.*, p. 37.
61. *Ibid.*, p. 13.
62. Gray (1997) *op cit.*, p. 2; (1995) *op cit.*, p. 89.
63. Gray (1997) *op cit.*, p. 148.
64. *Ibid.*, p. 142.
65. *Ibid.*, p. 81.
66. *Ibid.*, p. 45, 47.
67. *Ibid.*, p. 123.
68. *Ibid.*, p. 47.
69. *Ibid.*, p. 124.
70. *Ibid.*, p. 44.
71. Gray (1993a) *op cit.*, p. 122.
72. *Ibid.*, p. 103.
73. Gray, John (1997) 'After Social Democracy' in Gray (1997) *Endgames op cit.*
74. *Ibid.*, p. 23.
75. *Ibid.*, p. 36.
76. *Ibid.*, p. 17.
77. Gray (1993a) *op cit.*, p. 113.
78. Gray (1997) *op cit.*, p. 115.
79. *Ibid.*, p. 100.
80. *Ibid.*, p. 25.
81. *Ibid.*, p. viii.
82. Blair, Tony (1994b) *Socialism*, Fabian Pamphlet 565, London: Fabian Society.
83. Brittan, Samuel (1997) 'Tony Blair's real guru', *New Statesman*, 7 February, pp. 18–20.

84. Macmurray, John (1935b) *Creative Society: A Study of the Relation of Christianity to Communism*, London: SCM Press, pp. 69–70, 105.
85. Macmurray, John (1932) *Freedom in the Modern World*, London: Faber and Faber, p. 61.
86. *Ibid.*, p. 196.
87. *Ibid.*, p. 193.
88. *Ibid.*, p. 189.
89. Macmurray, John (1957) *The Self as Agent*, London: Faber and Faber; (1961) *Persons in Relation*, London: Faber and Faber.
90. Macmurray (1935b) *op cit.*, p. 118.
91. *Ibid.*, p. 162.
92. Macmurray, John (1931) *Learning to Live*, London: BBC, p. 24.
93. Macmurray (1935a) *op cit.*, p. 114–15.
94. *Ibid.*, p. 120.
95. *Ibid.*, p. 255.
96. Macmurray (1935b) *op cit.*, p. 158; (1931) *op cit.*, p. 31.
97. Macmurray (1935b) *op cit.*, p. 154.
98. *Ibid.*, p. 159.
99. *Ibid.*
100. Macmurray (1961) *op cit.*, p. 187.
101. *Ibid.*, p. 44–5.
102. Macmurray (1931) *op cit.*, p. 25, 34.
103. *Ibid.*, p. 12.
104. Macmurray (1935a) *op cit.*, p. 90.

NOTES TO CHAPTER 6

1. The Multilateral Agreement on Investment (MAI), due to be signed in April 1998, is an OECD treaty whose purpose is to remove from governments of member states virtually all powers to regulate foreign investment within their territories. It will open all sectors of the signatories' economies (except defence) to foreign investment, and will allow companies to sue local and national governments in international courts if they attempt to impose restrictions on companies. There is a lot of information on the MAI on the internet, or see *New Ground* 53, Winter 1997/8: 8.
2. Blair, 14 October 1996, speech at the CPU Conference, Cape Sun Hotel, Cape Town.
3. Mandelson and Liddle (1996) *op cit.*, p. 3–4.
4. Blair, 7 April 1997, speech at the Corn Exchange London.
5. Mandelson and Liddle, *op cit.*, p. 29.
6. Blair, 14 October 1996, *op cit.*
7. Mandelson and Liddle *op cit.*, p. 4.
8. Barratt Brown, Michael and Coates, Ken (1996) *The Blair Revelation: Deliverance for Whom?*, London: Spokesman.
9. Levitas, Ruth (1986) (ed.) *The Ideology of the New Right*, Cambridge: Polity.

10. Blair, 8 January 1996, speech to Singapore business community.
11. Blair, 29 January 1996, 'Faith in the City – Ten Years On', speech at Southwark Cathedral, London.
12. Wright, Tony (1997) *Why Vote Labour?* Penguin, pp. 56–7, 65.
13. Willetts, David (1996) *Blair's Gurus*; Willetts, David (1997) *Why Vote Conservative?* Penguin.
14. Willets (1997) *op cit.*, p. 11, 13.
15. Kelly *et al.* (1997) *op cit.*
16. Alistair Darling, *Ibid.*, p. 10.
17. *Ibid.*, p. 16.
18. *Ibid.*, p. 17.
19. *Ibid.*, pp. 18–19.
20. EPI (1996) *Employment Audit*, 2, Autumn, p. 1.
21. Gregg, Paul and Wadsworth, Jonathan (1996) 'Feeling Insecure?', *Employment Audit*, 2, Autumn, pp. 17–26.
22. Blair, 8 February 1997, speech to Labour's Local Government Conference; 16 April 1997, 'Seven Pillars of a Decent Society' speech at Harbour Lights Cinema, Southampton.
23. Meacher, Michael, *Guardian*, 14 March 1997.
24. Allan Black of the GMB *Guardian* 7 January 1996.
25. Peter Hain *Guardian* 7 January 1997.
26. Peter Hain *Observer* 22 December 1996.
27. Labour Party (LP) (1996d) *Learn as You Earn: Labour's Plans for a Skills Revolution*, p. 5.
28. Blunkett, 18 April 1997, 'Rights and Responsibilities', speech in Birmingham.
29. LP (1996d) *op cit.*, p. 9.
30. Blair, 21 January 1997, 'Making Britain Competitive in a Modern World', speech at the IPPR; LP (1997a) *Labour's Business Manifesto: Equipping Britain for the Future*.
31. LP (1996d) *op cit.*, p. 10.
32. Blunkett, 18 April 1997, *op cit.*
33. LP (1996d) *op cit.*, p. 3.
34. Blunkett, 18 April 1997, *op cit.*
35. LP (1996d) *op cit.*, p. 10.
36. Labour Party (LP) (1996c) *Lifelong Learning*, p. 4 (emphasis added).
37. Blair, 14 April 1997, '21 Steps to 21st Century', speech at the Barber Institute of Fine Arts, University of Birmingham; LP (1996d) *op cit.*, p. 10.
38. LP (1996c) *op cit.*, p. 7.
39. LP (1996d) *op cit.*, p. 18.
40. Blunkett, 22 January 1997, speech to the Excellence in the Early Years Conference, Congress House, London.
41. Mandelson and Liddle *op cit.*, p. 19.
42. Labour Party (LP) (1996f) *Labour and the Voluntary Sector: Setting the Agenda for Partnership in Government*, p. 7.
43. Mandelson and Liddle *op cit.*, p. 20.
44. *Ibid.*
45. Labour Party (LP) (1996g) *Strategy for Women*, p. 9.

46. Mandelson and Liddle *op cit.*, p. 125.
47. Blair, cited in *Ibid.*, pp. 47–8.
48. Jack Straw, *Campaign Roadshow* 29 April 1997.
49. *Guardian* 23 March 1995; Blair, 16 April 1997, *op cit.*
50. Labour Party (LP) (1996a) *Tackling Youth Crime: Reforming Youth Justice*, p. 12; Labour Party (LP) (1995b) *Safer Communities, Safer Britain.*, p. 1.
51. Straw, *Newsnight* 14 April 1997.
52. LP (1996a) *op cit.*, p. 16.
53. Mandelson and Liddle *op cit.*, p. 136.
54. LP (1996a) *op cit.*, p. 13.
55. Labour Party (LP) (1996b) *Parenting*, p. 18.
56. Labour Party (LP) (1996m) *Protecting Our Communities: Labour's Plans for Tackling Criminal, Anti-social Behaviour in Neighbourhoods.*, p. 3.
57. Mandelson and Liddle *op cit.*, pp. 135–6.
58. LP (1995b) *op cit.*
59. Labour Party (LP) (1995a) *Renewing Democracy, Rebuilding Communities*, p. 1.
60. LP (1996f) *op cit.*, p. 5.
61. *Ibid.*, p. 4.
62. *Ibid.*, pp. 7–9.
63. *Ibid.*, p. 8.
64. Blair, Tony (1994a) 'Sharing Responsibility for Crime', in Anna Coote (ed.) *Families, Children and Crime*, London: IPPR, p. 90.
65. Blair, *Guardian* 23 March 1995.
66. Margaret Beckett, *Election Call*, 14 April 1997; Alistair Darling, *Newsnight* 25 April 1997.

NOTES TO CHAPTER 7

1. Room *op cit.*
2. Castle, Barbara and Townsend, Peter (1996) *We Can Afford the Welfare State*, London: Security in Retirement for everyone.
3. Harriet Harman, 13 November 1997; speech at the Launch of the Centre for Analysis of Social Exclusion.
4. Hattersley, *Guardian* 26 July 1997.
5. Aitken, *Guardian* 7 August 1997.
6. Blair, *Sun* 29 July 1997.
7. Aitken, *Guardian* 7 August 1997; Brown, *Guardian* 2 August 1997.
8. Mandelson and Liddle *op cit.*, p. 17.
9. Hattersley, *Guardian*, 6 August 1997.
10. Blunkett, 25 February 1997; speech to the Raising Awareness: Combatting Inequality Conference, Institute of Education, London.
11. *Observer* 17 August 1997.
12. Mandelson and Liddle *op cit.*, p. 22.
13. *Observer* 21 December 1997.
14. *Channel 4 News* 6 September 1997.
15. *Guardian* 27 September 1997.

16. Blair, 2 June 1997, 'The Will to Win'; speech at the Aylesbury Estate, Southwark.
17. Brown, 26 March 1997; speech at the Forte Posthouse Hotel, Basildon; 11 September 1997, 'Good Work for Everyone', speech at the Churches Conference. Straw, 16 December 1996, 'Law and Order at the Crossroads', speech at the *Guardian*/LSE Conference, London School of Economics.
18. Layard, Richard (1997) *What Labour Can Do*, London: Warner Books, p. 72.
19. CSJ *op cit.*, Chapter 2.
20. LP (1996g) *op cit.*, p. 11.
21. Brown, 13 February 1997, 'The Anthony Crosland Memorial Lecture'.
22. LP (1996g) *op cit.*, p. 8.
23. *Ibid.*, p. 12.
24. LP (1996f) *op cit.*, p. 8.
25. *Ibid.*, p. 9.
26. *Ibid.*, p. 8.
27. Mulgan, Geoff (1997a) *Connexity: How to Live in a Connected World*, London: Chatto and Windus, p. 122.
28. Blair, 8 December 1997, 'Bringing Britain Together', speech for the launch of the SEU, Stockwell Park School, South London.
29. *Ibid.*
30. *Observer* 7 December 1997.
31. *Observer* 17 August 1997.
32. Perri 6 (1997b) 'Social exclusion: time to be optimistic' in *The Wealth and Poverty of Networks: Tackling Social Exclusion*, Demos Collection 12, London: Demos, pp. 3–9.
33. *Ibid.*, p. 8.
34. Kruger, Danny (1997) 'Access Denied' *The Wealth and Poverty of Networks: Tackling Social Exclusion* Demos Collection 12, London: Demos, p. 20; Perri 6 (1997b) *op cit.*, p. 3.
35. Mulgan, Geoff (1997b) (ed.) *Life After Politics: New Thinking for the Twenty-first Century*, London: Fontana Press, p. xviii.
36. *Ibid.*, p. 187, 189.
37. *Ibid.*, p. 190.
38. Mulgan (1997a) *op cit.*, p. 178.
39. *Ibid.*, p. 237.
40. *Ibid.*, p. 69.
41. Mulgan, Geoff (1997c) 'Think well-being, not welfare', *New Statesman* 17 January, p. 29.
42. *Ibid.*
43. Mulgan (1997a) *op cit.*, p. 67.
44. Mulgan (1997b) *op cit.*, p. 165.
45. Mulgan (1997a) *op cit.*, p. 227.
46. *Ibid.*, p. 129, 172.
47. *Ibid.*, p. 137, 227.
48. *Ibid.*, p. 184–5.
49. Lloyd, John (1997a) 'A plan to abolish the underclass', *New Statesman* 29 August, p. 14.

50.   Mulgan (1997a) *op cit.*, p. 202.
51.   *Ibid.*, p. 137.
52.   *Ibid.*, p. 185.
53.   Guy, Will (1996) 'Health for All' in Ruth Levitas and Will Guy (eds) *Interpreting Official Statistics* London: Routledge; Wilkinson, Richard (1997) *Unhealthy Societies: From Inequality to Wellbeing*, London: Routledge.
54.   Blair, 2 June 1997, *op cit.*
55.   *Ibid.*
56.   Blair, 24 January 1997, 'The 21st Century Welfare State' Social and Economic Policy Conference, Rijksmuseum, Amsterdam.
57.   Blair, 2 June 1997, *op cit.*
58.   Mandelson, *Observer* 17 August 1997.
59.   Blair, 29 January 1996, *op cit.*
60.   Harman, 13 November 1997, *op cit.*
61.   Brown, 11 September 1997, *op cit.*
62.   Mandelson, 14 August 1997, 'Labour's Next Steps: Tackling Social Exclusion', Fabian Society lecture.
63.   Harman, 13 November 1997, *op cit.*
64.   Plant, Raymond (1997b) 'The Labour Market, Citizenship and Social Exclusion', CASE Seminar, London School of Economics, 10 December.
65.   Campbell, Bea (1993) *Goliath: Britain's Dangerous Places*, London: Methuen.

NOTES TO CHAPTER 8

1.   Downes, David, *Guardian* 25 November 1997, 'Prison does wonders for the jobless figures'; Western, Bruce and Beckett, Katherine (1997) 'How unregulated in the U.S. Labour Market? The Penal System as a Labor Market Institution', paper presented to the American Sociological Association, Toronto.
2.   Finn, Dan (1997) *Working Nation: Welfare Reform and the Australian Job Compact for the Long Term Unemployed*, London: Unemployment Unit.
3.   Townsend, Peter (1996) 'The Struggle for Independent Statistics on Poverty' in Ruth Levitas and Will Guy (eds) *Interpreting Official Statistics*, London: Routledge.
4.   Perri 6 (1997b) 'Social exclusion: time to be optimistic' in *The Wealth and Poverty of Networks: Tackling Social Exclusion*, Demos Collection 12, London: Demos, p. 3.
5.   *Observer* 7 December 1997.
6.   *Guardian* 30 December 1997.
7.   Perri 6 (1997b) *op cit.*, p. 6; Schneider, Jo Anne (1997) 'Welfare-to-network' in *The Wealth and Poverty of Networks: Tackling Social Exclusion*, Demos Collection 12, London: Demos, p. 30.
8.   Perri 6 (1997) *Escaping Poverty*, London: Demos.
9.   Hall, Peter A. (1997) 'Social capital: a fragile asset' in *The Wealth and Poverty of Networks: Tackling Social Exclusion*, Demos Collection 12, London: Demos, p. 35.

10. Stewart, John (1997/8) 'And the SERA response', *New Ground* 53, p. 13.
11. *Ibid.*
12. Skjeie, Hege (1991) 'The Rhetoric of Difference: On Women's Inclusion into Political Elites', *Politics and Society* Vol. 19, No. 2, pp. 133–63.
13. Daniel, Caroline (1997) 'May the taskforce be with you', *New Statesman* 1 August, p. 29.

NOTES TO CHAPTER 9

1. Durkheim, E. (1964 [1893]) *The Division of Labour in Society*, New York: Free Press.
2. Gray (1997) *op cit.*, pp. 19–20.
3. Watts Miller, Willie (1996) *Durkheim, Morals and Modernity*, London: UCL Press, p. 246.
4. Soros, George *Guardian* 18 January 1997.
5. Durkheim, *op cit.*, p. 211.
6. Levitas, Ruth (1998) 'Will Hutton: Closet Durkheimian' in Paul Bagguley and Jeff Hearn (eds) *Transforming Politics: Power and Resistance*, London: Macmillan.
7. Watts Miller *op cit.*, p. 4.
8. *Ibid.*, p. 90.
9. Durkheim, cited in Giddens, Anthony (1986) (ed.) *Durkheim on Politics and the State*, Cambridge: Polity Press, p. 8.
10. Stanley, John L. (ed.) (1976) *From Georges Sorel: Essays in Socialism and Philosophy*, Oxford University Press.
11. Durkheim, *op cit.*, p. 17.
12. *Ibid.*, p. 16.
13. Durkheim, cited in Giddens, *op cit.*, p. 21.
14. Durkheim, *op cit.*, p. 242.
15. *Ibid.*, p. 2.
16. Pahl, R.E. (1991), 'The Search for Social Cohesion: from Durkheim to the European Commission', *European Journal of Sociology*, Vol. 32, No. 2, p. 348.
17. Lehmann, Jennifer (1994) *Durkheim and Women*, Nebraska: University of Nebraska Press.
18. Gilman, Charlotte Perkins (1966 [1898]) *Women and Economics*, New York: Harper Torchbooks.
19. Durkheim, cited in Watts Miller, *op cit.*, pp. 75–6.
20. Durkheim, Emile (1952 [1897]) *Suicide*, London: Routledge and Kegan Paul.
21. Durkheim, cited in Giddens *op cit.*, p. 31.
22. *Ibid.*, p. 238.
23. Durkheim (1964) *op cit.*, pp. 377–8.
24. Durkheim, cited in Watts-Miller *op cit* p. 254.
25. Fenton, Steve (1984) *Durkheim and Modern Sociology*, Cambridge: Cambridge University Press; Giddens (1971) *Capitalism and Modern Social Theory*, Cambridge: Cambridge University Press; Giddens (1978)

Emile Durkheim, London: Fontana; Lukes, Stephen (1973) *Emile Durkheim: His Life and Work*, London: Allen Lane; Pearce, Frank (1989) *The Radical Durkheim*, London: Unwin Hyman.
26. Lockwood, David (1992) *Solidarity and Schism*, Oxford: Clarendon Press.
27. Gane, Mike (1992) 'Durkheim: Woman as Outsider' in M. Gane (ed.) *The Radical Sociology of Durkheim and Mauss*, London: Routledge: 85–134; Lehmann *op cit*.
28. Watts Miller, *op cit*.
29. Westergaard, John (1992) 'About and Beyond the "Underclass"', *Sociology* Vol. 26, No. 4, pp. 575–87.

Select Bibliography

Andersen, Paul and Mann, Nyta (1997) *Safety First: the Making of New Labour*, London: Granta Books.

Barratt Brown, Michael and Coates, Ken (1996) *The Blair Revelation: Deliverance for Whom?* London: Spokesman.

Beresford, Peter and Turner, Michael (1997) *It's Our Welfare*, Report of the Citizens' Commission on the future of the Welfare State, London: National Institute for Social Work.

Blair, Tony (1994b) *Socialism*, Fabian Pamphlet 565, London: Fabian Society.

Campbell, Bea (1993) *Goliath: Britian's Dangerous Places*, London: Methuen.

Commission on Public Policy and British Business (CPPBB) (1997) *Promoting Prosperity: a Business Agenda for Britain*, London: Vintage.

Commission on Social Justice (CSJ) (1994) *Social Justice: Strategies for Social Renewal*, London: Vintage.

Dahrendorf, Ralf *et al.* (1995) *Report on Wealth Creation and Social Cohesion in a Free Society*, London: Commission on Wealth Creation and Social Cohesion.

Davies, A.J. (1996) *To Build a New Jerusalem: the British Labour Party from Kier Hardie to Tony Blair* , London: Abacus.

Dean, Hartley and Taylor-Gooby, Peter (1992) *Dependency Culture: the Explosion of a Myth*, New York: Harvester-Wheatsheaf.

Demos (1997) *The Wealth and Poverty of Networks: Tackling Social Exclusion*, Demos Collection 12, London: Demos.

Duncan, Simon and Edwards, Rosalind (1997) *Single Mothers in an International Context: Mothers or Workers?* London: UCL Press.

Durkheim, Emile (1952 [1897]) *Suicide*, London: Routledge and Kegan Paul.

Durkheim, Emile (1964 [1893]) *The Division of Labour in Society*, New York: Free Press.

Etzioni, Amitai (1994) *The Parenting Deficit*, London: Demos.

Etzioni, Amitai (1995 [1993]) *The Spirit of Community: Rights, Responsibilities and the Communitarian Agenda*, London: Fontana.

Etzioni, Amitai (1997 [1996]) *The New Golden Rule: Community and Morality in a Democratic Society*, London: Profile Books.

Fenton, Steve (1984) *Durkheim and Modern Sociology*, Cambridge: Cambridge University Press.

Field, Frank (1990) *Losing Out: The Emergence of Britain's Underclass*, Oxford: Basil Blackwell.

Field, Frank (1995) *Making Welfare Work: Reconstructing Welfare for the Millennium*, London: Institute of Community Studies.

Finn, Dan (1997) *Working Nation: Welfare Reform and the Australian Job Compact for the long term unemployed*, London: Unemployment Unit.

Gamble, Andrew (1988) *The Free Economy and the Strong State*, Basingstoke: Macmillan.

Gane, Mike (1992) 'Durkheim: Woman as Outsider' in M. Gane (ed.) *The Radical Sociology of Durkheim and Mauss*, London: Routledge, pp. 85–134.

Giddens, Anthony (1971) *Capitalism and Modern Social Theory*, Cambridge: Cambridge University Press.

Giddens, Anthony (1978) *Emile Durkheim*, London: Fontana.

Giddens, Anthony (ed.) (1986) *Durkheim on Politics and the State*, Cambridge: Polity Press.

Gilman, Charlotte Perkins (1966) *Women and Economics*, New York: Harper Torchbooks [1898].

Glucksmann, Miriam (1995) Why 'Work'? Gender and the 'Total Social Organization of Labour', *Gender, Work and Organization*, Vol. 2, No. 2, pp. 63–75.

Golding, Peter (1986) *Excluding the Poor*, London: CPAG.

Goodin, Robert E. (1996) 'Inclusion and Exclusion', *European Journal of Sociology* Vol. 37, No. 2, pp. 343–71.

Gray, John (1989) *Liberalisms: Essays in Political Philosophy*, London: Routledge.

Gray, John (1992) *The Moral Foundations of Market Institutions*, London: IEA Health and Welfare Unit.

Gray, John (1993a) *Beyond the New Right: Markets, Government and the Common Environment*, London: Routledge.

Gray, John (1993b) *Post-Liberalism: Studies in Political Thought*, New York: Routledge.

Gray, John (1996) *After Social Democracy*, London: Demos.

Gray, John (1997) *Endgames: Questions in Late Modern Political Thought*, Cambridge: Polity Press.

Gray. John (1995) *Enlightenment's Wake: Politics and Culture at the Close of the Modern Age*, London: Routledge.

Green Party (1993) *Manifesto for a Sustainable Society* London: Green Party.

Gregg, Paul and Wadsworth, Jonathan (1996) 'Feeling Insecure?', *Employment Audit*, 2, Autumn, pp. 17–26.

GUMG (Glasgow University Media Group) (1976) *Bad News*, London: Routledge and Kegan Paul.

Gutmann, Amy (1988) *Democracy and the Welfare State*, Princeton, New Jersey: Princeton University Press.

Hall, Peter A. (1997) 'Social Capital: a Fragile Asset' in *The Wealth and Poverty of Networks: Tackling Social Exclusion*, Demos Collection 12, London: Demos, pp. 35–7.

Hall, Stuart and Jacques, Martin (1983) *The Politics of Thatcherism*, London: Lawrence and Wishart.

Halsey, A.H. and Young, Michael (1995) *Family and Community Socialism*, London: IPPR.

Harker, Lisa (1996) *A Secure Future? Social Security and the Family in a Changing World*, London: CPAG.

Harker, Lisa (1997) 'New Paths for Social Security' in Alan Walker and Carol Walker, *Britain Divided: The Growth of Social Exclusion in the 1980s and 1990s*, London: CPAG.

Hutton, Will (1995a) 'High Risk Strategy', *Guardian* 30 October, pp. 2–3.

Hutton, Will (1995b) *The State We're In*, London: Jonathan Cape.

Hutton, Will (1996a) *The State We're In*, London: Vintage.

Hutton, Will (1996b) 'The Stakeholder Society' in Marquand and Seldon (1996) pp. 290–308.

Hutton, Will (1996c) 'Left with No Illusions', *Prospect* March, pp. 46–50.
Hutton, Will (1997a) 'Our Stake in Society', *Observer* 20 April, p. 29.
Hutton, Will (1997b) 'An Overview of Stakeholding' in Kelly *et al.* (1997) pp. 3–9.
Hutton, Will (1997c) *The State to Come*, London: Vintage.
Jones, Nicholas (1997) *Campaign 1997*, London: Indigo.
Jones, Tudor (1996) *Remaking the Labour Party: From Gaitskell to Blair*, London: Routledge.
Kay, John (1993) *The Foundations of Corporate Success*, Oxford: Oxford University Press.
Kay, John (1996a) 'The Good Market', *Prospect*, May, pp. 39–43.
Kay, John (1996b) *The Business of Economics*, Oxford: Oxford University Press.
Kelly, Gavin, Kelly, Dominic and Gamble, Andrew, (1997) (eds) *Stakeholder Capitalism*, London: Macmillan.
Labour Party (LP) (1992) *It's Time To Get Britain Working Again* (election manifesto).
Labour Party (LP) (1995a) *Renewing Democracy, Rebuilding Communities*.
Labour Party (LP) (1995b) *Safer Communities, Safer Britain*.
Labour Party (LP) (1995c) *A Quiet Life: Tough Action on Criminal Neighbours*.
Labour Party (LP) (1995d) *Excellence for Everyone: Labour's Crusade to Raise Standards*.
Labour Party (LP) (1995e) *A New Economic Future for Britain: Economic and Employment Opportunities for All*.
Labour Party (LP) (1996a) *Tackling Youth Crime: Reforming Youth Justice*.
Labour Party (LP) (1996b) *Parenting*.
Labour Party (LP) (1996c) *Lifelong Learning*.
Labour Party (LP) (1996d) *Learn as You Earn: Labour's Plans for a Skills Revolution*.
Labour Party (LP) (1996e) *Aiming Higher*.
Labour Party (LP) (1996f) *Labour and the Voluntary Sector: Setting the Agenda for Partnership in Government*.
Labour Party (LP) (1996g) *Strategy for Women*.
Labour Party (LP) (1996h) *A Fresh Start for Britain: Labour's Strategy for Britain in the Modern World*.
Labour Party (LP) (1996i) *Getting Welfare to Work: Opportunities for Lone Mothers*.
Labour Party (LP) (1996j) *Building Prosperity: Flexibility, Efficiency and Fairness at Work*.
Labour Party (LP) (1996k) *Labour's New Deal for a Lost Generation*.
Labour Party (LP) (1996m) *Protecting Our Communities: Labour's Plans for Tackling Criminal, Anti-social Behaviour in Neighbourhoods*.
Labour Party (LP) (1996n) *New Labour, New Life for Britain* (draft manifesto).
Labour Party (LP) (1997a) *Labour's Business Manifesto: Equipping Britain for the Future*.
Labour Party (LP) (1997b) *Because Britain Deserves Better* (1997 election manifesto).
Layard, Richard (1997) *What Labour Can Do*, London: Warner Books.
Lehmann, Jennifer (1994) *Durkheim and Women*, Nebraska: University of Nebraska Press.

Levitas, Ruth (1986) (ed.) *The Ideology of the New Right*, Cambridge: Polity.

Levitas, Ruth (1996a) 'Fiddling while Britain Burns: the 'Measurement' of Unemployment' in Ruth Levitas and Will Guy (eds) *Interpreting Official Statistics*, London: Routledge, pp. 45–65.

Levitas, Ruth (1996b) 'The Concept of Social Exclusion and the New Durkheimian Hegemony', *Critical Social Policy* 46, Vol. 16, pp. 5–20.

Levitas, Ruth (1998) 'Will Hutton: Closet Durkheimian' in Paul Bagguley and Jeff Hearn (eds) *Transforming Politics: Power and Resistance*, London: Macmillan.

Lister, Ruth (1990) *The Exclusive Society: Citizenship and the Poor*, London: CPAG.

Lloyd, John (1997b) 'Interview: Clive Hollick', *New Statesman* 24 January, pp. 18–19.

Lloyd, John (1997a) 'A Plan to Abolish the Underclass', *New Statesman* 29 August, pp. 14–16.

Lockwood, David (1964) 'Social Integration and System Integration' in George K. Zollschan and W. Hirsch (eds), *Explorations in Social Change*, London: Routledge and Kegan Paul.

Lockwood, David (1992) *Solidarity and Schism*, Oxford: Clarendon Press.

Lukes, Stephen (1973) *Emile Durkheim: His Life and Work*, London: Allen Lane.

Macmurray, John (1931) *Learning to Live*, London: BBC.

Macmurray, John (1932) *Freedom in the Modern World*, London: Faber and Faber.

Macmurray, John (1935a) *Reason and Emotion*, London: Faber and Faber.

Macmurray, John (1935b) *Creative Society: A Study of the Relation of Christianity to Communism*, London: SCM Press.

Macmurray, John (1957) *The Self as Agent*, London: Faber and Faber.

Macmurray, John (1961) *Persons in Relation*, London: Faber and Faber.

Macnicol, John (1987) 'In Pursuit of the Underclass', *Journal of Social Policy*, Vol. 16, pp. 293–318.

Mandelson, Peter and Liddle, Roger (1996) *The Blair Revolution: Can New Labour Deliver?* London: Faber and Faber.

Mann, Kirk (1992) *The Making of an English Underclass*, Milton Keynes: Open University Press.

Marquand, David and Seldon, Anthony (1996) *The Ideas that Shaped Post-War Britain*, London: New Statesman/Fontana.

Marshall, T.H. (1950) 'Citizenship and Social Class' in T.H. Marshall and Tom Bottomore (1992), *Citizenship and Social Class*, London: Pluto Press.

Morris, Lydia (1994) *Dangerous Classes: the Underclass and Social Citizenship*, London: Routledge.

Mulgan, Geoff (1997a) *Connexity: How to Live in a Connected World*, London: Chatto and Windus.

Mulgan, Geoff (1997b) (ed.) *Life After Politics: New Thinking for the Twenty-first Century*, London: Fontana Press.

Mulgan, Geoff (1997c) 'Think Well-being, not Welfare', *New Statesman*, 17 January, pp. 28–9.

Mulhall, Stephen and Swift, Adam (1992) *Liberals and Communitarians*, Oxford: Blackwell.

Murray, Charles (1990) *The Emerging British Underclass*, London: IEA.

Murray, Charles (1994) *Underclass: The Crisis Deepens*, London: IEA.

Oppenheim, Carey (1993) *Poverty: The Facts*, London: CPAG.

Pahl, R.E. (1991), 'The Search for Social Cohesion: from Durkheim to the European Commission', *European Journal of Sociology*, Vol. 32, No. 2, pp. 345–60.

Panitch, Leo and Leys, Colin (1997) *The End of Parliamentary Socialism: From New Left to New Labour*, London: Verso.

Pateman, Carole (1988) *The Sexual Contract*, Cambridge: Polity Press.

Pearce, Frank (1989) *The Radical Durkheim*, London: Unwin Hyman.

Plender, John (1997) *A Stake in the Future: The Stakeholding Solution*, London: Nicholas Brealey.

Room, Graham (1995) (ed.) *Beyond the Threshold*, Bristol: Policy Press.

Rowntree (1995) *Joseph Rowntree Foundation Inquiry into Income and Wealth*, 2 vols, York: Joseph Rowntree Foundation.

Shaw, Eric (1994) *The Labour Party Since 1979*, London: Routledge.

Showstack Sassoon, Anne (1996) 'Beyond Pessimism of the Intellect: Agendas for Social Justice and Change' in Mark Perryman (ed.) *The Blair Agenda*, London: Lawrence and Wishart.

Silver, Hilary (1994) 'Social Exclusion and Social Solidarity: Three Paradigms' *International Labour Review*, Vol. 133, No. 5–6, pp. 531–78.

Skjeie, Hege (1991) 'The Rhetoric of Difference: On Women's Inclusion into Political Elites', *Politics and Society*, Vol. 19, No. 2, pp. 133–63.

Sostris (1997) *Social Strategies in Risk Societies: Social Exclusion in Comparative Perspective*, Sostris Working Paper 1, London: University of East London.

Spicker, Paul (1997) 'Exclusion', *Journal of Common Market Studies*, Vol. 35, No. 1, pp. 133–143.

Townsend, Peter (1979) *Poverty in the United Kingdom*, Harmondsworth: Penguin.

Townsend, Peter (1995) 'Persuasion and Conformity: an Assessment of the Borrie Report on Social Justice', *New Left Review* Vol. 213, pp. 137–50.

Townsend, Peter (1996) 'The Struggle for Independent Statistics on Poverty' in Ruth Levitas and Will Guy (eds) *Interpreting Official Statistics*, London: Routledge.

Trades Union Congress (TUC) (1996) *Your Stake at Work: TUC Proposals for a Stakeholding Economy*, London: Trades Union Congress.

Walker, Alan and Walker, Carol (1997) (ed.) *Britain Divided: the Growth of Social Exclusion in the 1980s and 1990s*, London: CPAG.

Waring, Marilyn (1988) *If Women Counted*, London: Macmillan.

Watts Miller, Willie (1996) *Durkheim, Morals and Modernity*, London: UCL Press.

Westergaard, John (1992) 'About and Beyond the "Underclass" ', *Sociology*, Vol. 26, No. 4, pp. 575–87.

Willetts, David (1996) *Blair's Gurus*.

Willetts, David (1997) *Why Vote Conservative?* Harmondsworth: Penguin.

Wright, Tony (1997) *Why Vote Labour?* Harmondsworth: Penguin.

Index

6 Perri, 152, 153, 164

accountability, 29, 31, 75, 77, 80,
   115, 125, 173
Ackers, Louise, 26
Adonis, Andrew, 20
Aitken, Ian, 133, 134
Andersen, Paul, 34
Ashdown, Paddy, 43
ASI (Adam Smith Institute), 29, 31

Barclay, Sir Peter, 40
Barratt Brown, Michael, 78, 114
basic income, 101–2
   see also citizen's income
Beckett, Margaret, 32, 79
benefits, 10, 37, 41, 118, 132, 136,
   139, 141, 142, 143, 144, 146,
   150, 151, 153–5, 157, 161, 164
   in 1992 manifesto, 129, 131, 139
   in 1997 manifesto, 129 132–3, 139
   child, 5, 12, 129, 142, 143 144
   for disabled, 133, 142
   family credit, 140
   in-work, 5, 82
   income support, 129
   industrial injuries, 142
   jobseeker's allowance, 37, 141,
      160
   for lone parents, 5, 105, 133,
      141–2, 143
   means testing, 10, 16
   as moral hazard, 15, 17, 20, 146
   unemployment, 37
   working family tax credit, 5
   see also pensions
Beveridge, William, 49
Black, Allan, 118
Blackstone, Tessa, 33, 130
Blair, Tony, 1, 30, 31, 32, 39,
   69, 87, 90, 114, 128, 132,
   133, 140, 143, 175, 176, 177
   on 30/30/40 society, 52
   on community, 122–3

on crime, 123
on education, 129
on Hattersley and Benn, 134
on lone parents, 141, 142
on the role of government, 125–6
Socialism, 30
on truancy, 150
on underclass, 20, 155–6
on women and work, 146
on work, 138
Blue Circle, 118–19, 120
Blunkett, David, 120, 122
on equality, 134
on poverty, 135
Borrie, Gordon, 33, 113
Brittan, Samuel, 105
Brown, Gordon, 12, 105, 128, 132,
   134, 138
on equality, 135–6
on inclusion through work, 138–9
on lone parents, 141
on women and work, 146
Byers, Stephen, 148

Cadbury Committee, 55
Campbell, Bea, 157
   Goliath, 157
capitalism, 49, 50, 51–2, 54–7,
   67–9, 74, 102, 104, 105, 109,
   171, 180, 183–4, 187–9
CASE (Centre for the Analysis of
   Social Exclusion), 40, 148–9
Cash, Bill, 143
Castle, Barbara, 10, 132
Centre for Policy Studies, 29
Centre for Tomorrow's Company,
   86
charity, 125, 137–8
Charter 88, 31
child care, 5, 10, 24, 28, 140, 144,
   145–7, 150, 160, 162, 170, 192n
Chisholm, Malcolm, 105, 143
christian socialism, 30, 90, 105
   see also socialism; ethical socialism

churning, 161
Citizen's Commission, 33
It's Our Welfare, 33
citizen's income, 11, 36, 46, 87
  see also basic income
citizenship, 5, 7, 12–13, 16, 26, 44,
  46–7, 102, 103, 109–110, 126,
  128, 147, 158, 173–7
  active, 45, 46, 54, 125–6, 147, 158
  see also rights
class, 13, 19, 26, 28, 64, 106,
  108, 114, 183–5, 168
Clause IV, 1, 40, 49, 50, 190, 112,
  127, 175, 191, 133
Coates, Ken, 78, 114
Commission on Public Policy and
  British Business 4, 79
  *Promoting Prosperity: a Business
  Agenda for Britain* 79, 120
Commission on Social Justice 4,
  32, 33–40, 44, 49, 79, 144,
  156, 162, 195n
  *Social Justice: Strategies for
  National Renewal* 33, 38,
  39, 49
Commission on Wealth Creation
  and Social Cohesion, 4, 43–7,
  196n
communitarianism, 4, 45, 90–110,
  112, 127, 128, 168–9, 179
community, 2, 4, 12, 28, 34, 73,
  77, 78, 89–111, 113, 121–7,
  149, 155, 165, 168, 180
Conservative government (1979–97),
  11, 60, 128, 129, 143
Conservative Party, 1, 29, 104–5, 175
contracts
  relational, 72–5
  classical, 72, 73
Cook, Robin, 152
Coote, Anna, 32
corporate governance, 55, 74, 80
corporatism, 77–8
Corry, Dan, 32
CPAG (Child Poverty Action
  Group), 11, 165
  *Britain Divided: the Growth of
  Social Exclusion in the 1980s
  and 1990s*, 11, 12

CPRS (Central Policy Review
  Staffs), 29
crime, 17, 42, 46, 78, 121–5, 148,
  150, 166, 167
Crime and Disorder Bill (1997),
  125, 166, 167
Crosland, Anthony, 4, 113, 134

Dahrendorf, Ralf, 16, 43, 44
Dahrendorf report, the, 4, 43–7
  see also Commission on Wealth
  Creation and Social Cohesion
Daniel, Caroline, 175
Darling, Alistair, 117, 175
Davis, Sir Peter, 137
Dearing Report, the, 130
Demos, 29, 30, 31, 33, 89, 137,
  152–6, 164, 168, 175
dependency, 146
  culture of, 14, 15, 20, 100, 102,
  141, 144, 150–1, 154–5, 157
  see also underclass
devolution, 125, 173–4
Diana, Princess of Wales, 137–8
Dimbleby, Jonathan, 165
disability, 8, 26, 38, 133, 142, 171,
  174, 187
discourse, distinguished from
  ideology 3
Du Gay, Paul, 29
Duffy, Katherine, 20
Durkheim, Emile, 6, 22, 61, 178–86
  The Division of Labour in Society,
  178–80, 184
  Suicide, 183

economic inactivity, 36, 52, 61–3
education, 65, 79, 92, 93, 99, 109–10,
  124, 130, 149–50, 160, 166, 172–3
  higher, 82, 130
  nursery, 82, 140
  primary, 82
  private, 52 65, 68
  see also skills, training
Education Bill (1997), 172
employability, 4, 115, 118–21,
  128, 147, 150, 153, 156–7, 164
EMU (European Monetary Union),
  25, 68, 80

Environmental Task Force, 139
EPI (Employment Policy Institute),
 118, 120
equality, 12, 13, 47, 63, 65, 94,
 102–3, 105–9, 128–34, 136, 145,
 149, 153, 156–7, 185, 187, 188
 contrasted with inclusion,
 44, 63–7
 see also inequality
ESRC (Economic and Social
 Research Council) 148
ethnicity, 11, 13, 19, 38, 41, 44, 105,
 114, 148, 174, 187
Etzioni, Amitai, 4, 77, 89, 90–7, 100,
 105, 122, 128, 179, 185
 The Parenting Deficit, 89
 The Spirit of Community, 89, 92
 The New Golden Rule, 90, 92
European Social Policy, 23, 24
European Union, 21–6, 38, 51
 funds, 2, 22, 25

Fabian Society, 29, 30, 31
fairness, 99–100, 102, 114–15, 130,
 136
families, 38, 60, 94–5, 103, 108, 152,
 181, 183
 and social control, 5, 122
 see also parents, mothers, fathers
fathers, 17, 155
 lone, 10, 140–1
Field, Frank, 16, 17, 40, 43, 45, 142
 *Losing Out: the Emergence of
 Britain's Underclass*, 16
Fitzsimons, Lorna, 144
Foyer movement, 167
France, 2, 21, 22, 160
Freely, Maureen, 63

Gane, Mike, 186
GDP (Gross Domestic Product), 8,
 47
 and social security, 160
 see also wealth
gender, 7, 13, 19, 26, 38,
 46, 60, 61–3, 94, 101,
 108, 114, 174, 192n
Giddens, Anthony, 31
Gilman, Charlotte Perkins, 183

globalization, 35, 55, 84, 102,
 104, 117, 127, 135, 187
Glucksmann, Miriam, 8, 27, 146
GMB (General, Municipal and
 Boilermaker's union), 119
GNP (Gross National Product),
 and unpaid work, 47
Golding, Peter, 12
Goodin, Robert, 12
Government Statistical Services,
 29
Gray, John, 4, 31, 32, 89, 97–105,
 122, 128, 133, 134, 135,
 179, 180, 185, 187
 Beyond the New Right, 89,
 100, 102
 Enlightenment's Wake, 89
 After Social Democracy, 31, 89,
 102, 133–4
 Endgames, 89, 99
Green Party, 4, 86
Greenbury Committee, 55
Gregg, Paul, 118
*Growth, Competitiveness,
 Employment*, 23–4, 25

Habermas, Jurgen, 176
Hague, Douglas, 30
Hain, Peter, 119, 120
Hall, Stuart, 19
Halpern, David, 31
Handy, Charles, 116
Hargreaves, Ian, 31
Harker, Lisa, 12
Harman, Harriet, 32, 36, 132,
 133, 140, 141, 143, 144,
 145, 148, 149, 156, 174
Hattersley, Roy, 4, 113, 133–8,
 149, 187
Hayek, Freidrich, 103
health, 99, 172
Heseltine, Michael, 79
Hewitt, Patricia, 32, 33, 34, 144
Hills, John, 40
Hollick, Clive, 32
homework clubs, 150
Howarth, Alan, 142, 175
Humphreys John, 143
Hurd, Douglas, 45

Hutton, Will, 4, 25, 43, 45, 49–69,
    85, 86, 87, 92–3, 115, 116,
    132, 154, 169, 172, 180, 182,
    185, 186, 187
  on 30/30/40 society, 52–4, 68
  The State We're In, 49, 56, 64,
    66, 86, 118
  The State to Come, 49, 56, 66

identity, 60, 101, 154, 158, 174,
    180, 181, 182
ideology, 3
IEA (Institute of Economic Affairs),
    17, 29, 76–7
Individual Learning Accounts, 130
inequality, 7, 26, 38, 39, 41, 44–5,
    63–7, 136, 137, 170, 172,
    183–5, 188
  see also equality
inheritance, 66, 184, 185
Institute of Public Relations, 86
IPPR (Institute for Public Policy
    Research), 29, 32, 79–83, 175
Irvine, Derry, 105

Jacques, Martin, 30, 31
Japan, 36, 67, 76
Jenkins, Roy, 32
job security, 4, 35, 49–54, 58, 60,
    84, 93–4, 113, 117, 118–21
Johnson, Melanie, 1
Joseph Rowntree Foundation Inquiry
    into Income and Wealth, 4, 40–3,
    47, 49, 64, 196n
Joseph Rowntree Reform Trust, 32
Jowell, Tessa, 105, 148

Kay, John, 4, 71–9, 85, 86, 185
  *The Foundations of Corporate
    Success*, 71
  The Business of Economics, 76
Kennedy, Helena, 31–2
Keynes, John Maynard, 49
Kinnock, Neil, 1, 32, 34
Kruger, Danny, 153

Labour, old, 1, 30, 112–15, 133
Labour Party
  Manifesto, 1992, 129, 130, 131, 139

Manifesto, 1997, 116–17, 129,
    130, 132, 139–42
Lamont, Norman, 1
Lang, Ian, 1, 83
Lawson, Neil, 31
Layard, Richard, 142
Lehmann, Jennifer, 183, 186
Liberal Democrat Party 1,
    31, 32, 43, 175
Liberalism, 98, 14, 103–4, 113
Liddell, Helen, 137
Liddle, Roger, 63, 81, 114, 123
  The Blair Revolution, 63
Lister, Ruth, 13, 20, 149, 164–5
Livingstone, Ken, 143
Lloyd, John, 70, 79
Lockwood, David, 186
lone parents, 8, 10, 17–19, 36, 44,
    92, 94, 123–4, 133, 139–45,
    162–3, 167–8, 169
  see also benefits for lone parents,
    poverty, underclass
Low Pay Commission, 141–2
LSE (London School of Economics),
    31, 40, 148, 162

Maastricht Treaty, 26, 143
MacDonald, Calum, 105
Macmurray, John, 4, 90,
    105–110, 122, 188
Mahon, Alice, 144, 145
MAI (Multilateral Agreement on
    Investment) 113, 204n
Mandelson, Peter, 30, 63, 81, 114,
    123, 148, 149, 151–2, 156, 175
  The Blair Revolution, 63
  *Labour's Next Steps: Tackling
    Social Exclusion*, 30
Mann, Nyta, 34
Marquand, David, 43, 49
Marshall, T.H., 12–13, 44
Marx, Karl, 50
Marxism, 3, 113–14, 105
masculinity, 17, 42, 157–8
Meacher, Michael, 118
measures of inclusion, 164
Mellor, David, 175
Michael, Alun, 126, 148
Miliband, David, 32

miner's strike, 15
minimum wage, 5, 11, 39, 41, 55,
   79–80, 84, 136, 138, 140, 141, 163
Monks, John, 83, 176
Moore, Robert, 149
mothers, 155
   lone, 17–19, 142, 162, 167
   see also families, lone parents
MUD (Moral Underclass Discourse),
   2, 7, 8, 14–21, 40, 45, 101,
   110–11, 128, 138, 149–53,
   156–7, 159–77
Mulgan, Geoff, 30, 31, 152,
   153–6, 188
Murray, Charles, 17–18, 19–20, 163
   The Emerging British Underclass,
   17

National Insurance, 129, 131, 132
National Lottery, 138, 140
NEF (New Economics Foundation),
   86
New Deal
   Roosevelt's, 18
   New Labour's, 28, 128, 138–45,
   150 160, 161, 163
New Economy, 32
New Right, 14, 15, 32, 49, 76–7,
   89, 97–8, 103, 113, 114, 134–5
New Statesman, 31, 32
Newton, Tony, 1
Nexus, 29, 31, 32, 98
NHS (National Health Service),
   124, 172, 176

Offer, Avner, 62
ONS (Office for National Statistics),
   8, 47, 170
opportunity, 5, 24, 33, 34, 39, 45,
   47, 54, 115–16, 122–3, 127,
   128, 133, 136, 144–6, 149,
   150, 151, 156–8, 187
ownership, 55, 58, 68, 73–4, 114
   common, 1, 34, 133
   public 50–1, 113

Pahl, Ray, 182
parenting, 4, 60, 92
   full-time, 146

inadequate, 28, 93, 97, 123–4
   orders, 167
   as social control, 5
   and transport, 171–2
   as unpaid work, 10, 62
   as work, 95, 146–7, 154, 163, 167
   see also lone parents, fathers,
      mothers
participation, 10, 11, 35, 45, 54,
   101, 117, 128, 138, 149, 152–3,
   154, 159, 160–2, 164, 168,
   170–7, 178, 187
   income, 11
pensions, 5, 10, 41, 46, 52, 53,
   65, 117
   citizen's, 131
   in 1992 manifesto, 129, 131
   in 1997 manifesto, 131, 132
   private, 137
   see also Castle, Barbara
performative inclusion, 5, 45, 157–8
Perkin, Harold, 67
Plant, Raymond, 157
Plender, John, 69
political inclusion, 159, 173–7
poll tax, 15
Pollard, Stephen, 20
pollution, 171
Portillo, Michael, 1, 30
poverty, 2, 7, 8, 9–11, 13, 16, 19,
   23, 26, 38, 53, 101, 123, 132,
   134, 135–6, 138–9, 149–50,
   152, 153, 156, 160, 163–5,
   170, 188
privatization, 75

Radiohead, 49
Rayner Review, the, 29
RED (Redistributionist Discourse)
   2, 7, 8, 9–14, 35, 36, 37, 38,
   39, 40, 43, 44, 102, 110–11, 128,
   136, 149–53, 156–7, 159–75
redistribution, 5, 7, 10, 11, 32,
   34, 97, 102–3, 112, 131–8,
   149, 156, 170, 187
responsibility, 34, 63, 94, 97, 99–100,
   106–7, 108, 110, 115, 116, 121,
   123, 124, 127, 129, 146, 147,
   157, 164, 167, 185

Rifkind, Malcolm, 1
rights, 13, 26, 44, 45, 55,
    68, 94, 102, 185
    and responsibilities, 35, 54, 63,
        91, 112, 113, 116, 117, 122
risk, 53–4, 124, 132–3, 137
RMI (Revenu Mimimum
    D'Insertion), 21, 22
Robinson, Geoffrey, 31, 137, 148
Roche, Barbara, 148
Rogers, Jean, 162
Room, Graham, 22, 128
Royal Commission on the
    Distribution of Income and
    Wealth, 29, 40
Ruddock, Joan, 174
rural development, 171

Sawyer, Tom, 70
Scargill, Arthur, 70
Scruton, Roger, 103
Securities and Investments Board,
    the, 137
security, 34, 78, 103, 105, 118–20,
    153, 156
    as shifter, 121–7
    see also job security
Seldon, Anthony, 49
self, 107
    discipline, 93–4
    esteem, 59, 60, 101, 108,
        144, 145–6, 147, 154,
        157, 158, 159
    identity, 59, 101, 158, 181
SERA (Socialist Environment and
    Resources Association), 171–2
SERPS (State Earnings Related
    Pension Scheme), 131, 132
SEU (Social Exclusion Unit), 2, 5,
    31, 128, 138, 147–52, 159,
    164–8
SID (Social Integrationist
    Discourse), 2, 7, 8, 21–7, 35,
    37, 39, 101, 110–11, 128, 136,
    138, 149–53, 156–7, 159–77
Silver, Hilary, 6, 21
Singapore, 76
skills, 24, 65, 79, 82, 118, 120–1,
    135, 148; shortage 118, 120

Skjeie, Hege, 175
Smith, John, 1, 33, 34, 39
social accounting, 85–6
social capital, 168–9
social chapter, 80
social cohesion, 2, 6, 23, 35,
    41–2, 43–7, 103, 110, 116,
    122, 178–9, 182
    and growth, 43, 47
    incompatible with equality, 64
    inequality as threat to, 44–5
    and taxation, 66
social control, 4, 48, 61, 78, 93–4,
    95, 165, 168, 178
    families and, 122
social democracy, 4, 31, 33, 49, 98,
    102–3, 104, 114, 153, 187
Social Fund, 25, 129
social integration, 6, 35, 46
    work as, 36
socialism, 31, 33, 34, 49, 50, 104,
    130, 135; ethical 105, 113,
    christian, 105; state, 180
socialization, 91–3, 108
Soley, Clive, 144
solidarity, 22, 23, 25, 103, 108, 185–6
    Durkheim's concept of, 178–9,
        183, 185
Sorel, Georges, 181
Soros, George, 180
Spencer, Herbert, 180
stakeholders, 72, 74, 75, 80, 82,
    84, 117, 128
stakeholding, 2, 4, 43, 45, 49, 50,
    54–8, 63, 70–88, 118, 112,
    115–17, 127, 168–9, 179
    Stakeholder Capitalism, 117
    *Your Stake at Work: TUC
        Proposals for a Stakeholding
        Economy*, 83–7
Straw, Jack, 105, 122, 123, 124, 165
    on parenting orders, 167
    A Quiet Life, 124, 125
    Safer Communities, Safer Britain,
        124–5
    on work, 139
    *Tackling Youth Crime: Reforming
        Youth Justice*, 123
substitution, 161

taxation, 41, 67, 71, 116, 121, 128,
    129, 130, 141, 150
Taylor, Martin, 137
TGWU (Transport and General
    Workers Union), 33, 118
Thatcher, Margaret, 30, 31, 40,
    103, 113
Thatcherism, 4, 12, 20, 28, 97,
    113, 114, 133, 153, 187
think tanks, 4, 17, 29–33, 47
third way, the, 4, 6, 33, 49, 50,
    70, 83, 90, 104, 112–127,
    128, 153, 177, 180, 186–7, 188
Thompson, Tommy, 18
Thompson, Paul, 29
Tönnies, Ferdinand, 89
total social organization of labour,
    8, 27, 28, 63, 146–7, 183
Townsend, Peter, 9–11, 12, 15, 34,
    40, 132
    Poverty in the United Kingdom, 10
trade unions, 1, 32, 33, 43, 56–8,
    63, 68, 80–1, 87, 112, 114,
    116, 176, 182
Traidcraft, 85
training, 52, 65, 79, 120, 121, 129,
    139, 150–1
transport, 23, 149, 150, 159, 170–2
Tressell, Robert, 59
    *The Ragged Trousered
        Philanthropists*, 59
truancy, 148, 150, 166–7
trust, 45, 54, 68, 107, 168
TUC (Trades Union Congress), 4,
    70, 83, 86, 125, 176
    *Your Stake at Work: TUC
        Proposals for a Stakeholding
        Economy*, 83–7
Twigg, Stephen, 30

underclass, 14, 15–19, 20, 44, 53,
    100, 101, 152, 154, 155–6, 188
    see also dependency culture
unemployment, 35, 36, 48, 53,
    62, 65, 82–3, 101, 134, 138–9,
    148, 150–1, 156, 159, 160, 161,
    163
    benefits, 37, 65, 82
    and crime, 166

female, 46
    as insecurity, 120
    male, 46, 60–1, 157
    and truancy, 166
    see also economic inactivity
United Distillers, 118, 119

Wadsworth, Jonathan, 118
Wages for Housework
    Campaign, 170
Waldegrave, William, 1
Walker, Alan, 11, 12, 27
Walker, Carol, 11, 12, 27
Watts Miller, Willie, 179–80,
    183, 186
wealth, 41, 42–3, 47, 106, 109,
    137, 184–5
Webb, Steve, 143, 145
Weber, Max, 3
welfare reform
    Australia, 162, 195n
    Green Paper on, 5
    United States, 17–19, 160,
        162
welfare state, 4, 37, 93–4
welfare to work, 5, 28, 31, 128,
    138, 139, 140, 141, 142,
    159–63
Westergaard, John, 19, 188
Willetts, David, 49, 116
Wilson, Harold, 10
Wise, Audrey, 144
work
    ethic, 16, 17, 19, 66,
        108, 154, 162
    paid, 8, 23–4, 25, 27, 35–6,
        38, 39, 43, 58–9, 93–4,
        101, 102, 108, 112, 118–21,
        128, 131, 138–42, 144,
        146, 147, 151, 153–4,
        159, 162, 163, 167, 169,
        170–1, 180, 182–3
    lone parents and, 143–5
    and men, 60–1, 63
    redistribution of, 170
    and self identity, 59–60, 157–8
    as social integration, 47–8, 145
    and women, 61, 140–1,
        57–8, 183

unpaid 5, 8, 10, 12, 24–5, 35, 36,
37–8, 43, 47, 125–6, 131,
145–7, 159, 169–70, 180
child care, 28
domestic, 27
emotional labour as, 95
parenting as, 95, 146–7, 163

and private sphere, 46
voluntary, 4, 37–8, 125–6, 170–1
women, 61–3, 157, 172
workfare, 59
working hours, 9, 24, 38, 39,
60, 154
Wright, Tony, 116